PUBLICATIONS OF THE
DEPARTMENT OF SOCIAL AND ECONOMIC RESEARCH
UNIVERSITY OF GLASGOW

GENERAL EDITOR: A. K. CAIRNCROSS

SOCIAL AND ECONOMIC STUDIES

7

GLASGOW LIMITED

GLASGOW LIMITED

A CASE-STUDY IN
INDUSTRIAL WAR AND PEACE

BY

T. T. PATERSON
M.A., B.Sc., Ph.D.

Senior Lecturer in Industrial Relations, University of Glasgow
Past Fellow of Trinity College, Cambridge

CAMBRIDGE
AT THE UNIVERSITY PRESS
1960

331.1941
P29g

PUBLISHED BY
THE SYNDICS OF THE CAMBRIDGE UNIVERSITY PRESS

Bentley House, 200 Euston Road, London, N.W.1
American Branch: 32 East 57th Street, New York 22, N.Y.

©

CAMBRIDGE UNIVERSITY PRESS

1960

Printed in Great Britain at the Villafield Press, Bishopbriggs, Glasgow

CONTENTS

v

LIST OF TABLES

vi

LIST OF FIGURES

LIST OF PLATES

PREFACE

Glasgow is no mean city. Quite apart from its size—it used to boast being "the second city in the Empire"—it has an atmosphere quite its own—as distinct from London or Birmingham as Chicago is from New York or Pittsburg. There is a warmth of humanity, a generosity of heart, which well makes up for the squalor of the Anderston and Bridgeton districts, much more notorious to the Glaswegian than the ill-famed Gorbals. Here is slum-land, the home of the razor-gangs of the thirties, of men wild and seemingly untameable, yet capable of forming the core of a famous Highland regiment distinguished as a fighting-team in war. So, in peace, these men can fight in strikes, go-slows and other industrial 'delinquencies', yet can form the hard-working core of a manufacturing team when properly led.

It was this reality of living in Glasgow that I faced on deserting, after many secluded years, the ivory towers of Cambridge. Days spent in factories, and evenings given over to excursions into the wilds of the city brought me close into contact with the roistering gaiety of good men near to evil and poverty. Perhaps in this book I may seem to be more aware of their feelings, and somewhat more sympathetic towards them than I should be as an impartial observer; but I have tried, as far as I could, to keep these feelings out of my writing.

The book is about a factory staffed by nearly 300 men and women mainly from the Bridgeton district. It was brought to my notice by a former student and, it so happened, two of the managers had also been students of mine; so I was able to gain entry. As with most studies of this kind the firm must remain anonymous, though, I believe, there is nothing in this record which redounds to the serious discredit of any one person. It is a story of men working alongside each other, not together but wanting to be so, yet unable to find a way until they came, albeit quite unwittingly, upon a simple truth of all social activity. It is because of this that I have written the book.

For years the factory had been plagued with strikes, go-slows, low pro-ductivity and other industrial ailments prevalent in our society today. Then came a fairly sudden change to a state of peace, of production increased by over 80 per cent, of health and happiness of men. It was a change brought about not by buying men with money but by earning their loyalty, not by a change in machines but by a change in the relations among men. There seemed to be a lesson here in this small factory, a factory somewhat different from, and much more common than the large concerns normally studied by academics. It was a lesson to be learned only by looking at every possible variable in the social equation, examining as much evidence as could be

ix

gained without actually disturbing the factory situation by my own presence. For such is a fault of many observers of industry who enter factories and with questionnaires accost men, believing that the answers will give valid clues to motive. Either one has to be a participant observer or remain divorced from the work situation as much as possible so as not to affect it. The Hawthorne investigation demonstrated this adequately.

The story is about unskilled labourers, the "commonest" of "common working men", who showed themselves to be governed not alone by money, despite their obvious need for it, but by their conceptions of justice and fairness, and by their need for the warmth of working companionship. It is also the story of a manager who took up the challenge of industrial battle long waged between his predecessors and the workmen, and who, because of his own conceptions of justice and rectitude, won the battle in the end. Neither he nor his men were governed by economics, they were concerned with the morality of economics. Much of what I have to retail can be couched in clichés such as "a fair day's work for a fair day's wage", but this tells very little. I have tried to avoid such clichés or, when they have reared their unclear heads, I have attempted to make clear just what they mean. At the same time I have tried to avoid the jargon of psychology, sociology and labour economics since the story might be of use to managers and trade unionists who, justifiably, would find such jargon unpalatable and indigestible. Where it has crept in it is explained.

Because of the need for anonymity I cannot acknowledge, as I should so very much like to do, the help given me by managers, men and trade unionists during this study. Three men especially, the works manager, here called Anderson, one of the men, Maloney, and the trade union organiser, Macdonald, were most helpful. A fourth person, junior manager and my student, analysed one of the situations of work-group relations for me because I hesitated to go there and do it myself. To the most senior officials of the firm I am grateful for access to their files and records. Luckily I am able to record openly the generous and useful help I have had in conversations with my colleagues Professor A. K. Cairncross and Mr D. J. Robertson. But to Glasgow University I am most indebted, for, without the shelter of that ancient institution, without its peace, without the friendliness of its staff, and without its financial support (unavailable from any other source) I could have done nothing.

T.T.P.

CHAPTER 1

INTRODUCTORY

This is, first of all, a case-study. What can be learned from the case alone concerns only the case. However, if the conclusions on industrial relations are compatible with findings from other case-studies these conclusions can thereafter be stated as generalities. Such generalities may be of two kinds, principles and theories. By principles I imply what seems to be present in current American usage—modes of action. These principles are often enunciated in the form of injunctions, for example, "The manager should always be friendly towards his workmen"; or they may be stated as causal connections of behaviour, for example, "When a manager is friendly the workmen respond positively". Such principles do not tell 'why', they tell 'how'. By theories I imply 'why-ness', meaning explanations of behaviour, for example, "When a manager is friendly the men respond because . . . and provided, etc."; the explanatory clauses being universally applicable to that situation.

Three Parts of the book are given over to a statement of the case. The fourth Part is concerned with analysis in terms of what theories are available, and with extension of those theories in the light of the case. I cannot claim to have established universal application of these extensions. They are essentially cock-shies, but a cock-shy is better than no theory at all—it may, through its destruction, be the prime cause of establishing an unassailable truth.

The first Part sets the background of people and place, purely descriptive. The chapter on the Bridgeton workmen is a shortened version of a large psycho-anthropological treatise—a version which may well be criticised because of its shortness and inadequacy. But the description is necessary; indeed I should go so far as to say that any deep study of a factory must be prefaced by an outline of the belief system of the community from which its members are drawn. It will be quite clear to readers in England and elsewhere that the unskilled worker from Bridgeton is not the same as his occupational parallel to which they are accustomed. Nevertheless the generalised findings hold elsewhere. In other words, the variable that is the peculiarity of Bridgeton is cancelled out—but that variable had to be considered.

The second Part, the historical, is based upon three sources of information: face-to-face conversation with and verbally reported statements by the men involved, and written evidence. The written evidence is taken from the works office files, from files at trade union headquarters, and from letters to and from members of the factory and union. Throughout the book all statements in double inverted commas are direct quotations from these sources.

The writing of this historical account required strict selection from a mass of material, some of which had no relevance to the study though collected in case it might have had. The selection was on three bases: first, to give a coherently sequent narrative; secondly, to give all points of view in a specific situation; and thirdly, to cut the story short. It will be found that I have thus been able to utilise nearly every point presented in the narrative. As to its adequacy, this I tested by asking the works manager, the trade union organiser, and one of the men to read it and to comment. All considered it a full and fair summary with no omissions worth mentioning. On two very minor points they disagreed with me, and these I amended. The manager was of the opinion that I have leaned a shade towards the trade union side, probably because I have quoted more from the union files than from his office files. He still considered it a fair and just presentation, however. That I quote more from union files was due to the willingness of the union to give me access to everything I asked for, and to unwillingness on the part of the directorate of the firm to let me see 'confidential correspondence'. If I had been able to get at that correspondence I could possibly have given additional evidence on the directorate's attitude to problems of industrial relations.

The third Part, the statistical, is based on figures extracted from works office files. These figures are not complete. For example, I was unable to obtain the detailed statistics on absenteeism since the directorate took the view (which I still cannot understand) that their divulgence, even under the cloak of academic anonymity, was not possible in view of economic competition; this about figures for years past. When, after protracted correspondence, I finally obtained permission to look at the files I found that an over-zealous clerk had burned them "tidying up useless rubbish". This may seem a criticism of the directorate, but after this disaster they kindly let me go ahead. Nevertheless, I had lost data on labour turnover as well as absenteeism in that clerical conflagration.

The treatment of the statistics takes on two characteristics. The figures are graphically presented to show the relationship to historical events, for the numerical facts fit the story of changes in men's feelings and attitudes, a relationship which may be interpreted in terms of cause and effect. But the second characteristic is the demonstration of the association of changes in all the statistics and the historical sequence. It may seem that I use too much space in expounding this association rather than cause-effect, this totality rather than causality, but I have found it necessary to do so. For some people it is too easy, for instance, to say that accident-rate goes up because labour turnover has increased so that men new to the job are more

2

liable to sustain accident. It seldom strikes causality-minded observers that labour turnover and accident-rate may increase contemporaneously because of a factor or factors affecting both indices. It is too easy to say that absenteeism increases because men are less satisfied with the work situation, their so-called 'morale' is lower, when it may quite well be that morale is higher (as shown by other indices) or it may simply be that earnings are higher and men find it easier to stay off work, high morale or no. A single numerical index cannot satisfactorily be used to show what is happening in the minds of men; an association of indices is necessary, and also the relating of that association to verbal and other expressions of men's feelings. Dealing with these statistics I have avoided the fashionable use of statistical mathematics of the more abstruse kind, relying upon simple graphical and scatter-diagram methods of showing correlation.

The fourth Part is an analysis of the preceding Parts under several subject-headings. Here an attempt is made to understand the case itself in terms of simple known theory in psychology, sociology and labour-economics. For the last chapter I have no excuse except that I felt I had to write it. It is about management of men, which demands not merely technical competence but even more so, in my opinion, an understanding of moral judgment.

For several reasons this case-study has many advantages over the more complex systems usually studied, such as the Hawthorne, Glacier Metal, I.B.M., and so on. Here the men were all unskilled so that the difficulties of internal-differential wage-rates were reduced; nevertheless there were differentials according to occupation and these had their effect. During the period of five years examined there was no change in machinery or techniques, nor of types of product. There were, however, two fluctuations in markets. One was in demand for a certain product, a change which occurred after the major, critical period of experiment, and so had no effect on that experiment. The other was a change in supply of raw materials. This had little effect other than to heighten the tension already existing, and this effect soon passed, within weeks, when the market improved.

During the first nine months of the five-year period the factory was in charge of a manager who "cracked up" on account of the poor industrial relations. For the rest of the period the factory was run by a works manager, Anderson, whose adjustment to the situation, and whose relations to the men constitute the major source of interest—there was, therefore, no change in management during the important years.

The method of manufacture was essentially mass-production of large batches, coming off machine-lines working on a continuous three-shift cycle, day and night. The products could be altered according to sales demands, but these alterations did not require any big-scale change on the lines, rather some relatively minor adjustments. Nevertheless such alterations could cause

3

trouble, but the relation of alteration to resultant trouble was easily comprehended. There was only one change in the method of deploying men, and this will be shown to be of considerable importance.

There were two main production-lines. The troubles that beset the factory had their roots almost wholly in one of these lines. The one change in incentive, a matter of great import, affected them both; the products were somewhat different but the methods of production were comparable; the line in which trouble lay was 'treated' by the manager, the other was not; hence the second line acted as a control on the experiment made on the first. Both lines occupied the same building and so the men were close enough in contact to be able to talk and otherwise 'communicate' with each other. This may be regarded as a serious deficiency in control-experiment relations but, as will be shown, it was a situation that illuminated some very interesting problems. The manager, senior foreman, and foremen were the same for both lines.

In order to avoid the difficulty that always arises when experiments and observations are made, the difficulty of estimating the effect of the observer upon the observed, I kept away from the work floor. So my information was *a posteriori* to some extent; but *a priori* as well, since future moves were mentioned in my presence. I gleaned my information either in the manager's office, or at a meal or meeting with him, in the trade union headquarters where I was always made as welcome, and in homes and pubs with the workmen. They had no clear idea of what I was after other than that I was interested in "what kind of work" they were doing, and in industrial relations generally. For the same reason, to avoid disturbing the work situation, I did not use the questionnaire technique. That might have aroused the same kind of reaction as was met by a colleague working in a Glasgow shipyard—the men threatened to throw him in the river. Besides, I have found that the questionnaire technique, at least among Scotsmen, seldom reveals motive. In any case I was getting a free expression of feeling without the use of a questionnaire, and, since the statistics and my notes seemed to be compatible, I feel the avoidance of the questionnaire was justified. Similarly, much though I should have liked to do so, I could not use psychological tests for personality. This certainly would have added considerably to the value of my observations, but it just could not be done. I could well imagine how some of my Bridgeton men would have reacted to a Thematic Apperception Test or even an ink blot; and I could not afford, once having got well on with the study, the possibility of everything being made useless.

So my statistics are not the usual psychological and sociological kind. They are the plain statistics of any factory, productivity, spoilage, labour turnover, accident-rate, sickness, absenteeism and lateness. Perhaps because of that, managers, who may find it worth while reading this book, will be encouraged to use such statistics close to their hands in watching their industrial relations; for, as I hope to show, such statistics are good indicators of the state of industrial relations, and are much more dependable than hearsay, guess, and intuition, which is what most managers seem to rely upon.

PART I. THE PLACE AND THE PEOPLE

PLATE I. A crumbling tenement in Bridgeton

CHAPTER 2

DRAMATIS PERSONAE

Bridgeton lies in the east end of Glasgow and, like most east end districts of large cities, it has the character of near-slumland. But it is not as depressing as the slums of continental cities nor of those of New York and Chicago; for the majority of buildings were put up when Glasgow was at the height of its prosperity last century, and they were well made, of stone, and with rooms of fairly large dimensions. It is a district of long streets of well-proportioned three and four storey frontages, one entrance (called a 'close') for from six to sixteen flats, the characteristic Glasgow 'tenement'.[1] What is missing mainly is good sanitation. Though each flat or sub-flat has water piped in, the closet is external and shared by the occupants of as many as four flats. At the back of each tenement, that is the block of flats served by one close, there is a communal wash-house in which laundry is washed on a rota system. The 'drying-green' is usually an earthen enclosure used as a play-place by children and as a dumping-ground for tin cans and empty whisky bottles.

Between such tenements there survive a few pre-tenement houses, small-roomed, thick-walled and decrepit, built in the eighteenth and early nineteenth centuries. And scattered through the district are factories, foundries and mills whose smoke-belching stacks thicken the layer of black grime that encrusts the good stone of the tenements, and bring down a fog, almost of London type, between the River Clyde to the south and the rising ground to the north where runs the Forth and Clyde Canal. There are not enough of these factories and mills to give work to the population of Bridgeton. Many find work outside the district, some even travel as far west as John Brown's shipyard at Clydebank fully ten miles away; for that yard was, at one time, on the river near Bridgeton and migrated downstream before the present generation, which still continues in the fathers' ways.

At one time these tenements were occupied mainly by the skilled Glasgow engineering tradesmen and shipyard workers. But these men have migrated to more status-giving outer districts of the city nearer the newer factories, or to between-war housing schemes on the outskirts. Their places have been taken principally by unskilled men less able, during the between-war period, to afford the shift, and now awaiting their turn on an enormous list of applicants for houses in the new districts where the City Corporation is

[1] If the close is lined with white porcelain tiles it is known as 'a wally close', and the inhabitants have higher status.

9

desperately building to wipe out the slur of "the worst-housed city in Europe".

The Bridgeton people are mixed in origin, Glasgow Scot and Glasgow Irish. I use 'Glasgow' to distinguish the Scots and Irish peculiar to this city, for the Glasgow Scot is not at all like his national brothers of the neighbouring city of Edinburgh or of the east coast and Border country. Nor are the Glasgow Irish the pure and unadulterated Irish of Eire. These Glasgow 'working men' have been described, with some reason, as the "cockneys of Scotland". I can do no better than to quote a Highland Scotsman with the gift of words, Moray McLaren[1]:

The 'working class' Glaswegian has many qualities in common with the true Cockney. He is humorous, self-reliant, and self-sufficient, and often has an odd Scottish equivalent of the Cockney's perkiness. Like the Cockney he is very fond of enjoying himself on high days and holidays, going about in droves of his own kind with much display of colour and music. He is, however, more emotional or sentimental, as you will, than the Cockney. [But he shows] an agreeably sentimental melancholy [, and] unexpected sad grimness [which the Cockney never has. There are certain characteristics of Glaswegians as a whole,] warmheartedness combined with a love of combat and dispute, liveliness, a lively curiosity, and a capacity for intellectual activity combined with an odd streak of complacency, real generosity in material and spiritual things combined with a very material respect for wealth, a love of sentiment that it would be unfair to call sentimentality, combined with a sharp practicality, a love of, or at least a respect for beauty in art, combined with a native coarseness in custom and expression, a warm, deep and indeed infectious love for their city that sometimes expresses itself in a prickly and uncertain defensiveness about it, and finally a patriotic love for Scotland and Scottish things, a distrust of English manners and ways and politics combined with an exceedingly wistful pride in the title of the 'Second City of the Empire'.

Myself I doubt if the Bridgeton working man has "a capacity for intellectual activity", but there is no doubt that he can talk knowledgeably about politics. Nor would "respect for beauty in art" be a Bridgeton characteristic but undoubtedly there is a "native coarseness in custom and expression", and most certainly a dislike of things English. (Anderson, the manager in the factory to be described, was English.) Otherwise Moray McLaren has given a delightfully accurate 'snapshot' of the Bridgetonian.

The dislike of things English is a common Scottish attitude but it has been strengthened in Glasgow by the Irish element. "The Irish element", says McLaren, "has helped to make the Glasgow character and has contributed to it some of those qualities which we admire in it. Would the Glasgow liveliness and vitality be quite so lively and vital without the admixture of Irish blood? Would the celebrated 'Glesca' type which is the joy of music-hall audiences, and the repetition of whose terse and witty sayings fills so many columns of the Glasgow press, be quite so much himself without that

[1] *The Scots*, Pelican, London, 1951, pp. 90–97.

10

faint but pervasive touch of Irishness in his speech and manner? And finally, has not the Irish element contributed largely to the reputation of the Glasgow soldier in warfare of which Glasgow is justly proud?"[1] Bridgeton has much of this Irish element.

The main influx of the Irish into Glasgow began with the great Irish famine of the 1840's when so many emigrated to America. Most emigrants, however, came to Scotland prepared to take the most menial jobs for the lowest of wages.[2] The great majority were Roman Catholics who herded together in the poorest quarters and tended to intermarry and have large families. On the whole they remain the poorest of the 'working class', taking the lowest paid, unskilled jobs. They are not upwardly mobile in the 'status rat-race'.

These 'small, dark men', the Irish, after three generations are now British citizens, but they retain affection for the land of their forefathers. Their "convivial violence" is, on the whole, restricted towards their own people and towards their hereditary enemies, the Protestant Irish of Ulster, 'Orange-men' who migrated with them. The battles between these groups are notor-ious[3] and probably more fierce than in Ireland itself. The split, epitomised in religious differences, has spread to other social institutions, not the least important being that of football. For here in Glasgow, football is a social institution.

Of the two most prominent football teams in the city, one, Glasgow Celtic, as its name betokens is Irish in practically every way. Its team flag is Irish green, its jerseys too. The majority of players bear Irish names. The other team is Glasgow Rangers, supported by Protestants, sporting a blue flag and jerseys—the St Andrew's cross of Scotland is blue and white. When these two teams join battle on the field so do their supporters, and blood is shed on the spectator embankment during the match, and in the streets and pubs afterwards. This battle of the teams has come to be known as "the auld firm", a day of tribulation for the police force. On this football institu-tion has centred many of the fierce loyalties of the Glasgow working man, and his football has become of great consequence to him, a subject of perpetual discussion and argument, more important still with the innovation of 'the football pools'. It is also of economic importance to him for he must, perforce, spend money to see a match to be able to talk about it, spend money to meet his cronies in the pub to share his knowledge of it, and have enough to try his weekly luck on 'the pools', that ever-beckoning, elusive road to a life of luxury and ease.

[1] McLaren, ibid., p. 94.   [2] Oakley, C. A., *The Second City*, London, 1946.
[3] As a student in the late 1920's, I experienced this at first hand when working during vacation in a Glasgow factory. As a Protestant, I was called upon by a rosette-wearing Orangeman to join in a set-up fight behind the foundry wall.

In the industrial world, the Glasgow Irish are not strong trade unionists like the Glasgow Scots. They are not the people from whom sprang the leaders of militant trade unionism and of the labour movement; men like Keir Hardie, Smillie, Kirkwood and Maxton. Nevertheless they have something of the same Celtic fire, that sense of righteousness in belief in the equality and difference of men which activated such great trade unionists and which gave U.S.A. its John L. Lewis and Philip Murray. They do not lead the Glasgow Scot, they follow, and follow impetuously as is their nature. From the Scots they have learned the tradition of anti-authoritarianism which, to my mind, is the outstanding trait of the Clydeside working man so often called "Red". The strong Roman Catholicism of the Glasgow Irish does not permit them to be "Red"—nor are the Glasgow Scots "Red" for that matter.

This anti-authoritarianism springs from the core of Clydeside industry, the shipbuilding. The character of the product, the ship, cannot lead to continuous employment, so there is frequent dismissal of men who must seek work elsewhere until another ship is at that stage of construction when they can be again employed. It is thus "a hard industry", and the employer, the source of authority, incurs the odium of the men so forced to migrate in and out of shipbuilding. And it is the unskilled or partly skilled labour which suffers most, labour so often Glasgow Irish, migrating from job to job, into factories, back to the yards, and again to the factories, carrying with them this sense of employer injustice, and infecting other labour. They may have learned that this is the way of shipbuilding and do not much mind their mobility, but they cannot forget or dismiss the sense of their being pawns in the hands of a seemingly immoral management. This kind of work life, a permanent insecurity of occupation, and a smouldering dislike and distrust of the employer and managerial class, has a profound effect upon the man— and upon his family too, for he takes home his feelings of frustration and insecurity, and vents them upon his kith and kin. It is not to be wondered that his children, reared in such an atmosphere, perpetuate the attitudes so transmitted.

In the Glasgow Irish household the father plays a much more dominant and domineering rôle than the Glasgow Scottish father. This may seem antithetical to the general concept of the Presbyterian household with its accent upon the stern, unbending authoritarian father. But it is so. The woman has a large say in the economy of the Scottish household. For example, it is very common (how common I cannot say *precisely*) for the Scotsman to hand over his pay-packet to his wife on a Friday pay day. From it she extracts his "pocket-money", "cigarette-money", and "beer-money" and hands this to him, keeping the rest. In the Irish household the man hands to his wife what he considers is necessary for her housekeeping and which may or may not cover more than just food and other necessities. The historical background to this cannot be enlarged upon here, suffice to say that the Irish 'system' stems from the age-old Irish agricultural tradition—well described by Arensberg in his studies of the Irish community in Eire—whereas the Lowland Scottish importance of the wife in economic control has its roots in another culture, the North Sea Littoral, which is essentially a fishing culture.

The Roman Catholic Glasgow Irish father is probably more of an autocrat than the Protestant Glasgow Scot—this can be seen in the 'idealised' family scenes from local playwrights, and in 'newspaper strips' which are so popular. The child, brought up in this atmosphere, sees the father as a source of unbending power (and of physical force frequently employed), as a giver of all sustenance, doled out by the mother accordingly as the father provides. Sometimes he does not. He may be a conscientious provider for his family, but the 'improvident Irishman' often squanders his wages on beer, liquor and racing, and brings little to the house. A circular system of pawning domestic goods and trading the pawn-tickets is practised in these tenements by the neighbouring womenfolk who seem to accept this as a normal way of living. After all, it is what they have been accustomed to. The woman has little or no say in what the lord and master of her household does with his earnings or himself, despite a frequent and lively use of female vituperation. She may herself seek solace by vicarious identification with players in "the picters", the cinema, while her children roam the streets to battle for themselves. Her husband's round of non-working life is also fairly circumscribed. Two or three visits to the pub each week with "a big do" on Friday pay-night, and a Saturday night "after the match" to talk football; and politics, for here in Glasgow politics is important, tied up as it is with religion and nationalism. Not all the men are like this; many are conscientious father-providers, but almost all are autocrats in their own, domestic, sphere of authority.[1]

In this atmosphere the small boy-child, still on his mother's knee or clinging to her skirt, sees the father as an all-powerful figure, meting out punishment from great strength, and the source of reference for authority in behaviour—"be good or else your father will . . . , etc." What is right is the father's word—the law. Yet in such an atmosphere uncertainty reigns. There is no regularity of feeding, as prescribed by modern medical men pandering to the needs of a middle class, but the more primitive technique of feeding when food is available or when the child yells for it long enough. Even then the child may not get it. He learns to take what he can whenever he can get

---

[1] The ensuing description of the development of the Bridgetonian may appear to have little to do with his behaviour in a factory. But it has, as I propose to show in analysing that behaviour.

13

it. His mother is no certain tower of refuge. There is the emphatic law of right in the father but little complementary law of good in the mother. (It is small wonder that in the adult stage the man seeks for his own personal good and rejects the power of the law.)

In the period between knee-child and immediately pre-school age the boy finds himself cast on to the street to spend his time with his 'eeldons'[1] in play. He is now more mobile and so can avoid more often the supreme power of the father whose authority, however, is still effective. At the same time the boy finds his mother rejects him more and more, not only to look after a younger child, but to send him "out of the way" while she carries on her work, escapes to a make-believe world at the cinema, or gossips with neighbours leaning from adjoining windows, "a good hang-out", to translate from the local dialect. Uncertainty continues and he becomes more aware of the dichotomy between father and mother.

His play centres round football mainly, and some more primitive child games. The football is not a team game but one of indiscriminate kicking, egocentric in character; there is no organisation but an elementary form of coherence in which each child plays for self-pleasure, yet, in the doing, commences to recognise the differences in character and temperament of his playmates. This can be beautifully seen in street play and in school playgrounds. There are no 'leaders' in the usually accepted sense of that word, there is more of a 'pecking order'. The order does not seem to depend on brute strength or size but on aggressiveness and belligerence. A small, wiry fellow will often be seen to start up some game, or to change a game, and larger boys to follow suit. This kind of elementary grouping, not organised and with no explicit purpose, I have called 'turbate',[2] and I shall refer to it again. It is the most primitive form of the social group as distinct from the crowd. It is the group wherein personality differences first begin to have significance.

The school child from five to about eleven or twelve years, develops his learning of social living still further. He learns from his father, from his elder brothers and from example of his senior playmates that he must be "tough", that fighting on the drop of a hat or any other form of challenge is a recognised social activity. He learns to jeer at strangers and at any who do not conform to his conception of "toughness". He is no longer egocentric; he conforms to his play-group and therein finds a security of unity. The group's norms become his. No longer is rule external and sacred, vested in the father, it is now vested in the group as well. His games, especially football, are organised and become central in his boy thinking. The game-group is structured according to the part each has to play in the game,

---

[1] The Scottish for 'same age grade'.

[2] Paterson, T. T. and F. J. Willett, Unofficial Strike *Soc. Rev.* XLIII, 1951.

though the rôle-takers are decided (subconsciously) on a basis of personality fitness. And with this structuring of play-groups, and the demand for conformity, there comes a developing interest in rules and regulations. Games will be stopped to settle arguments on the 'fairness' of behaviour, with seeming heat and aggressiveness, loud shouting and threatening gestures, and, inevitably, a battle. There is intense preoccupation with what is 'right' in the sense of being 'fair', which means that a framework of values is conceived against which behaviour is judged. The rules, which constitute the value system, are the play-group rules or the gang rules, neither written nor explicit, but clearly perceived nonetheless. These rules, which vary from gang to gang, are necessary to the game or to the gang-behaviour as the boy senses them, but the reason for such rules is not rational—as their variation demonstrates. This kind of social group, more advanced than the turbate, I have elsewhere named 'gregal'.[1] Whereas the turbate group can roughly be said to be irrational and unorganised, the gregal group may be described loosely as irrational yet organised.

To indicate a line of thought to be developed later—the turbate form of group is typical of pub-life, the gregal group is typical of the pre-adult street gang and of the factory work groups. It is in the gregal group that the Bridgetonian learns the use of the word 'fair', and it is the work group which decides the values behind what is 'fair' in the factory. By very reason of its social origin 'fairness' has a high emotional content so to speak, so that, to the observer (who often is the manager) fairness may be illogical. On the other hand, it may appear logical to an observer who sees it as satisfying needs arising from belonging to a work group. And 'fairness', since it stems from group activity, is regarded as 'right'.

As the boy fends for himself on the street he is also subjected to another discipline in school. Here he meets a new external power, the teacher (almost always a woman) who, by right of being the teacher, has power to compel the boy to do things that he may not want to do. This is the ordinated society,[2] of purposive social groupings, therefore rational and organised. Here the boy finds a totally different atmosphere from that of the gang. Compulsion and repression, normal concomitants of the ordinate group, symbolised by the teacher, have to be countered. The boys "gang-up" on her, depending upon whether she is "a soft mark" or a stern authoritarian. The gang, if the class is allowed to sit where it likes, will retire to the back away from the 'strong' teacher and collect in the front near the 'weak', where they can flaunt their anti-authoritarianism and even break out in rebellion. For the teacher to avoid what is normally called "insubordination", she must be, in the eyes of the boys, "fair". By that they mean no favouritism or unjustifiable punishment. Punishment that is deserved is never objected

[1] Paterson and Willett, op. cit.　　[2] Paterson and Willett, op. cit.

15

to, and the boy who does object comes under the taunt of "cissy" or "no sport". In objecting to favouritism the boys seem, as far as I can make out, to be concerned with equality of treatment.

In the same vein they look askance upon "the swot" who studies too hard. Either he is trying to curry favour or else he is not conforming to the standard practice, the norm of his gang. A boy who does well because he is clever, without swotting, is accepted. Difference is allowed, inequality is not. (So in a factory a man must not labour too hard, but if he is clever and makes more money because of his skill, not his labour, then he is permitted to do so.) Here the boy is learning to be more concerned with what his group (gang) thinks of him rather than with worthwhile activities of a more self-gratifying nature. This makes for serious difficulties should the boy come from a household where the pattern is more truly Scottish than Irish. In the Scottish household work is considered 'good'. The adjective 'hard-working' is almost always prefixed by 'good', or else it is tacitly understood. To do well at school, for education is also 'good', is another belief in the Scottish household. Doing well is allowed by the gang but not 'hard-working'. So the boy, if he is that way inclined, surreptitiously does his 'hard-working' in order to do well, and will be one of the first to shout "Bah! Swot!" at another, for it is "right", according to the gang mores, that a boy should not swot. This clash of 'good' and 'right' the boy carries with him into adult life.

Adolescent, he apes his elders, smoking, going to the football match, lounging, frequenting billiard saloons because he is barred from the holy of holies, the pub. And he clashes with that other great external authority, society, in the form of the police. It is the law of his gang and his neighbourhood which matters to him, not the law of the nation. He is judged by his neighbours not by the nation. Sent here by "they", the policeman is punitive, not protective. The neighbourhood is protective, even though, as his mother did, it may reject him when he seeks security in it. He needs to "go about in droves of his own kind".

Leaving school as early as he can (at 15) he looks for work to yield him a living, for his parents "expect some good of him" as the expression is. He is approaching man's estate which is symbolised by a man's wage and the right of entry to the pub at eighteen. His emancipation is completed about nineteen to twenty-one when he becomes, to all intents and purposes, a lodger in his parents' house, that is if he has not already married. This final stage is almost always accompanied by a "dust-up", a kind of expected ritual quarrel, which symbolises the mother's desire to keep him tied to her, and his desire to escape finally. Before this break he is expected to accept his father's continuing domination even though he may resent it and be able to retaliate physically. After this break the father's authority is dispelled and the young man is free to "dree his ain weird", to settle his own fate. And this he does by becoming, as his father before him, authoritarian yet anti-authoritarian, individualist yet closely conforming to the demands of his group, more concerned with what people round about think of him than with struggling to remove himself to another society, more concerned with being "a' richt" (a "regular guy") than with getting up in the world and so being a non-conformist, for being "a' richt" makes life in the pub and the factory so much more easy and pleasant.

THE MANAGER AND TRADE UNION ORGANISER

It is a most difficult situation for me to describe these men well enough to give the reader a fair conception of them. I had thought at first to let the historical details produce their own picture, but the inevitable happened. My own impression of these men, in my company, was quite different from the men's impression of them; certainly their behaviour towards the men was not what it would be towards me. I can, therefore, give an impression that the reader might have got, not what the men got. (This is forced upon me since the men altered their views about the manager considerably.)

Anderson, the manager, was in his middle thirties, a medium tall man, lean, with a longish face and features, eyes somewhat deep set and dark as was his hair. He had a quick manner; I would not call it nervous but rather one giving the feeling of energy, of wanting to get things done, of (perhaps) a little intolerance of that which could stand in the way of getting things done. I would guess him to be what psychologists would call an extrovert. He talked quickly and emphatically, and would cut across another's talk to take up an idea he seized from that talk. That means it was easy "to make contact" with him. He was receptive of ideas, but tended to be impetuous in following them up. He was a sound and qualified engineer who made engineering and management a whole-time job, day and night.

I was convinced that he was sincere in his approaches to the men even at the most exasperating times. A quickness of extrovert temper, unalloyed by any fine sense of humour, did not make things more easy for him, and this, coupled with a fluent command of non-parlour language, did not appear to make him quite the 'ideal' managerial type. But as Maloney, one of the men, said, "Mr Anderson's bark is worse than his bite". It was not the form of the language but the content that mattered, and, as it so happened, to these men long accustomed to anything but mealy-mouthed language, the use of "bloody" as an emphatic rather than an expletive or epithet, was normal. The same could be said of their interpretation of the rest of Anderson's language. I did note that he never used words taboo to the men. This he may have learned during the war—he was certainly aware of their character. His impetuousness, ruggedness, downrightness, was not everybody's "cup of tea". Myself, I liked him.

Macdonald, the trade union organiser, was altogether different from Anderson. Nearly twenty years older than him, he was tall and fair, heavily built with steady eyes, slow-spoken, quiet-mannered. Slow to take up a difficult point, but steadily capable of hammering away until he got it, he would discuss any matter of industrial relations in a most illuminating fashion. For he was one of the old-guard trade unionists, had always been one, with a steadfast belief in unionism and the benefits it has gained. His trouble, and he had plenty of it at Glasgow Ltd, was that the men he stood for did not always stand for him—not an uncommon complaint voiced by trade union officials. Nevertheless, he was completely convinced that, however much he privately disagreed with the men he represented, their belief was what mattered. I would go so far as to say that he was as professional towards the men as a lawyer towards his client—and this will appear in the story. Given a cause he was most tenacious and, if the worst came to the worst, he was quite capable of replying to Anderson in terms as colourful. I should imagine, though I never saw it, that he could show considerable anger if driven to it. His wry sense of humour kept this from occurring too often in situations tending to temper-losing but requiring tact and restraint. Everyone had good to say of him.

CHAPTER 3

THE FACTORY

Two main types of product were manufactured by Glasgow Ltd and these are here called *bigparts* and *weeparts*.[1] There were twelve variations of these two types but the differences were minor. Both were usually sold completely assembled, but the constituent portions were also sold to other establishments for assembly there. A section of the factory was set aside for the finishing treatment of non-assembled weeparts (N.A.P.); this work was done by women, and it was part of the factory system which is of little or no interest to this study, except that when demand for the non-assembled weeparts increased the manager had to decide how much he reduced the production of assembled weeparts, which is a main concern of the study.

There were, therefore, essentially two production-lines; and these were a curious mixture of new and old techniques. Raw materials were prepared and fed into the "new" section, the lines of machines which almost automatically roll, press, weld, grind and bore. The "old" section of the line was assembly, which was done entirely by hand. In factories in other parts of the United Kingdom and America similar assembly work is mechanised but, after the change which is to be described, the old method in Glasgow Ltd was found to be nearly as profitable. By the time of writing the line has just become wholly mechanised.

Apart from one change[2] on the weepart production line during the two years, 1948 to 1950, described in Part II, there was no variation in specification of either product—they were completely standardised. So, because the demand did not vary outside fairly narrow limits, they were produced on a maximum-minimum stock basis.[3] The system was essentially mass-production in large batches, and on each of the two lines, simple though they were, mass-production techniques were used. Their simplicity made easier the understanding of the managerial process and industrial relations. The usual problems of mass-production lines, monotony, effect of changing work-load, incentives, human relations and supervision, were also easier to understand in such a simple set-up, the more so because machinery, techniques, and physical conditions did not alter throughout the five-year period to be considered in detail.

---

[1] The nature of the products cannot be divulged, nor details of techniques, in the interests of anonymity.　　　　　　　　　　[2] The temporary manufacture of longparts.

[3] Production was not governed immediately by demand. A minimum stock was held ready to meet demands, and a maximum level was set in order to limit capital thus tied up.

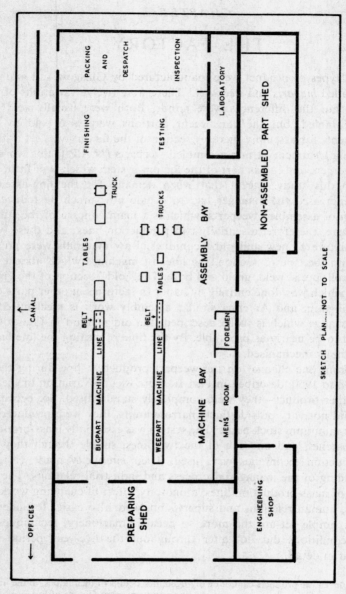

Fig. 1. The factory lay-out.

The flow of production was preparation → machining → assembly → finishing → storing and despatch; and the building was laid out accordingly. The raw materials were brought into a preparing-shed, where they were inspected, cut, and then prepared for feeding into the machines. The men in the preparing-shed worked on a variety of jobs, and were paid a time-rate with bonus for tonnage handled. This tonnage depended upon what the machines took, whether they worked at a high or low rate, and since the rate depended upon the efforts of the machinemen and assemblers, the earnings of the preparing-shed men depended marginally upon the efforts of these others. Seven or eight feeders-in wheeled the prepared parts into the machine-bay and fed them into the machines at the behest of the machine controllers.

In the machine-bay were the two long machine-lines, each largely governed by a machine-controller. He was usually seated at a control desk at the end next the assembly-bay where he could watch the speed of work of the assemblers and adjust the rates of the machines accordingly. His duties also included seeing to the setting of the various controls along the machine line, and on this setting depended, to a great extent, the quality of the finished product. He had, in a way, authority over the feeders-in since he told them at what pace to supply the line. But this was an anomalous authority since the feeders-in were directly responsible to the foreman who frequently oversaw the controllers' work, giving advice and orders. The two machine-lines were somewhat similar and controlled in the same fashion.

The bigpart machine-line fed its products, which were comparatively large and heavy, on to a wide conveyor belt which extended into the assembly-bay. At the end of the belt the part rolled on to a table where templates and other gear were removed with the aid of small machines. It was then lifted on to a table where it was dressed, lined up and finally machined. This machining could also be done (if special orders required) at an adjacent table or in the so-called "bigpart area" of the finishing-shed. A trucker wheeled the parts into the finishing-shed where they were heat-treated, tested, coloured, coated and dried, before being sent into the packing- and despatch-shed.

The weepart machine-line fed its products on to a conveyor-belt which was not so big as that on the other machine-line; the parts were smaller and came off the machines at a correspondingly higher rate. The parts were picked up in turn by two men who came from each of three groups of four assemblers, and were placed on a trestle-table adjacent to each of three assembly tables. After they had been assembled, dressed and completed they were placed on waiting trucks to be taken to the finishing-shed by the truckers.

Both machine-lines were run on a three-shift continuous cycle. Seven feeders-in supplied both machines, and there was a machine-assembly foreman for each shift. The General Foreman could come on any shift, usually the day-shift, so that he could supervise maintenance and also the non-assembled weepart shed (shut down at night); but occasionally he turned up on a night-shift if mechanical or other trouble was anticipated. He was expert on the machine side. There were, of course, the various preparatory men as well, and truckers, finishers and other occupational groups, but they do not much concern us.

Only the bigpart and weepart machinemen and assemblers are to be considered. They were paid a basic wage-rate of so much per hour, and their earnings were increased by an incentive bonus calculated on a piece-rate (payment-by-results—PBR). For bigpart, and separately for weepart, men the bonus was calculated on output of all three shifts over each week; that is to say, it was a three-shift pool-bonus scheme. (The feeders-in benefited correspondingly.) It meant that even though one shift were to work especially hard its members would not earn more than the members of the other shifts. To calculate the bonus a standard rate of output, so many tons per week, was taken as the norm, 60, and rates were measured against this. (Allowances were made for mechanical breakdowns.) For every unit-increase in productivity above 50 the bonus was increased by one farthing per hour.

In calculating final bonus a deduction was made for spoilage, measured by tons of spoiled parts as a percentage of tonnage handled. Since it was total tonnage handled, including spoiled parts, upon which the assemblers were paid their bonus, and since the total spoilage was revealed only at inspection, this index was a measure (inverse to productivity) of the skill of the assemblers. In order to save materials spoiled parts were not scrapped but dismantled and sent back to the preparing-shed.

Inspecting took place in the finishing-shed. Apart from inspection for spoilage, statistically-selected samples were examined for quality of materials. The management had devised a measure of relative quality expressed as an index higher than a standard of unity, and taken to the third decimal. It is unnecessary to expand on this index, but it was essentially a measure of the skill of the machine-controllers, who were paid a penny an hour more than assembly men. There was no adjustment of pay if quality varied.[1]

There were fifteen men on each shift on the bigpart line, four distributed along the line, from the feed-in to the controlling-point, including the controller. Ten men worked in the assembly-bay and bigpart area of the finishing-shed, and one trucker-cum-crane man manœuvred the parts from the bay to the shed.

The line-men could move up and down the line watching machines and keeping in touch with the controller, but the eight assembly-men were

[1] Unfortunately I was not allowed access to statistics on quality. All I could gather was that quality improved contemporaneously with the striking increase in productivity which was the most remarkable of the changes to be described.

comparatively distant from each other. They worked in pairs at opposite sides of the part, which kept them about ten feet away from each other. Since the machine-bay was not screened off from the assembly-bay the noise of machinery made speech at this distance difficult. The men had to shout to each other, and to the controller to whom they usually signalled by gesture. This difficulty was not so pronounced in the finishing-shed. It was only when each pair passed a part to another pair for treatment that they could converse ordinarily, and then each only with the man on the same side. There was a leading man in the gang of assembly men. The line men were not under his jurisdiction but under that of the foreman.

On the weepart line there were several crew compositions. The crew at the time of writing consisted of twenty-four, that is seventy-two for all three shifts. At one time this was as high as eighty-six and has been as low as fifty-four. For each shift there were nine men on the machine-line proper, including the controller; and on the assembly there were three gangs of four with three spare men for either line or assembly work.

The line-men, working on either side of the portion of the line which they watched and dealt with, could move up and down fairly easily, but communication was not easy because of the noise. The noise was bad enough in the assembly bay, but was not so overpowering, and the assembly-men could talk with more ease. Each gang of four assemblers worked close enough to be able to talk to each other, and to gossip as they worked. Their job was physically hard, an aspect of its unskilled character, but this did not prevent them from laughing and joking as they went at it. Occasionally, one gang would stop working while the others continued; sometimes the stoppage was purely the result of lack of parts from the conveyor belt, but each gang took turn to stop and rest. This resting was not allowed to continue too far—the other two gangs saw to it that the third did not slack. In this way, the weepart assembly-men had the breaks necessary in such a strenuous job, and a spare man could be brought in to relieve any man who seemed unable to cope with the prevailing tempo of the work.

The machine-controllers on both lines were constantly trying to speed up the flow of parts, but the reaction of the assembly-gangs on the two lines was quite different. On the bigpart line the parts flowed forward on the belt, piling up against preceding parts if these had not been removed. Since the parts were heavy and there was great difficulty in removing them from such a "jam" the conveyor pair of the assembly-gang made strenuous efforts to prevent this state of affairs. "I can fairly make them sweat", said a bigpart controller. On the weepart line the assemblers resisted controller pressure by refusing to handle what they considered to be too heavy a load. The controller had to conform to the pace set by the assemblers. If the work piled up due to controller pressure the foreman would be forced to order him to desist otherwise work would stop. The foreman could not order the assembly-men to take whatever came off the machine-line. There were also differences between the two lines in attitude to work, which will be described at a more appropriate point.

The machine- and assembly-bays were overlooked by the foreman's office which was placed at floor-level just on the line between the two bays. The foreman's duties also included overseeing the N.A.P. shed so that he was not constantly present in the two bays. The Works Manager's office and that of his Production Manager and clerical staff were outside the factory building itself, nearly 100 yards away, so that the office staff were seldom seen by the factory staff, and the manager was not always "on the spot".

There were ten shop stewards, all in the same union, one for bigparts, three for weeparts, two for the shift-workers in the finishing-sheds, one for day-workers and women, one in the stores and despatch-shed, one in the laboratory (which was big for a factory of this size) and a chairman. They were appointed by the usual formal democratic election.

PART II. HISTORICAL

INTRODUCTION

Not long after the end of the war, productivity being low and labour turnover high, an incentive scheme was introduced at the factory. This apparently did little to help either and brought with it a series of strikes and other disturbances which led to the removal of the manager in 1950, and to his replacement by another, Anderson. This historical section is concerned mainly with that background to Anderson's arrival, and with his effort to raise productivity. As for most managers, productivity was central to all his thinking. It did rise, dramatically and suddenly, in 1952, and from that time has remained high, and unaccompanied by strife. The cause of this change is the theme for study.

This Part is intended to give a picture of what happened in the form of a plain non-statistical narrative of the sequence of events as manager and men appeared to see them, of their reaction and counter-reaction. It seems that Anderson was not much affected by historical background, but the men were. This is not uncommon. A study of even a comparatively well-run enterprise like I.C.I. shows that managers tend "to act upon incident rather than upon precedent", as one of my research students so aptly put it. This seems to me to be a failing of managers. History has a lot to teach commanders of men whose memories of events, especially emotionally charged events, are not apt to disappear like straws in the passing wind of time.

The change, which is of so much interest, came about unexpectedly. Indeed, it was not until I called Anderson's attention to it that he recognised something vital had happened at a critical period. This is the stuff of history. Great events are recognised by the participants only after they have passed through them and can look back as a kind of detached observer of themselves. Or else the events are to be seen at their happening only by the unbiased observer removed from all participation.

CHAPTER 4

BEFORE ANDERSON'S ARRIVAL

Up to 1946 there was no incentive to special effort by the workmen on weeparts; there was no piece-rate system, no bonus scheme; the men, unskilled, were paid according to a national time-rate. In June 1946, a payment-by-results scheme (called a bonus scheme) was introduced, stated as 3½d. per hour to be paid when productivity reached a 60.[1] The payments were to begin with a penny per hour when a 50 was reached, with an increase of ¼d. per hour for each unit increase in productivity thereafter, "irrespective of the number of workers employed on the process". Prior to inception of the system, productivity was about a 26. The scheme had no significant effect on productivity, which reached a 35 and 40 in several weeks during the last part of 1946. It reached a 44 in the first week of 1947 but at once reverted to between a 35 and 40.

In the second week of February the men were told that a new product, longparts, was being introduced which meant a change on the machine-line and tables. The effect of this information was immediate. The men already having apparent difficulty in increasing productivity and so "making bonus" instituted a short go-slow in protest at what they thought was likely to make good earnings even more difficult to achieve. They worked the full hours, but productivity dropped from a 40 to a 19. This recovered by March when mixed longpart and weepart production commenced. There was an immediate drop in productivity culminating in a strike just before the Easter weekend. Productivity rose sharply as the men adjusted quickly to the change and, with 100 per cent longpart production, reached a rate similar to that before its manufacture started. Nevertheless, they did not seem to make any further headway and dissatisfaction was expressed in a short, sharp strike, a "down-tools", in May. Thereafter, productivity began to rise rapidly and immediately to a 40 and, four weeks later, to the bonus target of a 50.

But this gain was short-lived. Three weeks before "The Fair", as the mid-summer holiday is called in Glasgow, a falling-off in demand for longparts required mixing production with weeparts. That meant allowances for waiting-time when machines were altered, but they were not sufficient to bring earnings to an acceptable level; they were "not fair allowances". As longpart production dropped still further, dissatisfaction grew and culminated

[1] This figure represents the weight of output assumed as normally produced per hour, and is an index common in work study and analyses. In most factories, as here, the figure is usually preceded in speech by the indefinite article.

in a strike in the middle of August. It was a short strike, about one shift, but apparently it had the same effect as its predecessor for, in September, productivity began to rise, even on weepart production alone.

Sales Department were "on their toes", and in November brought in some "solid orders" for longparts. The line was altered to longpart production at once. This time it had no apparent effect on the men whose productivity continued to rise as it had been doing since the strike. They were now steadily "making bonus".

The beginning of 1948 brought continuation of the steady increase in productivity on 100 per cent longpart manufacture. But production on longparts was suddenly cut to an average of about 15 per cent in February; and productivity dropped. This recovered when 100 per cent longpart production was resumed in March; and the rate of improvement increased until, in May, productivity reached its highest level for the year, a 67.

In the first week in June the men were warned that, after the Fair holiday, longpart production would be reduced. There was an immediate "down tools" for a few hours in protest, and thereafter productivity started to fall away rapidly right up to the week before the holiday.[1] In that week no bonus was earned with productivity at a 40. This decrease in effort continued after the holiday—again an abnormal phenomenon for, in the previous three years, productivity increased on the men's return. Longpart manufacture was now varying between 10 and 15 per cent of the total each week. Another short protest strike in the third week in August emphasised the men's difficulties in making bonus. Their productivity figures rose slowly, but the complaints about machine changes for longpart manufacture were rife.

By the autumn weekend holiday, longpart production was practically nil and productivity started to rise, reaching a 63 for October. Then about 5 per cent longpart manufacture was demanded by 'Sales' at the beginning of November. Again productivity fell, accompanied by a short protest strike in the middle of that month. There was little improvement until January, 1949, when longpart production finally stopped. For the next few months weepart productivity remained fairly constant, about a 57.

It was during this period of 1947 to 1948 that the Trade Union began to organise in this factory. By 1948 over 80 per cent possible membership had been achieved and the local district organiser started to take an active part in men-management relations. Prior to 1947 the manager had refused to have the union in the factory. (Of this period, 1947–48, there is little in the trade union files because, so I was told, the organiser was "mainly trying to make gentlemen's agreements—but the managers were not gentlemen!")

Productivity remained stable around a 57 for the first six months of 1949,

[1] It is usually expected that men work harder to make more money in anticipation of the holiday—usually, that is, in mines and in engineering works.

but in May signs of discontent began to appear. Union membership started to decline rapidly. The factory secretary wrote to his headquarters that the union were "on the verge of losing 100 members" and only thirty were paying their dues. The district organiser, Macdonald, met the men and by June practically the whole of the factory had resumed or assumed membership.

Absenteeism began building up after the 1949 Easter holiday and was strongly marked before and after the Fair holiday at which time productivity fell to a 46. The ostensible cause was suspicion in the minds of the men that they were not being paid a bonus comparable to that being earned by similar workers elsewhere. Accordingly the union organiser made enquiries of his opposite number in a similar factory in England where the men, it was found, appeared to be paid the same bonus for only two-thirds of the Glasgow output per hour. This brought about a meeting of the acting manager (in the absence of the manager himself) with Macdonald and the factory union secretary at the end of July.

The acting manager (Bulgin) did not make clear to the men that their information was distorted. In the English factories the basic rate was the same as in Glasgow Ltd, but, because of greater mechanisation the English workers could make more. (This had not been taken into account in setting the rate at Glasgow.) Instead of making this point Bulgin complained bitterly about the weepart workers. "They stop twenty minutes before time,[1] take ten minutes off for tea breaks and leave paper and tea-leaves all over the place." "They are going slow." "Some want to make the bonus and some don't." "There are too many dud parts, badly milled and off line—losing 6 to 8 per cent on rejects." "The crews are not doing as much as they used to."[2] "The leading men are not doing their stuff." He threw out the demand for the same rate as the English factory but suggested that the production could be raised by staggering the crews at meal intervals, two crews off and one on, so that the machines could keep up continuous working. "You can't stop the machines and keep quality." He wanted a "fair do from the men" for he "gave them a fair do." (He did not ask whether the men thought it 'fair'.)

The resentment against the manager—and against the senior foreman who was anti-trade-union—culminated in a strike in August two weeks later, but the men had to go back without satisfaction of their demands for a higher bonus, and agreed to the managerial scheme. A month later, in September, the factory union secretary could write to the branch that there was "quite a lot of unrest", and in October could report that "no material change had

[1] Lateness on arrival was also high.
[2] During 1949 there had been a change in number of men on the tables at the end of the weepart line. The two gang per shift system was changed to three gangs of four men each per shift. Bulgin complained that he was not getting greater total production as he had expected from this increase.

taken place". Nevertheless, productivity was rising, and in November was higher than it had ever been, a 69. This was partly due to slight changes in line techniques as a result of a simple methods study. Labour turnover had increased alarmingly. The exact figures for the weepart line alone are not available, but for the whole factory the proportions of the force employed leaving each *month* were, for that year, consecutively (per cent): 12·5, 15·8, 24·9, 20·7, 20·1, 20, 26·9, 37·5, 8·5, 8·5, 6·4, 6·8. The maximum in August is remarkable for any factory, even for Glasgow Ltd.

These complaints about bonus earnings, from bigpart men as well as weepart men, seemed to stem from dissatisfaction about differentials. Thus Maloney, a prominent weepart man, pointed out to Macdonald that workers not on the production lines were making bonuses of 20/- to 35/- per week, whereas the weepart men were getting only 15/2d. (He blamed this on the machines.) But there was still the feeling that men on the same job in other factories were being paid more. The demands for adjustment were intensified.

Bulgin met the weepart and bigpart men at a meeting in the canteen the third week in December, denied their allegations and refused their demands. He threatened closing down the works, saying that the factory was "small beer" in a large concern and that its closure would not be a loss. "No draught would be felt", he said.

This did nothing to make the men feel any better about the situation and, just over a week later on the last day of the year, a weepart man wrote the union organiser that the management had cut the previous week's bonus, their calculation being different from that of the men.[1] He continued, "the place is in a ferment over this and other things". "The men were inclined not to start today. In fact it took some persuasion on (the foreman's) part to get them started. I am afraid there will be a showdown after the holidays." The union membership, he said, was falling off a little.

The year 1950 opened with Macdonald asking that the weepart men be upgraded in rate of pay—pointing out the differential between them and those men not on the production line. As Maloney wrote him at the end of January, "Up to around three years ago our job in Glasgow Ltd carried 1½d. above the basic but the basic increased while our rate stood still. Two months later the weepart men discovered that the basic got 1½d. which brought them up to the same." The organiser also pointed out to management the differential between the weepart men and operatives elsewhere. The directorate of the firm invited him to see the operatives at another factory working on a fully mechanised line, not partly as at Glasgow Ltd.

Productivity still remained at a level of about a 63 but the grumblings

---

[1] The men had included three hours on a Saturday morning—at an 83—as a full day's work, but the management had not done so. Note that the line even at that time was capable of producing at this high rate.

continued and discipline worsened. Two men, for example, were sacked on that account in January. Then the manager put his foot in it. In the second week of February, Maloney wrote the union organiser: "As you know when Mr Raymond[1] left here, he instructed us to get in touch with you if our bonus should fall. I am afraid that time has now come. From when Mr Raymond left, up till last week, things had been going splendidly, our percentage figures had been steadily rising, three weeks ago we reached a 70 and a fortnight ago a 69. We were aiming to keep these figures that way but Mr Bulgin had other ideas. For the first three days of last week our figures averaged a 69 then Mr Bulgin introduced that old bone of contention the dual boring unit and our figures slumped for the rest of the week, not through the fault of the men, but certainly through that of the unit. We finished up the week with an average of a 63 the lowest since Mr Raymond's visit."

The previous manager had realised the inequity of penalising the men for mechanical faults. This manager did not: "After having seen the unit working and producing almost nothing for two hours he said the men need not worry; as he would not penalise them for the fault of the unit. Now Mr Bulgin, anticipating trouble, called in O'Donnell and I last Monday. He explained to us that as there were certain types being made on the triple boring unit that he did not want (though he admitted that export would take them, but that did not satisfy the home customer), and others which he wanted that he could not get he would have to change the unit, he said we could not always work with the triple unit. His first proposition was that we use a triple unit on the night-shift. We reminded him that we had an agreement made with Mr Raymond that a triple unit would not be worked unless in conjunction with the side-assembly and he dropped the point. He said they have teething-troubles with new units in every factory and they would have to persevere with the dual unit. We asked that some concession be made until the unit was working properly as was made by Mr Raymond. His reply was that it was all right for fly-by-night Raymond to give concessions but he wasn't holding the baby.

"He reminded us that if the men were not earning bonus they could not expect to be paid it. I pointed out to him that if the bonus figures averaged a 69 for the first 3 days that was 5¾d. per hour the men had earned it, but they had to lose it through the fault of the unit. He was quite adamant and would not look at our side of the case at all. Then he broached the question of the single boring-unit. We said we had no objection to working this if he adjusted the bonus scheme to meet the single unit, otherwise he could scrap the whole scheme. He said they do this in other factories. We pointed out to him that it entails twice the labour to work the single unit in Glasgow Ltd as it does elsewhere, as the machinery does it, but he just brushed that aside.

[1] A previous manager now visiting-inspector from Head Office.

Well we left with a firm conviction that he is out to bust our bonus whether we like it or not. The men are not satisfied to produce a 70 half the week then see it taken from them the other half. So they have told me to inform you of the facts and get a meeting with Mr Bulgin."

Bulgin persisted in putting in his scheme in the third week of February and the weepart men, who had been working at a 72 on Monday and a 68 on Tuesday walked out on Tuesday evening. The night-shift did not start nor the day-shifts on Wednesday. A meeting held by Macdonald on Wednesday voted to return to work, 80 for and 6 against. Nine men "lifted their books" that week.

Macdonald, with Maloney and O'Donnell, met Bulgin. As the men saw it, production was going up in that they had to handle greater numbers of pieces but, since management calculated the bonus on weight, the bonus was not increased correspondingly with numbers. It meant an increase of about 33 per cent in the number of weeparts per shift with the triple unit and they wanted the appropriate proportional increase. Bulgin was adamant, accused the weepart men of trying to bring out the bigpart men on strike with them, and denied their allegation that he was "interested only in money and not in men".

Macdonald at once got in touch with the Works Director, writing, "The basic for the bonus with the triple unit must be revised". "The rate for the machine is too high and the present bonus system seems to be a reduced quantity alongside more physical efforts as far as the weepart men are concerned." "The matter is urgent," he added, "there is plenty of trouble at the works."

And there was. The rest of the week was quiet, but absenteeism was high the following week. The next week ten men left, some dissatisfied with the wages and conditions and others sacked for indiscipline. Most of these men were newcomers of a few weeks, but some had been in the job for periods relatively long for this occupation with a high labour turnover of short-service men. Three more left before the month was out. During April and May twenty weepart men left, again some of them of comparatively long service. A wave of indiscipline broke out in June, three men leaving in one day at the beginning of the month, saying the wages were unsatisfactory; and five were sacked for disobeying orders.

In May union membership began to drop off and by the beginning of the Fair holiday in July, "the whole business fell flat", according to the factory union secretary. The men were saying that the union was not worth supporting because it did not seem to be getting anywhere in its fight on the bonus for weeparts.[1] But the union was not inactive. Macdonald was busy establish-

---

[1] The whole factory was thus influenced by the weepart trouble even though neither bigpart men nor others had been brought out on strike.

ing his case, by reference to other factories, that the weepart men were being underpaid.

The last week in June, immediately prior to the Fair week in July, productivity dropped sharply to a 51. On their return to work the weepart men did not pick up their former rate, and for about three weeks productivity remained less than a 50.

Maloney, now armed with data on what other workers were getting, approached one of the foremen, Wilson. Wilson had accidentally dropped the information that Glasgow Ltd had higher productivity than any other comparable factory. So Maloney tackled him with this, saying that Bulgin had hidden this from the men. "Was it true or not?" But Wilson said it was the same as at X (where the same kind of work was carried out). "Then," said Maloney, "would you believe it if I showed it to you in black and white, typed out?" "I won't believe it," replied Wilson, "even though it is in type." Whereat Maloney produced the document. Wilson retreated from his original position and emphatically denied all knowledge of what was done elsewhere. This, to Maloney, was clear evidence of what he called "jiggery-pokery".

The men then started a "go-slow" which lasted for the first two weeks in August with productivity rates of a 28 and 45. The manager tried to get over this impasse by increasing the number of men on each table by one, that is, to five each. The men told him, "wrap the scheme round your bloody neck", but it was put in. It had no effect, for productivity did not go beyond a 51 the following week. Twenty-seven men left during these August weeks, some of them comparatively long-lived members of the weepart crews.[1]

During the go-slow, spoilage increased to an exceedingly high figure, to as much as 11 per cent, but in the beginning of September it dropped as productivity rose to a 67, thereafter levelling to about a 64. And contemporaneous with this improvement was the removal of the manager "on a nervous breakdown". He was a man "who gave promises without doing anything about them". He was "not a man to be trusted".

Anderson took over at the beginning of October, 1950.

---

[1] Note that, as the effect of this increase of manpower at the tables shows, it was not the speed of the machine line which was hindering the attainment of the bonus but the effort at the table end.

CHAPTER 5

ANDERSON ARRIVES

During the first three months of Anderson's reign productivity remained fairly constant between a 61 and a 65; but trouble was brewing. The weepart men were demanding a change, and wastage, labour turnover, and accident rate were slowly rising. As Anderson saw it at the time, the bonus scheme as an incentive was "eminently unsound"—he was listening to what the weepart men had to say (see below). So he wrote his Directorate at the end of December with suggestions to review the incentive scheme:

(1) He proposed to cut down the size of the weepart gangs from 5 to 4. "It occurred to me", he wrote, "that by reducing personnel, and in effect paying the redundants' wages to the personnel who were retained, the latter could earn sharply increased bonus." He believed that the machines could not be speeded up sufficiently to provide the greater number of men with an adequate reward. There was also the thought in the back of his mind that he could "cut down the high cost of labour turnover" even though he recognised that the core which remained "had been poisoned".

(2) Instead of calculating bonus as weight of material passing through the machines as a total for all the crews, he proposed to count the number of parts made by each shift and, multiplying by an appropriate conversion factor, calculate the weight of material produced by each shift. That is to say, he intended making numbers of parts produced (easily comprehended by the men) the criteria of bonus earning; rather than a weight which the men could not comprehend. Indeed, this followed the line of argument used by the men in comparing their productivity with that of other shifts, the number of parts made per shift.

There was no positive reaction from the Head Office but Anderson persisted, spending many months in arguing his proposals with his superiors.

The feelings of the weepart men were expressed by the secretary for the shop stewards in a letter to Macdonald in January 1951. He summarised bonus earnings made in the various occupations in the factory which showed that the weepart men were plainly making much less than their efforts justified. He went on:

Now we in the production end on weeparts have had meetings galore with managers and others, as you yourself know. They have always promised to have this rectified but nothing seems to come of it. These bonus figures are not an isolated instance, they are the true position of what is happening week in and week out.

It is farcical when men on actual production receive a bonus only equal to a quarter of the men handling the stuff made by them. Then they have the cheek to ask why are the men discontented on the job. As the final unit gets off-true we lose production.[1] We are lucky if we make a 60 and when Friday comes we are throwing away the bonus we have earned, as sometimes we drop as low as a 30. It only takes one bad shift to knock a good week's figures haywire. There seems to be a dead set against the weepart side in this shop. They are the only ones who fight to better their conditions and the only ones who get nowhere. There is content everywhere except here because the men have got something for their labour.

At one time . . . the men on this job had 1½d. above the basic and this coupled with their shift percentage made them the highest paid men on the shift. Nowadays, their rate is the basic and their earnings the lowest of all. When the bonus scheme was introduced it was for weepart men only as an inducement to keep them on the job. Now they are the only ones who don't get a bonus irrespective of the fact that the output of the machines has increased by over 50 per cent. When we have good figures it is pointed out on our bonus slips that our bonus would be a lot better if we had not so many rejects, but they won't admit that the weight of this came from inferior parts made by machines driven at an excessive speed.[2]

This brought Macdonald into action. He wrote Anderson and pointed out some of these discrepancies, little knowing that Anderson, of his own accord, had become aware of them and was taking action. Macdonald also questioned what would happen when the fifth member of a gang was absent— was his wage split among the others, meaning, if four men did the same job as five, would the total wage of the four equal that of the five? This, of course, was akin to what Anderson had been thinking when considering reduction of personnel.

One of the first things Anderson began on his arrival was a ritual of taking the leading men to see what had been done during the previous twenty-four hours—by this means knowledge of the earnings of all three shifts was passed to each shift and, so he thought, would inspire a spirit of competition. He added to this technique by putting up a chart to show everyone the same thing. In January Macdonald requested that this be stopped. "There should be no competition within the factory," he said, "there should be co-operation of the men, and as a union."

February saw nearly a ten-unit increase in productivity over January— though labour turnover remained the same. But accident rate and absentee-ism began to rise. Apparently the rising accident rate excited a feeling that the effort to reach the high bonus was causing the accidents. On 22 February "the men refused to work under the so-called dangerous conditions".

Anderson was sympathetic. As he said, a 70 productivity gives the men

[1] Said Anderson, referring to this complaint, "In my view this was simply one of the symptoms of the deep feeling of injustice and sense of exploitation which at that time permeated the minds of the weepart personnel".

[2] This was the ostensible basis of the rejection by weepart men of the controllers' attempts to go fast.

35

6d. per hour but "the men had to handle nearly 50 per cent more and got only 13½ per cent extra money".[1] He was still fighting to alter the bonus scheme in some way or another. He wrote to the Head Office pointing out the gross irregularities between the weepart bonus scheme and that for other schemes operating in the factory. For example, stock-room and despatch were making 9d. to 1/- an hour, bigparts and dipper (colouring-coating) were making 8d. to 9d. per hour, but weeparts made 4½d. per hour. He went on, "It is not possible to run constantly at much more than a 70, therefore 6d. an hour is the absolute maximum the weepart men can expect to make". He was appalled at the rising wastage. There was no positive answer from Head Office.

At the beginning of March 1951 the Works Director and some of his underlings visited the factory and told the manager that there was a shortage of some essential raw materials, and that production would likely be cut. The men saw the Works Director "and his stooges" around the factory, "and were not impressed", as they made clear to Anderson in their own inimitable fashion. Anderson pointed out to the Director that, despite shortage of raw materials, he could raise productivity to an 80 with his proposed scheme.[2] But this seemingly did not convince the Head Office. Productivity now began to fall and dropped to a 60. Wastage was leaping upwards and labour turnover began to rise; nine men left that month.

April was a difficult month to say the least. Accident rate shot up and wastage was still rising. In the first week Anderson commenced altering the tables, and the arrangements at the end of the weepart line, in order to do without two men, in other words, going ahead on his own in order to put into practice his plan to increase productivity. He also tried staggering the meal breaks so as to keep the machines running constantly, and tried shutting the machines down for half an hour—which is what the men preferred. Indiscipline was rife and little incidents occurred (such as switching off all the factory lights) which showed the manager in no uncertain terms that the men were dissatisfied. "There's been no discipline in this factory for five years", he said—an expurgated version of a longer comment.

Productivity dropped to a 47 in the second week of April and in this week came the first of two strikes. On the 13th the weepart men downed tools for nearly two hours, complaining about the machine supply and demanding a penny per hour addition to their bonus. There was confusion about productivity and production. The men felt that the lowered productivity (and therefore bonus) was entirely a matter of reduced raw materials affecting the quantities coming off the machine. Whereas it was compounded between

---

[1] I do not know how he made this kind of calculation.

[2] Note that the productivity was not affected by production; in the sense that Anderson thought he could produce less at an even higher rate—and therefore cheaper.

productivity and spoilage which was mounting rapidly.[1] According to Anderson, the bonus on the available production was being shared among too many men.

The manner in which this 'down tools' came about seems worth while recording. Maloney described it thus:

Me and my mate were on the machines when Macrae[2] comes up to me. He'd got the rest of the weepart men together in the canteen. I couldn't leave the machines so I wasn't there. And he says to me, 'We've had a meeting and we're going to Anderson for a bonus'. So they went. I wasn't going.

So the next day Anderson came to me and says, 'I know now you're the cause of it'.

'Cause of what', says I.

'Your mates say you're the cause. You're not letting enough parts through to them', he says.

'First I've heard of it', says I.

'Well Macrae says it', says he.

'Oh! He does, does he! Well I tell you I can give him all he bloody well can take', I says.

'Aye, that's what I think', says Anderson.

But I told him straight he'd get a 60 and no more. And he says that would be good enough, he wouldn't expect more.

And there was Macrae starting his shift at an 80.

The weepart crew was disunited.

On 20 April the weepart men again went on strike and this time walked out. Macdonald met them at the top of the road leading to the factory. He partially convinced them they should return until negotiations were finished, but on the 21st only six hours were worked. He next met all three shifts in the recreation room and advised them to return because he proposed to negotiate a reduction of three men per shift, two men off the machine line and one off transport (then two per shift). The men at first refused but finally agreed to his negotiating with the manager and to give the scheme a week's trial. On going back they spoke outrightly to Anderson, "You've got us up to a decent bonus and now we're having to cut it"; "it isn't your fault" (referring to the drop in supplies) "but give us 2d. and it'll be all right". He had wanted to give them this—which was about 1d. more than they were getting—but he had to refuse since he had no authority from Head Office to accede to their demands.

He was sympathetic, as his attempts to alter the scheme show, but he did little to avoid the strike which he had foreseen. "The strike could have been averted", he said, "had I conceded them the extra 1d. per hour bonus, but I refused this." In a way he was deliberately allowing the strike to develop, and said, "If they don't have it now, they'll have it sooner or later; let them

---

[1] Showing their efficiency was lowered—spoilage was deducted from the totals upon which productivity was calculated.   [2] One of the assembly stewards.

get it out of their system". Nevertheless, throughout the trouble, he remained aware of the justification for the men's complaints. He was quite explicit about it, "This cheese-paring, though small, means a hell of a lot to the workmen".

The men returned to their labours but not to work, for they began at once a go-slow which lasted for the next three weeks while Anderson and Macdonald negotiated the change in crews. Productivity was below a 40. At the same time the dissatisfaction was expressed in straightforward desertion. Six men left on the week of the strike, twelve the following week and nine the week after that. In April month twenty-four men left, and in May nineteen. This was a large slice of the weepart crews but Anderson did not object to this because he thought it would be "a good way out of the difficulty" of reducing the labour force. The more men who left the fewer would hold to the idea of the larger work-gang and what it had entailed. Besides which, "there are certain elements who are ringleaders and agitators", and he could "eliminate those elements who would upset the new scheme[1] . . . by suggesting that it would slog their guts out".

After the negotiations were completed Maloney wrote Macdonald:

About the works, well, a good many men took their books and a good deal of new labour has been started and a good few of them have lifted their books too— 5 men got their books, they must have a bigger turnover of men here than they had in the 8th Army. How they get away with it is beyond comprehension. The week before last with 3 gangs of three on, our bonus was 7d. Now that was gained with new labour against one snag and another and by the end of that week we had got the feel of things and were ready for a go next week on the same terms. And that we did in no uncertain manner. After Sunday night 10 to 6, Monday, our figures on the board read 81. We were out to raise this figure which we very easily could do, but Mr. Anderson had different ideas. They started experimenting with the machine end which caused our figures to drop. Then when they were tired of this they put on the single boring unit on the Wednesday. That meant a bigger production of parts to reach bonus figures, but I think we shall be around 7d. again. We started off again this week with the triple boring unit and again they tried changing the machine end. I don't know how it will turn out.

The high labour turnover bothered Anderson and he used it as an excuse for requesting Head Office to increase the bonus earnings. In the middle of July he suggested "offering better earnings so as to attract a better class of labour instead of nomadic riff-raff". He softened the request by the further suggestion of "forfeiture of 1d. per hour for every $\frac{1}{4}$ per cent waste over basic", even though, at that time, spoilage was decreasing. He was still very sympathetic towards the men on the weepart line. "They have to work very hard indeed . . . their rate of pay should be, if anything, at the higher level among the factory workers as a whole. This is the heart and core of their

[1] Reduced personnel with same total bonus.

grievances and until this is settled there may be little prospect of finding a solution to this grievance which has beset Glasgow Ltd ever since the bonus scheme was introduced".

Immediately after the Fair holiday in July, productivity began to regress. Probably machine inefficiencies had some part in this regression, for a great many mechanical and electrical faults had to be attended to. Nevertheless, theoretically this should have had little or no effect on productivity which was calculated on the actual number of hours worked by the men.[1] But, in the state of mind of these men, waiting for repairs to be made must have been very irritating.

This state of mind is reflected in other indices. The accident rate rose rapidly—the greatest number of accidents ever reported in the factory occurred in June—and the labour turnover increased sharply. All these troubles continued high into August.

Overt trouble broke out in September. On the 8th five men walked out, and on the 9th the weepart men refused to work the relief system at meal times. On the dayshift of the 12th there were not enough men to work more than two gangs up till 8 o'clock (the result of two-hour lateness, or absenteeism). On the 13th only two gangs were present and they refused to do the work of three, leaving the parts lying on the floor. Finally the machine-line had to be stopped for half an hour at a time. A go-slow started and lasted into the first week of October. Wastage shot up to an alarming height. Labour turnover maintained its disheartening rate, but fortunately injuries began to decrease.

The manager was now in the position of being able to force the hand of Head Office. Orders could not be filled, and other sections were being affected; costs were rising. With this lever, in much correspondence with Head Office, he drew the Works Director to the factory in the first week in October—the go-slow was still 'on'. There he presented an ultimatum—the Head Office must recognise that he could not obtain higher productivity unless a new incentive scheme, such as the one he proposed, be given at least a trial. And he threatened resignation.

The scheme was finally agreed at the factory there and then, and, at the end of the week, a full statement was posted up, the scheme to be in action pending the authorisation by the Managing Director. The changes were threefold: (1) calculation of bonus was to begin at a 40; (2) the bonus was to be increased; (3) the number of men employed was to be allowed for, i.e. the fewer the men the greater the bonus for the same production.

Thus eighteen men on one shift crew, beginning at a basic bonus of 5½d. at a 40, would get ¼d. for every rise of one unit, making 8d. at a 50 and 1/- at

---

[1] At a later period, when productivity was much bigger, mechanical inefficiencies of a greater order had no effect on human efficiency.

39

a 66, and so on, upwards. Twenty men beginning at a basic bonus of 4d. at a 42 would get 6d. at a 50 and 10d. at a 66, and so on, upwards. The calculation of productivity for different shift size was based on numbers of parts produced, multiplied by a conversion factor to give weight handled, this weight to be related to the standard or 'normal' weight expected off the machine-line by adding a percentage corresponding to the difference between the shift size and a 'normal' shift size of 24, e.g., for an eighteen man crew the percentage would be $33\frac{1}{3}$ per cent.

This bonus scheme was a copy of one employed at an English factory which Anderson had lately visited. He told the men that he was introducing it "off his own bat", that the Managing Director had not finally approved it, and that he wanted to prove to him that the scheme was "better than the previous monstrosity". "You'll make a shilling an hour bonus", he forecast to the weepart leading men. They accepted it on trial knowing that Head Office had to give a final decision. They did not say anything to Macdonald.

The second week of October, thirteen men were declared redundant, and Anderson got rid of those whom he considered to be "bad elements", not necessarily those who had last been hired.

The men were waiting for the Head Office *pronunciamento*. And it came in the third week of November. The principles of the scheme were agreed to, but there was a cut of $\frac{1}{4}$d. an hour, the promised shilling was to be $11\frac{3}{4}$d.! It was "a criminal mistake" growled Anderson, adding a lot more. And the men blamed him for the cut—"Anderson's let us down. As soon as he gets us going he cuts us down". (This was despite their relatively low productivity of a 45.) "This began an outbreak of another period of distrust of the Head Office and even of me", complained Anderson. Yet productivity rose in December. Labour turnover, which had dropped after the introduction of Anderson's scheme, remained low, and wastage dropped rapidly. Accidents however, jumped sharply, and a flood of complaints was tabled by the leading men. Not only were the machines at fault and also ancillary equipment and materials, but ventilation was bad, tea water was not hot enough, the canteen bread was stale, penalties for bad time-keeping were too severe, and such like.

During the period of the go-slow, right as from the summer, the union membership had declined. The men had not even bothered to tell Macdonald about the new bonus scheme which, as was proper, he should have "vetted". He learned about it only in the last week in December from Anderson. He suspected that Anderson was aware of the union weakness but, in fact, Anderson was quite ignorant of it.

Anderson was resuscitating Joint Consultation in the Works Council but Macdonald objected to this, for a clause in the constitution permitted non-union men to be elected and this would weaken still further the union's bargaining power in the factory. He would not support or accept any decision the Works Council, so formed, would come to. Anderson tried to assure him that the Council would not discuss any question governed by the agreements between the firm and any trade union, but Macdonald would have none of it. He felt something was wrong. On the one hand Anderson was telling him "how happy all the men are", and on the other hand there was a feeling among the solid trade union men in the factory that Anderson was anti-union. Maloney wrote Macdonald, "I have no notion of letting the union drop in this shop. He may have swung the men to his way of thinking, that is, that a union is not worth one damn. I have a few dependables in here that I can rely on, and only await my opportunity. It is galling to think a few keep a union going for the benefit of the many, but if it's that way it's got to be, we cannot help it, anything is better than letting Anderson have his way." That traditional trade union attitude seemed justified in this situation.

The year 1952 began with this feeling of suspicion of Anderson's motives. Productivity had not yet reached a 60 and the manager was trying in several ways to increase it by new methods, and minor mechanical changes. Against such a background Maloney wrote Macdonald: "There has been that much chopping and changing that there was nothing static from week to week. I could not let you have the position from one week to the other because it was always explained that these measures were only temporary, but now things have taken a definite shape and I can see the drift of Mr Anderson's moves, now that he has informed you that he has gained a revision of the bonus scheme let me explain the position to you. He may have gulled the workers in his own mind but they are not all as dense as he imagines."

Then ensued a complicated, and somewhat confused, analysis of Anderson's believed malpractice. The gist of it was this. He had cut production by reducing the number of assembly men from three gangs of four to two gangs of four on each shift, i.e. from a twenty-four man crew to eighteen. The 'normal' of a 60 for *machine productivity* was estimated on what twenty-four men could take. For the eighteen-man shift an allowance of 33 per cent was to be given calculating on the machine productivity, i.e. if the machine with eighteen men produced the same as with twenty-four men, *man productivity* should be $(60 + \frac{1}{3} \times 60) = 80$. But, argued Maloney, Anderson was taking the 'normal' of machine productivity for eighteen men as 75 per cent of the twenty-four man machine productivity, that is a 45; and Anderson was calculating the man productivity as $(45 + \frac{1}{3} \times 45) = 60$. In other words, only if eighteen men, *working much harder*, produced per shift the same as twenty-four men previously, would they get the same total bonus. Maloney went on:

Anderson, by keeping to machine figures is blinding the men to the fact that he is making them do the work of the other gang. Eighteen men on a shift here producing the same as eighteen men in the other factories,[1] making a 60, are only at a 45. The men here fell for his scheme and went hell for leather into it.

Take the number of men 18 as against 24, that is 6 men knocked off allow them six men £6 a week on an average; and at that, it won't be far out, that is a saving to Mr Anderson of £36 per week, divide that £36 among 18 men it gives them a bonus of £2 weekly but our bonus never reaches that figure. So you see Mr Anderson has got higher production at lower cost. Now that I have exposed his scheme you can tell him the next time you are talking to him that there is no revision on the bonus, it is the same old suit under a new coat.

In other words, this was the same kind of suspicion that had antagonised the men against Bulgin. This was in answer to Macdonald's amazed letter that he had only then—beginning of January—received word of the new bonus scheme. This was a measure of the break that had taken place as a result of the fall away of union membership. As he said, "Why, oh! why didn't they ask me first? They accepted this scheme without consultation with me, and the whole matter was a 'fait accompli' by the time I got knowledge of it. Meantime, some new men had been taken on who rolled their sleeves and broke all-time records. Eighteen men are doing what twenty-four used to do. But, as Maloney says, they don't get what was saved." "I know, of course, that this kind of thing won't last but I have to pay out enough rope to let the manager hang himself."

By February the reorganisation of the union membership in the factory was developing under the hand of Maloney. It got to the stage that he suggested making it a district branch in itself which would strengthen the union hand in negotiation. It certainly would keep the management-controlled Works Council in order.

Macdonald was now in a stronger position to join battle with Anderson. First he tried to upgrade the weepart assembly rate. "It would be impossible", he said, "for the employers to find weepart assembly men if the present basic wages being paid weren't boosted by the bonus earnings, and I repeat that weepart assembly men without skill would make it quite impossible for any of the team on the weepart line to earn other than basic wages." This attempt failed. The reply from the Works Director was, "no great skill is needed to become an assembly man as compared to a controller; it takes one day or less to train an assembly man". The only admission from the firm was that the job was physically heavy.

Then Macdonald came back on the bonus scheme and made two points with Anderson. Firstly the new bonus scheme was not yielding the earnings that were anticipated, and it was admittedly a temporary scheme. Anderson

---

[1] Anderson's only comment to this was that at other factories mechanisation made the difference in rate. At no time did he answer this accusation of making an unfair misuse of the difference between machine and man productivity rates, forced upon him by Head Office pressure.

rejected this, saying that it had so yielded. This was maybe true for him as a manager but it certainly was not for the men, as Maloney's letter showed. But Macdonald persisted that, "the wages paid have been dropping since the new bonus scheme, and it has been a net gain for the firm. The wages of the men taken off have been saved and weepart production has been kept at a much higher level without compensating remuneration to the men involved in this extra productivity."

The Works Director, challenged by Macdonald, replied, "You over-rate the trouble. During recent months, output per man-hours has increased and the percentage waste has declined". This was true, for eighteen men were doing more than twenty-four during the spring and autumn. What he did not add was that the men were being paid on the machine output and not the man output. "Someone has given you only half the story", he went on and, unconsciously stating the crux of the matter, "when the bonus scheme was first introduced in 1946 the number of men was eighteen per shift. From time to time concessions were made by way of appeasement till there were twenty-five men per shift at which time the men were still not satisfied. It became apparent that the individuals wanted a bigger pay packet. This was offered last October by arranging the bonus scheme so that payment to the individual increased as fewer men did the work. Since 15 October the bonus earnings have averaged 9·2d. per hour. Compare this with the average for 1950 which was 3·8d. per hour and 1951 (January to September) which was 2·2d. per hour." This was adequate "compensating payment for extra effort".

This is as clear a statement as could be of the difference in outlook between the *Head Office* management, and the men. It is as if the directorate said, "we increase the bonus only if *production* goes up; and production is measured by machine output". The men's attitude is, "we work much harder, that is, our productivity is greater whatever the production may be, so we expect a proportionally higher bonus". Anderson, caught between these upper and nether millstones of attitude could only say, as he did, "This bonus I've introduced has, in point of fact, given the weepart men higher bonuses than they have ever earned before because the basis of the new scheme gives at least some recognition of the manual work put in". The indicative words of Anderson's remark are "at least".

CHAPTER 6

THE CRITICAL YEAR

From November 1951 on until spring 1952 Anderson was fighting against the suspicion and ill feeling. He fell back upon the 'tricks' of management that so liberally bespatter the 'text-books' of advice to managers. Joint consultation was one method, and his drive to form the Works Council was the result. He tried 'better communications', for it was then fashionable as the key to all problems of industrial relations. He posted production data on the notice-boards—"I've tried to give them the meaning of the firm"; "I've tried to educate the union and the shop stewards in production possibilities". He put up cuttings from newspapers, quoting what the firm was doing; and when the inevitable queries and criticisms of high profits came up, he answered them as best he could, explaining the position of the Sales Manager and the need for production. But he was rejected. The Works Council had no effect and the notices on the boards were burned—"the night-shift put their cigarettes to them".

He tried all kinds of schemes "to take the hard work out of the job", such as providing the assembly men with lighter finishing equipment, adding to the machine-line so as to cut out part of the assembly process, speeding up the machines so as to give as much as the assembly could take (hence no "waiting time"), and reorganising the layout of the tables. But, as he said, "I've five years of 'worker frustration' to contend with and none of my physical improvements reaped much reward".

There was much insubordination, and four men were sacked for indiscipline during this period, not the nomadic riff-raff he decried, but men who had stuck out months of frustration. In February accidents, wastage and labour turnover began to rise but productivity remained steady despite the reduced crews.

The condition of uneasy equilibrium was upset in March, Anderson's own action precipitating a crisis. Early in the year he had called the leading men to his office and expressed himself about the spoilage, in cogent terms (of which he was a master); and apparently he thought he had obtained their agreement to the levy of fines for rejects. On 10 March Macdonald saw Anderson about this and pointed out that the leading hands had had no authority to agree to anything: indeed these men were indignantly rejecting Anderson's claim that they had agreed to fines. (This matter came to a head a month later.)

Macdonald went back to the deeper problems—increased production (meaning productivity), lower spoilage, yet bonus smaller. The promised shilling bonus "had not matured". He pointed out that extra men had been included in the bonus scheme, and they should have been on a special bonus-rate of their own. Anderson replied that they had been included in his own interim bonus scheme of October last, and had not been included in the Head Office scheme of November. He was prepared to remove them from the scheme.

Anderson, as "bloody-minded" as the men by this time, blamed one crew for reducing production. Macdonald promptly retaliated by blaming the foreman in charge; and it turned out that, after all, it had been "the pleadings of the foremen" that had brought about an increase of one man to the shift despite Anderson's reluctance to putting on any more men. Anderson complained bitterly that productivity had not yet reached a 60. Whereupon Macdonald questioned office figures compared with those kept by the men themselves. Moreover, he went on, the weepart men wanted three gangs on each shift because the rate at which they were working was having an adverse effect on their health. Anderson agreed to the addition of another gang. He could well do this, having already removed the extra men, wherefore production could go up without increase in productivity and therefore bonus. The men saw this point too, and the apparent managerial willingness had little effect on their attitude towards him. Finally there was a problem of the running of the machines during meal hours. Too many parts were being piled up for the men to return to—and this, they demanded, must be kept to a minimum. Anderson refused—"the meal-time running was essential to the efficiency of the machines", and that had already been agreed to.

The men were not at all satisfied with this, and their disgruntlement grew. That same week productivity started to fall and spoilage jumped sharply. In the following week the men stopped work because there were too many parts waiting for them after their tea. On 21 March the afternoon shift downed tools at 6 o'clock, and the night-shift refused to work. The morning-shift of weepart men, and of bigpart men too, did not start when they arrived. The whole factory stopped and a strike meeting was held. Macdonald was hurriedly called in. Then, as Maloney said, "a deputation of about twenty went in to see Anderson with their chests stuck out". (Maloney was one of them!) "Anderson and Macdonald sat there bawling each other down." But finally Anderson agreed to Macdonald's demand that only the agreed minimum of parts would be made during the meal-break. The morning shifts began work at 10 o'clock.

The foreman had "sent the shift up the road" which the men deemed a lockout, and therefore demanded pay. But the Works Director refused, and, said Anderson, "That was no lockout, the shift foreman had been brutally rude to the weepart men on account of their eternal grumblings so the men put on their jackets straight away and 'walked out' on their own accord."

To get over the problem of meal-time running, Anderson thought to increase the speed of the machine-line between breaks. During the spring holiday (beginning of April), he tried it out, finding a potential productivity of an 80. "After the test the night-shift was best. The foreman ran it at an 80 on his own and this started the ball rolling, and several shifts did it", he said. Then he added, "The fermenting fear seems to be there still and it wouldn't go". "I don't understand it, the 8d. seems satisfactory, compared with the other groups." Then, later, "You can imagine the men saying to themselves, in the mood they're in, 'Ah! *THEY*'re going to sweat the blood out of us by making the machines turn off more stuff, and then *THEY*'ll reduce our bonus again' ". He was quite right, only the men put it in much stronger terms. April's productivity was 53, and May's the same.

It was in the last week of March that Anderson started working out a scheme of speeds and times (i.e. methods) which formed the basis of a later change. He broached it to the weepart shop stewards, but their reaction was what might have been expected. On 30 March the secretary wrote Macdonald:

We had a pow-wow on Tuesday with his nibs about certain matters with the same old results. On his way home from England he hit on something which he thought would solve everyone's worries. I enclose herein a copy of his brilliant idea. No doubt you will spot his move like we did. This is only a stunt to get the machines running again at tea-break. Rest assured on it, that machines have run for the last time during our meal-time. A 90 would not kill us but the only way that they could get the parts off the machine line would be to run it during the break so ''nuff said'. Mr Anderson did not seem very elated when Bro Maloney proved to him that the wonderful bonus scheme of October which he alleged came from his own head is in fact a very old scheme which is still in progress, at X.[1] We broke up with Mr Anderson suggesting another peace-talk at a later date expressing the opinion that only O'Donnell and myself need attend but you can depend on it that whenever we meet him to talk bonus we will not be without Maloney, the only man who can match our friend Anderson at figures on weeparts.

They weren't the only people suspicious of Anderson. Replying, Macdonald wrote referring to the proposals, "I presume, however, it will be full of monkey business as per Glasgow Ltd incorporated".

At the end of March the union membership was over 200 and the factory had been constituted a district. Maloney's dream had come true. A stormy meeting, to elect shop stewards, also had strengthened the union's position for the stewards' committee was left in no doubt about the feeling of the factory after the strike. There had been a tendency to regard the union as "the weepart union" because weepart men's complaints occupied most of the negotiating time; but at this period there was trouble concerning other

[1] See p. 40. It was a scheme from elsewhere. Anderson had said he put it in 'off his own bat', meaning without Head Office permission.

factory personnel, questions involving two-shift working, questions of big-part bonus, questions about bonus for preparatory workers, and the women in N.A.P.[1] had their complaints as well. The district secretary felt confident enough to demand from Anderson that he do something about non-union employees, join the union or get out—and "give them a week to do it!"[2] Macdonald could also request the election of the Works Council in terms of the original constitution, for he could now be certain none but union members would be elected. (Anderson got out of this by reminding Macdonald that elected delegates at the first meeting decided unanimously to postpone the fresh election for a year—a decision resulting from union pressure.)

The district committee studied the Works Director's letter which rejected the union organiser's claim about weepart bonus. "The hard fact", as these men saw it, was that they were working on a machine rate which was set for a third more men. The Director had stated that "when labour was short only, the line was worked at two-thirds. During this time Mr Anderson paid a tempory bonus, roughly calculated on two-thirds of the potential output." "But", retaliated the Committee, "there are no more men on the job today than there was in October. On the bonus only is there an increase in men, not on the job, for the increase includes two extra men." It was a case, as they had seen it for so long, of fewer weepart men doing more work and not getting the increase in bonus appropriate to the change. The firm was making profit out of their extra work; but the men weren't.

Another bone of contention was the amount of spoilage. Anderson was being pushed by his Head Office, apparently as a matter of policy, in "a drive against waste", even though the level of spoilage was no higher than it had been a year previously. Beginning in January he had instituted a system of fining, the fines to be deducted in calculating productivity, and therefore not appearing on the wage-packet statement. As already said, the men became aware of the deduction of these fines about the beginning of March, and Macdonald protested, on behalf of the leading men who protested that they had not agreed to the fine. Macdonald then made his first demand for return of fines imposed in January and February. The answer was an unqualified but colourful negative.

There was even a sting in the tail of the answer, for Anderson said there would be no fining but that the men would gain precisely nothing by it—indeed would lose a little because he would henceforth be more scrupulous with allowances for mechanical breakdowns and allow only the exact time lost in production.

In the last week of March Head Office complained again about spoilage. On the fifth of April Anderson ordered his foremen, "even at the expense of production spoilage is to be cut down". The drive to reduce spoilage

[1] Non-assembled parts.   [2] This is the classic demand on Clydeside—the union shop.

47

was increased, but in the second week of April it had climbed as high as it had been just before the last strike.

On the 14th Anderson posted a notice—"the position is so grave that the Shift Foremen have been instructed to dismiss those employees who are proved responsible for this slip-shod work". "In brief, it simply means that either the weeparts are assembled to the standards expected or you lose your job and, finally, this notice applies *ONLY* to those weepart men who let the side down." At the same time he wrote to the district secretary, Macrae, pointing out that he (Macrae) and his crew had been very much at fault, and, "in most factories you and your mates would have been dismissed for such bad workmanship"; he went on, threatening dismissal, even though it was the district secretary he was addressing. This notice and letters cut no ice; spoilage did not decline appreciably.

Then to the further exasperation of the manager, Macdonald retaliated with a report that a district meeting claimed a recovery of the fines already deducted. Anderson replied; "The fines you mention are purely fictitious, in actual fact, and I think you'll agree with this when I tell you the average actual production efficiency for the weepart line for the last four weeks has been 53·55, whereas the average efficiency on which bonus has been paid amounted to 57·06."

Two weeks later, on 11 May, Macdonald again protested. He reported the result to a district meeting in these words: "I couldn't get Mr Anderson to give me a direct affirmative that fines had been recorded and deducted, and he kept on saying that it was purely a fictitious measure kept on for the purpose of holding waste down to 2 per cent. In view of the fact that I couldn't make sense of this proposition I've asked Mr Anderson to let me have some figures for January and February to prove his contention." "I may say I'm definitely worried about this as I would be bound, in the interests of this district, to report the matter formally to the Legal Department of the union and let them take the necessary legal action against Glasgow Ltd.[1] But I've got to keep in mind my experiences at the factory to decide which would be the best policy for us to pursue, as there could be no question that if we take legal action on the fines position labour relations between ourselves and the firm would definitely harden against us and would be to the ultimate detriment of our members there."

He left this decision to be made by the district committee, advising against legal action if the fines hadn't been too gross. This was a frame of mind that could only have come about in the situation of stress which, at this period (May), was increasing.

Anderson was aware of the strength but not the weakness of Macdonald's

---

[1] Macdonald had protested to Anderson that the fining was an infringement of the Truck Act.

position and, the day following his meeting with Macdonald, he wrote that he had "investigated the matter of the fines imposed in January and February". He made the point that the fines deducted in January and February were paid back in "over-generous allowances for certain stoppages in production", giving calculations to the second place of decimals and to 1/8th of a penny. He then showed that he had retaliated, as he had threatened to Macdonald, by cutting out the fines in April but reducing the allowances, the net result being that the men had earned less in April.

This statement only worsened the situation, for the men could take only one meaning out of it. Anderson did not make allowances for mechanical inefficiency in calculating bonus according to agreement; and he had subtracted fines despite his strenuous denial that they were fictitious.[1] Then when he saw that the fines were causing trouble he had to hold his hand, beginning in April. But that would have increased costs. So, instead of fining the men, he reduced allowances for "mechanical inefficiency" and was "now more scrupulous with allowances for mechanical breakdowns". Macdonald and the men, therefore, had the probability of successful legal action, but the net result would be still "more strictly controlled" allowances, and worsened relations. Macdonald bided his time.

Spring was a period of tension. The district secretary wrote Macdonald in the beginning of May: "I was in the factory today and it is one hotbed of trouble. The weepart men are up in arms about the 'brilliant idea' of three men on the job while one helps out on the line." (Anderson was trying to make up for the extra men being taken off the weepart bonus list, and the men would not have it.) There was also trouble about shift-working of other occupations. "I caught a very strong smell of 'go-slow' all through the factory", he went on, "and my opinion is, there is going to be a very big blow-up pretty soon." He asked Macdonald to come down for "the men are really at the collar just now". Productivity remained at the low ebb of about a 53, accident rate was beginning to rise, and spoilage and labour turnover were climbing. Absenteeism was high; in one April day alone nineteen hours were lost as a result of absenteeism and shifting of personnel to make up.

June was a crucial month. Management as well as men were now in a frame of mind when the slightest incident was a potential cause of trouble.[2]

---

[1] The loss of bonus earnings due to spoilage was posted up regularly every week—but it did not include a statement as to what loss was due to fines. Anderson's use of the word "fictitious" was most unfortunate. He meant (and I am sure of this) that the reduction was not real since he made up for it in other ways, by "over-generous allowances for certain hindrances to production". He commented—"my 'fining' tactic was a psychological idea which misfired. I wanted to make the men see that waste costs them money as well as the Company". Psychology should be left to psychologists, it seems.

[2] Anderson, on one of his occasional surprise visits during the night-shift, met an angry crew who threatened to throw him into the canal.

Conversely any sign of easing of the tension was welcomed. In the last week of May productivity rose to a 59 and this was hailed by management as a good sign. Next week it was back to a 52.

On the morning of the second week in June the new production manager, Brown, talked with the weepart men who mentioned that "they'd sooner work four in a gang". This was the size of gang used in some other factories, and Brown put it to Anderson who took action at once. The shop stewards of the two day-shifts, Macrae and Gordon, were called in during the afternoon for discussion of the idea, and the talk was quite amicable. (Both sides were looking for a way out of the stress of stalemated desires.) A proposition in general terms (increase of three to a crew, and a recalculation of bonus) was agreed to, and the stewards said they'd bring it up at the district meeting on the 20th, with the idea of putting the change into operation on the 25th. Anderson set to that afternoon and evening to work out in detail what the change would entail.

The next morning, the 11th, he called in Brown right away and went through the scheme. He met Macrae and Gordon in the afternoon and put his argument this way, with the aid of many figures: If the twenty-four men crew produced as much as they did before the bonus scheme came in they would make a 74, which would give a bonus of 10d. per hour. But if they increased that output by $7\frac{1}{2}$ per cent they would make an 80, and so one shilling per hour. What he did not say was that he was proposing a reversal to the *status quo*, that is before the crew was cut to eighteen. His appeal was almost exactly that which he had made at the inception of his bonus scheme, even to the shilling per hour bonus as a target and a prize.

But the shop stewards wouldn't have it. They recognised, even without Maloney's help, that the bonus scheme was not altered. There seemed to be too little return for the extra work, and besides, so they argued, the machine-line couldn't give enough for an 80, it would have to run through meal-times to produce what was wanted. "All right", said Anderson, "but I'll show you that you *can* make the extra money and you *don't* need to slog your guts out." He had in mind a speeding-up of the machines, and forthwith he and Brown planned to try and run the line at an 80 between 9 a.m. and 5 p.m. the next day, the chief foreman to act as controller.

On the 12th, while Anderson drew up a new system of work-times, Brown supervised the speed-up experiment which the stewards had willingly agreed to, since part of their platform of complaints was that the machines could not produce enough. The morning shift didn't like it, they felt that they were being rushed, but the afternoon shift took it in their stride. "They sat down at times waiting for the parts to come", said Brown delightedly. So it could be done. The stewards came in, accepted Anderson's amended working system, and said they'd take it up with the branch meeting as soon as possible. They were non-committal.

Anderson's account of the system was couched in sympathetic and conciliatory terms. He gave a financial statement of the weekly production performance showing to what extent the weepart earnings were affected by working two gangs instead of three during the hours when non-assembled parts were drawn off to go to the N.A.P. finishing shed.[1]

The average production efficiency over the past six months has been no higher than a 56·5 and this has been gradually declining during the past two months, for the average production efficiency for the months of April and May was only a 53. This decline in output clearly reflects the results of shutting the machine-line down during the meal-breaks; also the advent of warmer weather has naturally contributed to the decline.

[He quoted rise in wastage from $2\frac{3}{4}$ per cent to over 5 per cent.]

It is evident, then, that the Management is asking too much of the weepart men; under the present system they cannot assemble in a shift so many parts free from blemishes; indeed, they cannot accept all the parts the line could give them, etc.[2]

Therefore, always bearing in mind one of the over-riding considerations in this business—the maintenance of a contented labour force—the twin problems of raising and holding the total volume of production and reducing and holding the total spoilage down to a level of something like 1·8 per cent must be tackled another way, which is to put more men on assembling weeparts and to lift the production to accord with this increase in the strength of the total personnel [i.e. three gangs of four men each (as the men had proposed)].

[His scheme, he said, would work the line] more in keeping with its true productive capacity, [and waste] should fall considerably because the weepart men would not have to assemble so many parts per crew and, since they would be able to spend more time assembling each part, blemished or defective production in this section would be negligible. Under the new system the machines would not shut down over the meal break. In the event of absenteeism, a team of assemblers must be prepared to work for a while at least with 3 men if necessary. An opportunity of earning a bonus of $10\frac{1}{2}$d. per man is now made available—remember that the potential rate of production has recently been raised by one-fifth in increasing the machine speed to this extent—and $8\frac{1}{2}$d. per hour bonus is the absolute minimum which should be earned.

On the 13th Anderson called in his foremen and explained the proposition. Meanwhile the shop stewards and the men were conning the new proposition and were not much taken by it. Their main suspicions were primarily on what they'd get for the extra effort. There was the business of running the line during the meal hours—for they'd suffered in the past from foremen

[1] His new system of working was based essentially on a re-timing of this so that the night-shift (which always had plenty of reserve in hand, finishing at least an hour before the whistle) could carry more of the load previously carried by the day-shifts, which had to work much faster to make a good rate during those hours when non-assembled parts were not being drawn off. .

[2] I.e. he admitted line-rate did not govern the speed of the men's work.

who seemed too anxious to pile up parts during the break—and there was no guarantee that the line would provide enough parts to enable them to make the promised bonus of at least 10d. an hour. So, on the 15th Macrae wrote to Macdonald:

Things have broken with a rush on the weepart job owing to an expert having been sent up from England [by this he meant Brown]. I enclose the new bonus scheme which has been arranged and can tell you that the weepart men are 100 per cent against. I'm afraid the argument would be too lengthy to put on paper but have been assured of a big turnout on [the next district meeting]. Mr Anderson has obliged by holding back the new scheme for a week until we can get our house in order concerning it. [He added that] the bigpart boys are in their seventh heaven. [Their bonus earnings were now over 1/- per hour.]

On the 17th Anderson again met the shop stewards, reassured them that the machines could produce the parts and that there was plenty of materials available. The shop stewards agreed on the 18th to try the system for a six-week period provided the district meeting agreed, the system to start on Monday, 23 June. The next day productivity was practically an 81 and Brown attempted time study in the afternoon. The men wouldn't have it and threatened to down tools. On the 21st the shop stewards were again called in and Anderson again explained the system, especially the changes on the morning shift. Macrae was accompanied by Maloney and Gordon. They took up the question of four men who would have to go on to one of the special products for a little, pointing out that they'd drop 13/- a week. Anderson promised to rectify this (the final scheme included it) and indeed these men would probably make a little more than the others. This conciliatory attitude on Anderson's part was reciprocated, but suspicion remained. Macdonald seemed satisfied that the proposed system was an improvement, and, though his suggestion to Anderson that they meet and discuss it was put off by Anderson, he did not object. The men had unanimously agreed to the six-week trial period.

During the first week of negotiations, the week ending the 15th, productivity leapt ten units to a 62, and during the next week of continuing negotiation it went to a 63, *an improvement even before the system had been put into operation*. Productivity had not been so high since the year previously.

The system started with the night-shift on Sunday, 22 June, and Brown came in to see how the men were doing. They had started well and seemed to have enough time to assemble carefully and so avoid waste. The week went well, waste dropped at once and productivity jumped to a 70.[1] "This is the best scheme of its kind that has yet been introduced by Glasgow Ltd", said Macdonald, and Macrae could echo his words with "the weepart

[1] This even though five new men started that week, replacing five who had left because of the approaching change.

52

assembly at present is a sort of convalescence". But there were two flies in the balm of this new ointment.

The first trouble was an old one—foremen. Ackroyd, the senior foreman, had always been a "management's man" and, especially during Bulgin's time, was always suspect. Maloney described him as "a polished type who'd promise you the world, at the same time putting a knife into you behind your back". He had been the hand of management until the advent of Anderson who preferred to come down into the shop himself—despite the threat to throw him into the canal. He tried to ingratiate himself with Anderson but the latter knew it, saying, "the trouble with Ackroyd is that, though he knows the machines inside out, he doesn't know these men. You see, he's English". (So was Anderson!)

The other foremen were not 'polished' by any means. Simpson for one, had started as a truck driver, found himself thrust on to the machine-line in a period of high labour turnover, became a machine controller, then was elevated to foreman—this before Anderson's time. He, like the other foremen, was aggressive. During one of the periodic struggles about meal-time working he was heard to say, "You'll bloody well do this whether you like it or not".

In this new system of working the foremen had an opportunity of expressing this aggression. During meal-time breaks they themselves went on the line so that the men would return to find a "mountain of parts" waiting for them. To clear this up either they had to work exceedingly hard or the line had to stop on their account and they would not be paid for that stoppage. The machines could be run at a slow rate (and it was most desirable to keep them running) but, the men argued, "why shouldn't it run slow during the meal-times?" The situation was made the more tricky because the men on the bigpart line had "gone mad on bonus to the extent of skimping meal times". Said one weepart man formerly on bigparts, "skimping meal hour and taking my meals on top of the job is against my principles. I decided to get out of it". (Bigpart men were making about 1/2d. per hour at this time.)

The shop stewards protested violently about this "pile-up" at meal-time break but, since they were not yet achieving the output Anderson had hoped to get from his scheme, he was unwilling to take action that would keep the men still further from his target. "The previous week they had hit a 70— why did they not continue and make even higher rates?" He had already shown them that a crew could easily do an 85 (which was true because the night-shift crews could do a 90 on a shift and be finished an hour before time, usually because "they had done enough" or, with the tongue in the cheek, "there were no bogies to carry the parts"). However, still struggling for the harmony he had glimpsed for a short and heavenly few days, he said he would be prepared to stagger the meal-time breaks for the three gangs. That would

53

keep the line running and there should be no pile-up. The men turned this down flat, and Macdonald was with them on this point, to the extent that he suggested the bigpart men "should be restrained" from showing a bad example. They were!

As the second fly in the ointment, Anderson received orders from Head Office that a modified weepart of smaller size had to be made in larger numbers to satisfy orders—Sales pressure. This meant continuous production and therefore the handling of greater numbers to maintain the same tonnage productivity. The night-shift could do it, and did do it easily, completing their quota by 5 o'clock. But the other shifts, with non-assembled parts to be drawn off, and other changes, did not like it. Moreover, the speed of the machine had to be increased, and as the tooling deteriorated so the quality decreased and made the job more difficult. Anderson could do very little about this except keep maintenance men working at high pressure. He had to obey Head Office commands however much they were then making his carefully laid scheme "gang agley".

Macdonald came in to see him and present the men's complaints. Anderson, irritated by the apparent failure of his scheme, by the apparent intransigence of the men who had concurred in it, and by the pressure from on top, was in no mood to be conciliatory. Macdonald finally told him that if he continued production of the modified weeparts he'd have a "sit-down" strike on his hands; and at this Anderson lost his temper. Macdonald had to leave and Anderson followed him to his car, there continuing his vehement protests. An attendant shop steward proposed to "bash 'im". Nevertheless, Macdonald still said it was "the best scheme of its kind so far if it weren't for these drawbacks".

Productivity dropped to a 61 the first week in July. But Anderson's trouble was piling up on him. The bigpart men had been working at record rates during June, averaging a 94, so much so that some were finding it a bit heavy. The production control slipped—a matter of finding space at the right time for all that was produced. The bigpart men had to slow down through no fault of their own and the stewards protested to Anderson on Friday, 5 July. This, combined with the meal-time break forced upon the bigpart men by the weepart crew, brought their productivity down to an 84, and the week following it was little better.

During this second week of July the trouble among the weepart men again became overt. On the 9th Anderson posted a list of men selected to clean down the machines at the beginning of the Fair holiday week. The shop stewards demanded that all the men be taken on during the first Monday and be paid double time, "or else you'll get nobody at all—and we'll stop now". A hurried telephone call brought Macdonald post-haste that afternoon, but he was adamant at the meeting with Anderson. It was a deadlock.

Later, outside the meeting, Macdonald convinced the men it would be impolitic to strike just before the Fair, so they agreed to Anderson's request the next day.

But underneath was smouldering discontent and on that very evening the night-shift decided to go slow "because it was too low a bonus last week", and "there's something fishy about this". Macdonald hurried down again and remonstrated with them, but it was of no avail. Only two gangs turned up on the night-shift on the 11th, and both day-shifts went on a go-slow as well, some of the men leaving before closing time, on holiday to nurse their complaints against their return.

CHAPTER 7

THE CRISIS AND AFTER

The men returned on 21 July still decided on a go-slow. Their productivity that week was a 26 and, as luck would have it, a main shaft broke providing a good excuse for the low output. Absenteeism also accounted for part of the loss.

That week-end Anderson went on "a badly needed" holiday[1] and Bulgin came in as interim manager. So August was approaching with a go-slow policy and a manager suspected and rejected. Macdonald also had gone on leave and another official, Richards, took his place. But Macdonald had left some advice to the men who, incensed with Anderson because they thought he was pushing them too hard, were all for striking. This advice was—"Refuse to strike, work to rule, don't do anything silly, stop reading papers, and at least go through the actions of work". Which they did.

On Tuesday, 29 July, Brown, the production manager, met the shop stewards and discussed the future of the scheme with them. This was a calm meeting (Brown was not an object of their odium). The stewards said nothing of their work-to-rule decision but blamed the low productivity on controllers, that is, on the machines. There was certainly some reason for complaint because there were several faults in the line, shearing units were going wrong, and the input end was jamming.

The next day, at a quarter to two, just before the afternoon shift came on, the shop stewards demanded that the line be stopped so that both shifts could meet—"and we're bloody well going to do it whether you allow it or not". The line was stopped—"No allowance for that stoppage", said Bulgin to the men, which he need not have said—the men did not expect it.

There was a ten-minute meeting of the shifts, quick and to the point. They decided to make their "go-slow" official as from the next morning, and presented Bulgin with two demands: (1) They wanted the previous week's bonus to be made up with an allowance similar to that which had just been granted the bigpart men for machine faults; (2) and in any case they didn't like Anderson's new scheme—"to blazes with it".

Bulgin and Brown (with the attendant Ackroyd) argued with the stewards the rest of that afternoon but got nowhere. It was the sixth and last week of the trial period for the scheme.

On the morning of the next day, the line speed was cut; the go-slow was on. Ackroyd told the foreman to make the controller speed up the line—

---

[1] Anderson told me that he nearly had "a crack up".

56

but to no avail. Brown rang Anderson on holiday to get his advice on what to do before telling Head Office. "Be firm" was the gist of the advice. By afternoon there had been no change in the weepart output. The line itself was running well, the parts were coming off in first-rate quality, and the foreman was instructed to run it at normal speed, booking any periods during which the line was stopped. It would stop only because the assembly men would not take the parts, so this was tantamount to saying that they were going to be penalised for not working at normal speed.

On Friday, 1 August, the shop stewards said they would work only at a 30 until the scheme was altered. Bulgin pleaded with them to stop the go-slow until Anderson or Macdonald returned, for this go-slow was hardly justified. The stewards were adamant, so Bulgin telephoned Head Office. The reply was, in effect, that they should have "a show-down". The men were separately and individually to be asked: "(1) Do you associate yourself with the information given to the Management this morning, that the output of the Weepart Line is to be restricted to an efficiency of 30 units, which, as you know, is about half normal production? (2) Are you prepared to work in future to the reasonable instructions of the Management?" If the man answered the first question in the affirmative he was to be told that "his services were no longer required". If, on the other hand, he answered the second question in the affirmative, "he would be retained under the present arrangements".

In the afternoon Bulgin started to put this order into operation by having the men sent in individually to his office for interview. The shop stewards immediately stopped this. "If you've got anything to say, you can say it to us." When they were told that Head Office had ordered it they then insisted that Macrae should be present at the interviews, and if Bulgin wanted to carry out the procedure properly Richards was available in Macdonald's absence. To have these interviews without first consulting the trade union was contrary to agreements between firm and union. (The Works Director tried to cover his action in avoiding procedure by writing Macdonald that day saying what he proposed to do—having done it—even though he knew well enough that Macdonald was on holiday.)

Bulgin backed down and agreed that he would wait until the following Monday, the end of the six-week trial period, to meet Richards and the shop stewards. Meanwhile the men agreed to work at a 40, this after "Bulgin practically went on his bended knees to beg us to make enough even to cover overheads", said Maloney.[1] Head Office, told of this agreement, concurred but insisted there should be no retraction of the new scheme.

On Monday of the following week, 4 August, the men were still going

[1] Telling about this incident later, Anderson remarked, "the men put the fear of God into Bulgin".

57

slow, working at a 26. A piece of scrap metal was dropped into a feeder during the night-shift, breaking a connecting rod at the input end of the line, and it had to be stopped for replacements. Nobody knew anything about the matter.

That afternoon the meeting with Richards and the shop stewards started at a quarter past two and went on until seven o'clock. The main theme was that the scheme had "promised" the men 8d. or 10d. an hour bonus and they were not getting it. Richards seemed to be under the impression that this had become a "fixed amount of bonus". The stewards were "dissatisfied with the set-up" and made no bones about it that unless the bonus promised by Anderson materialised, or some adjustment was made, they would continue the go-slow. The adjustment first demanded was average bonus for the two weeks previous to the go-slow; then this was reduced to one week. Bulgin would not give in, could not give in, in view of Head Office directions. The stewards finally asked that bonus calculation should commence as from that night so that the day's go-slow would not affect the week's bonus. This too was refused. "No concessions were made", said Bulgin in an uncompromising manner. The final agreement, which was put up to the men on shift, and apparently agreed to, was "that all Shop Stewards, having met the Division Secretary along with the Management, ask all employees to carry out normal production on the understanding that immediately Mr Macdonald and Mr Anderson return the operation of the bonus system would be examined at local level. We appeal to all members to stand by this request."

But the men did not, despite their apparent agreement to the resolution. That week productivity was only a 42, though rising towards the end of the week. There were several complaints about the line and its efficiency. The foremen were trying to boost productivity by taking a hand in the controlling, a forcing measure which the men rejected by slowing down or idling. Bulgin had to reprove the foremen, telling them that they must not work while the men stood around. By the following week the men had decided to increase productivity. "The Manager and Mr Macdonald will be back this week; we'll get something settled then." Productivity that week was a 61.

Anderson returned on 1 August. Macdonald came back at the same time, and immediately went down to see the men. Simultaneously they wrote each other. "During our absence", said Anderson, "the weepart personnel have been behaving in a most impossible manner and the time has now come for the bonus scheme to be thoroughly understood by you so that we can reach a clear decision as to the future course of events at this factory", and asked for urgent arrangement of a meeting. Here Anderson recognised the desirability of using union authority in order to carry out his plans, yet he said to me that he thought the union was against the men and that the men were not with the union.

Macdonald wrote Anderson, "I have now to say that the men have reviewed the position in its (the bonus scheme's) ninth week of working and they are not at all satisfied that the new scheme is coming up to its initial expectations". He too asked for an early meeting. He also wrote Head Office asking for the attendance of the Works Director.

Anderson and Macdonald, with their attendants, met on Monday, 25 August. The question discussed was whether the scheme could work or not. The union argument was that the line could not provide what was needed. Anderson said it could and proposed to show it could. The whole discussion was conducted in an amicable fashion. That afternoon Anderson ordered Ackroyd to control the line himself from 9 a.m. to 4.30 p.m. each day for the rest of the week. Anderson and Macdonald had a private talk after the meeting and they agreed "come hell or high water, there were going to be no more strikes in this factory". (It seemed to me that both had had a most refreshing holiday.)

The next day Anderson issued a notice to his foremen which began, "As I have repeatedly warned you during the past few months, the trouble with the weepart personnel can be traced to one thing and this is the inability of the line to give an adequate overall volume of production. The time has come for us to maintain and improve the techniques of the line-control so that we become accustomed to weekly productivities of the order of at least a 77", and which finished with figures to show this was quite possible. Productivity that week was a 72. At the same time Anderson sacked Simpson, the foreman, whose blustering, aggressive behaviour towards the men had certainly been no help in these troubles. Macrae, the shop steward, also "left", as Anderson and others put it. There is reason to believe that pressure was applied by union as well as by management, for Macrae's handling of union subscriptions was not regarded in a favourable light, to say the least.

Macrae's place as a shop steward was taken by one O'Brien. O'Brien was a comparative newcomer whose rise to this position of influence was meteoric. How it came about is unknown. Maloney, questioned on this, described O'Brien—"He was a caulker in the yards during the war. Made big money". "He's a man that always wanted something for nothing." "He works about three days in the week." "He's a real Red." Anderson sized up O'Brien. "O'Brien always opens his mouth more than the others." "The trouble is that he is a darned sight more articulate than his foreman." "He's an arrogant type, walking about with his hands in his pockets—he's even got the nerve to talk back to a controller."

The week following the Anderson-Macdonald pact, O'Brien and other stewards came to Anderson to protest about the meal-time working. Anderson in no uncertain manner (and this is a mild understatement) told O'Brien what he thought of him as a trouble-maker, and that he proposed to get rid of him at the first opportunity. He, Anderson, had done all he could, given them all the chances they needed, their own organiser (Macdonald) had agreed the scheme could work, it had been shown to work—O'Brien and others like him were trouble-makers and would be treated as such whenever the chance arose. "O'Brien", said Maloney, "sat there with a smile on his face and said nothing"; and Anderson "was right not to sack O'Brien, for that would have made him a martyr". Anderson was by this time firmly of the belief that management was becoming stronger than the union, meaning by that, the shop stewards.

Productivity that week was a 70 and the following week a 71. The bonus was now nearing what Anderson had promised and the men expected. The improvement in productivity continued. The morning shift of the first week in October reached an 87. The next day that same shift complained about the difficulty "in making bonus". "The complaints", said Brown, "were petty", mainly concerned with the quality of parts off the line. O'Brien and Maloney saw Anderson that afternoon and made the complaint official, and pointed out that the previous week's bonus was not what they thought it should be. Anderson carefully explained what allowances had been made and why, but O'Brien remained suspicious. (There had been an increase in spoilage the previous week.) However, the weepart men seemed more easy in mind and finished the first week in October with a 78, even though three men left and had been replaced by newcomers.

The following week eight men left. Two of them were dismissed for in-discipline, and the others went because "the work was too heavy". Nine left the following three weeks for the same reason. Nevertheless, some shifts reached an 89. The average for the month of October was a 76, which was higher by far than it had ever been. But in November productivity fell and Brown seemed to think "there's a lack of interest in the weepart men". Even so, he could also say, "At long last the labour seems to be reasonably satisfied with their money". Spoilage kept on dropping and labour turnover improved.

The relations between Macdonald and Anderson were now much better. Both were striving to keep the peace. The vexed question of the Joint Works Council was a case in point. The election was held at the beginning of October and, though there was apathy, "lack of enthusiasm" said Brown, only thirty in the whole factory failed to vote.[1] The nominees had been put forward in the same fashion, questioning of the men by foremen. Macdonald did not raise objections on this occasion, he merely asked that next time "facilities should be given for the union branch to nominate members". Since the nominees were all union men in any case, it hardly mattered. The factory was now virtually a union shop.

[1] Brown himself went round to collect the votes, so that this result is not surprising.

But Anderson's troubles continued. Sales wanted an increase in non-assembled parts (N.A.P.) and the order came from Head Office early in October. At the same time labour turnover in the N.A.P. shed increased and, as the month wore on and November came, fewer recruits were available. Indeed, the coming of one recruit was of sufficient importance to merit special mention in management conclaves. N.A.P. had to be increased, so he called together the leading hands in weepart assembly and asked their help. He proposed that one gang of the assembly men be taken off assembly and be employed in N.A.P. The men were non-committal about this and went back to their assembly, to increase productivity for December to a 77.

On 22 December Anderson called in the leading men and shop stewards and presented to them his difficulty—demand for N.A.P. products and fewer personnel in that department—would they help? Again they were non-committal. "We'll have to think about it." That meeting was probably of some consequence for later events. Anderson described it to me in his usual colourful terms:

I'd sent for a couple of leading hands to come and see me about the N.A.P. business and the necessity for finding alternative employment for one gang of weepart assembly-men during daytime when N.A.P. parts were taken off the line. I'd previously spotted O'Brien and summed him up. Anyway, instead of a couple of leading hands coming to my office, in walks the bold O'Brien looking frightfully important and feeling every inch the 'exdominus', followed by the 'mimetic'[1] leading hands.

At once I shouted, 'I sent for two leading hands not the whole fucking factory'— and to O'Brien, 'who the bloody hell are you?' This shook him to the core and you could see him deflate so suddenly that for a split-second I felt sorry for the little rat. Almost with tears in his eyes he told me that he was the Convener of Shop Stewards. I replied to the effect that I wished somebody would tell me of these 'appointments'. He was no good, after this little opening gambit, at that meeting. He was really deflated—'lost face' with the group he represented.

Well, we had another meeting. Now, up to that time, I'd deliberately set about the problem 'according to the book', with liberal and free consultation, presentation of production data and so on—all in the most friendly manner. Yet despite all this O'Brien announced at the close of this last consultation, 'We agree that you have a case but we're just bloody well *not* going to go on to N.A.P.'

In the third week of January 1953 the situation was becoming desperate for Anderson so he wrote Macdonald that he proposed employing the third gang from 7.30 a.m. to 11.30 a.m. and from 12.30 p.m. to 4.30 p.m. on N.A.P. work. "Obviously", he wrote, "I would infinitely prefer the weepart men to accept these new arrangements, rather than have them forced upon them and I should be grateful for your good offices to this end." Later in the week O'Brien and another steward went to Macdonald's office and discussed

---

[1] These terms came from my teaching, and are defined in Paterson, T. T., *Morale in War and Work*, Max Parrish, London, 1955. (See here, p. 171.)

the matter with him. He advised caution and "see what it's like". That week productivity was an 83 even though several men were off sick and reliefs had to be brought in.

There was a lot of talk going on about the proposed scheme due to be put into operation on the Monday. The discussions were so open that Brown was driven to note it as remarkable. He thought the scheme would go through because "the unstable elements" had left. These were the men who "lifted their books" in November because the work was too heavy.

The scheme came into operation on Monday, 26 January. By ten o'clock in the morning the weepart assembly men had stopped work. (Anderson was quite convinced this was O'Brien's doing, for O'Brien had stayed over from night-shift in order to talk to the morning-shift—"and he brought out the bigpart men as well"; that line stopped at eleven.) The foremen kept the weepart line ticking over in order to supply the N.A.P. department. All the men on strike met as a district meeting, but no decision was made on the next step. The men remained on strike. Said one to Chalmers, who had come to take over from Brown, "we want to be with our mates". Anderson sent word to the shift foremen that four men, including O'Brien, were "undesirable types and should be dismissed".

On the Tuesday morning a meeting of all union members was called at 10.30 a.m.; Macdonald had come as well. Anderson seized this chance to speak to all the men of the factory together. He started off with facts and figures to illustrate to them what his aims were, for them and for the factory as a whole. He wanted a contented labour force which meant strong management, skilful supervision, and high bonus earnings; and earnings could be got only by increased production and improved productivity. He was frequently interrupted by newcomers but these he silenced with a "what the hell do you know about this?", and belittled them as loud-mouthed freshers among men of long standing who knew what he was saying and so gave him a hearing.

The stewards replied—the manager was always using squeezing tactics to suck more out of them for no extra. Anderson reassured them. There was absolutely no question of the Management tampering with the existing bonus scheme—such action would be dishonest and only a fool or a knave of a Works Manager would even contemplate doing such a thing, that any Works Manager worth his salt knows that his men can't be fooled, that unless the Works Manager and his men trusted one another they all might as well pack up. He told them the Board had said that it could not go on tolerating the labour trouble at Glasgow Ltd and that unless things settled down properly under Anderson the Board would close down the factory and have done with it. He then turned to attack O'Brien who "was showing off" and said that if O'Brien had worked at Glasgow Ltd for a couple of years instead of only for weeks he might know what he was talking about. He and three other "undesirable types" were sacked—"and get out", he finished.

Then Macdonald took over, arguing convincingly that the weepart men would suffer no loss going to N.A.P. since they would be paid the bonus they would have made on assembly. Moreover, the scheme was interim until sufficient recruits were found. Anderson chimed in to add that he would be prepared to withdraw the dismissal notices "if the men decided to be sensible about the matter".[1] The meeting agreed to go back to work at 2 o'clock, but it was not until the night-shift came on (10 p.m.) that weepart assembly was resumed. The bigpart men had returned at 2 p.m.

On the Wednesday a weepart crew started on N.A.P. and Brown had the impression that the men seemed interested. But the productivity that week was only a 46. The men got into the swing again the following week, productivity was a 74, and thereafter it continued rising—apart from the usual loss in the spring holiday week.

Anderson wrote Macdonald on the Wednesday:

Since it seems impossible to have a few moments with you alone in which to chat over things, I would like to get a few thoughts down on paper so that you can consider these and let me know your views when next you visit these Works. In the first place, I would like you to know that I appreciate the efforts you made on Tuesday to appease the outraged feelings of the weepart men. It is a very exhausting business and I do thank you for your personal help in this matter, but I cannot understand why you allow the Shop Stewards to create these turbulent situations which take up so much of your and my time and nervous energy to settle. For example, the small change in working conditions which led to this week's upheaval was placed before and thoroughly discussed with the Shop Stewards, and Leading-hands, as long ago as the 22 December, and yet in the intervening period not a single gesture or response came from that side.

This week's incident is a classical example of Shop Stewards taking the law into their own hands and causing interruption to the country's much needed production and undermining the goodwill between Management and men at this Factory. It has always been my understanding that any stoppage of work which is not authorised by the Trade Union is unofficial and as a general rule the Management refuses to discuss the cause of the complaint until employees get back to work. It distresses me to discover no sign of conducting disputes in this manner at Glasgow Ltd, and we always have to have a stoppage of production whilst the subject of the dispute is being discussed and settled. This is a costly business for the men as well as for the Company, and I would like to see the Shop Stewards at this Factory more closely controlled and disciplined than they are at present. It is not right that the good relations between you and me should be periodically upset by the irresponsible behaviour of certain Shop Stewards, who apparently like to exercise their feeling of authority.

[1] He said later, "I'd been a bit hasty in issuing dismissal notice to *all* the ringleaders when I knew only too well who was the real nigger in the woodpile. I was, therefore, easily persuaded to withdraw the dismissal notice knowing that I would in due course get rid of the O'Brien in a more subtle manner"—and this he did that month.

From this moment onwards the weepart men seem to have settled down. Their productivity climbed steadily and occasionally they reached a 100. Their bonuses increased and so they could afford to take time off. Absenteeism, which had declined with improving productivity, now started to increase and by September Anderson was forced to put up a notice threatening penalties (including no Sunday overtime) if he could get no men on the Saturday for necessary running and maintenance. Even Head Office felt the necessity to send a letter of congratulation to the weepart men because of their remarkably high productivity.

Industrial relations continued good, all decisions worked out at Anderson-Macdonald level. There was a slight mistake in interpreting a national award on holidays with pay owing to a misreading of the award but this cleared quickly without any setbacks in productivity. There was one small trouble about rates for cleaning down machinery and this too was quickly adjusted. Macdonald, more than ever before, recommended members of his union to ask for jobs at Glasgow Ltd.

The weepart men had settled down to an average productivity of about an 85 and the district secretary wrote Macdonald in June 1953 that "the future of the district hinges on the claims of the bigpart men" (not weepart men). These claims were for arrears on overtime, and were also satisfactorily settled. The union was now so strong that "the closed shop" was suggested to Anderson, who turned it down flat.

In March 1954 Anderson, who had become accustomed to a very low level of spoilage, complained to Macdonald that it "was three times what it was at the end of 1953". There was one slight clash between a steward, Tully, and Anderson, when the former complained about too high a line speed. Anderson felt that Tully was a bad element. "He oozes arrogance, truculence and self-complacency." This complaint brought about a meeting between Anderson, Macdonald and the shop stewards, for Tully's shift refused to work an extra half-hour of short specification weeparts at 6.30 a.m. The original arrangement had been 7 a.m. This was settled on the old question of amount to be taken off during meal-time breaks.

The manœuvres to control the Joint Works Council went on but caused no trouble. It was merely pleasant skirmishing.

PART III. STATISTICAL

INTRODUCTION

Part II has been concerned mainly with an anecdotal description of the attitudes, opinions and explicit motives of the men of Glasgow Ltd expressed in speech and writing. But, as in most studies of the human enigma, such overt motives do not provide satisfactory explanations of the events. They certainly could not explain the most striking feature of Glasgow Ltd's history, the change from industrial war to peace. These overt motives, it must be presumed, are sometimes (perhaps often) rationalisations of covert motives either vaguely conceived or unconsciously felt.

Part III is concerned with a description of facts that can be considered as more objective "measures" or indices of behaviour, productivity, quality of work, labour turnover, accidents and health. It is from such indices of behaviour that deep-seated motives may be inferred for, unlike speech and writing, these facts tend to be less coloured by what men believe to be logical thinking; some are certainly the outcome of non-volitional behaviour. Nevertheless, the inferences of motive drawn from these facts must remain to some considerable extent subjective, though it is hoped that the treatment, mainly statistical, leads to a maximum of objectivity.

The productivity index is here taken as a base of reference for all other indices, since these indices were considered by the manager mainly in terms of their effect on production and productivity, the central themes of all factory thinking. The relation between productivity and spoilage is taken first, for these indices governed earnings, so much a bone of contention between manager and men.

The major conclusion from Part II is that prior to autumn 1952 there was industrial war, and after that peace. In Part III the numerical facts corroborate this historical finding, and are found to be indices of variation in the struggles of war and in the stability of peace.

CHAPTER 8

PRODUCTIVITY AND SPOILAGE

PRODUCTIVITY

Productivity, as already pointed out in Chapter 3, was taken as the rate at which materials came off the machine-line during the time the line was working. A rate of weight per hour, given the figure of 60, was adopted as a standard output for the line in normal working efficiency.[1] Allowances were made for mechanical deficiencies, the same allowances that were made in the calculation of bonus earnings. Productivity was, therefore, a measure of the materials passing through the machines and hands of the men, a measure of production per hour.

There were several reasons for using this index. First, it became possible to compare the two lines, bigpart and weepart, and also to make comparisons with similar factories elsewhere. Secondly, the size of the work-group altered thrice during the period described, hence, if productivity were measured as output per man-hour, there would be considerable variation leading to much difficulty in comparison. There would also be the variable of absenteeism and this could not be accurately assessed in its effect on man-hours worked. This very problem of man-hours against weight handled was a major source of contention at Glasgow Ltd. By taking weight-production per hour as a measure the man-power changes could be calculated as a simple ratio of numbers of men. As will be seen, however, the changes in man-power had little direct effect on production per hour. The effect was indirect—the result of grievances about rates paid for extra labour.

Thirdly, changes in type of product made comparative calculation of productivity in man-hours difficult. There were three major types, the demands for which were changing rapidly according to orders placed by the Sales Department. Because of the three-shift pool-bonus system, and since, on part of both day-shifts (not the night-shift) some of the weepart production was drawn off to the non-assembled weepart shed, N.A.P., the rate of parts per man-hour was bound to vary considerably. Nevertheless, when the weepart men talked of output, they did not talk of bonus gained but of production as, "we've done so many parts and that's enough". They considered the three shifts as a team of three units, each shift setting the target it felt physically capable of achieving, but always near to what other shifts could achieve.

[1] This is a method common in ergonomic analysis for mass- and batch-production lines.

It was known for the night-shift to work at such a rate that they could finish their quota by 5 a.m., an hour before breaking off. (Note here, again, that the line rate did not govern productivity.) On the other hand, should the previous day-shifts have been somewhat behind, and this was known to the night-shift, the latter would make up the leeway.

This was operative rate-fixing, but of a peculiar kind. The three groups didn't have the time to discuss or settle the rate, since the shift going off stopped work early in order to give the engineer in charge opportunity for maintenance. They had left the assembly bay before the men coming on were in place. The leading men, it seems, fixed the rate, and, of the three leading men of each shift, one seemed to be the communicant of production, and attitude. Maloney was one of such key people.

How remarkably effective the rate-fixing was can be gauged from the following figures, Table 1, a random sample.

Table 1. *Productivity of each Weepart Shift in Six Successive Weeks*

Week	'A' Shift	'B' Shift	'C' Shift
1	86·09 (2–10)	85·96 (10–6)	85·65 (6–2)
2	86·42 (6–2)	79·32 (2–10)	82·01 (10–6)
3	77·71 (10–6)	87·95 (6–2)	79·09 (2–10)
4	67·62 (2–10)	78·93 (10–6)	79·12 (6–2)
5	86·10 (6–2)	71·06 (2–10)	84·73 (10–6)
6	83·64 (10–6)	87·03 (6–2)	75·75 (2–10)
Average	81·26	81·71	81·06
Night shift (10–6)	80·67	82·45	83·37

The total output of all three shifts for each week measured against the standard, ironed out these differences. Similarly, by taking a monthly efficiency measured in the same way (a four-week running mean), a figure was obtained which tended to reduce differences arising out of the rota of shift changes.

Fourthly, the weight per index was a clear indication of the effect of changes in machines and methods. For example, the effect of introduction of longpart manufacture in 1947 and 1948, involving such changes, could be measured properly only in terms of weights handled. Lastly, since the job of assembly involved hard physical labour, mainly the lifting and moving of heavy parts, this index was a measure more of effort than of skill—the job was within the class of unskilled labour previously mentioned.

In practice the technique is batch-production but, by calculating in terms of weight of production per hour, the whole process, on both lines, could be viewed as a mass-production technique. This it essentially was since the batches were large. Productivity could be calculated as numbers of finished products per hour, but it would be impossibly complicated. Indeed, the method was tried by management in calculating wage payments, but the men suspected such calculations liable to error, and rejected them. Nevertheless, they themselves knew from shift to shift their rate of work by gauging numbers completed, and on this basis could adjust what they determined should be a "fair day's work". At the end of the week, however, they made their final estimate of earnings in terms of productivity as used here.

For four years prior to Anderson's arrival, and throughout the period discussed, there were no changes in machinery other than the small adjustments made by Anderson, already mentioned. The machine variable is therefore minimal.

The productivity index can suitably be examined as in periods before and after Anderson's arrival, that is, 1946 to 1950, and 1950 to 1954.

Period 1946–1950 (Fig. 2)

From the inception of the bonus scheme in 1946 there was a rise in productivity through 1947 into 1948 when a period of equilibrium appears to have been established continuing into mid-1949. The rise is broken by two sharp drops in productivity (March 1947 and July 1947) clearly related to the go-slow and strikes brought about by the introduction of longpart manufacture. This relationship yields to examination in detail.

Longparts were larger and required more material than weeparts; and were considerably heavier. If they came off the line at the same rate as weeparts (measured in numbers per hour) the productivity was greater. The difference would be in weights handled, a difference in physical effort; hence, to achieve a bonus-making output the part-rate for longparts need not be much increased over that for weeparts. Therefore it must be assumed that the men, in late 1947, during the interruption of longpart manufacture, and again in 1948 after cessation of longpart production, had become so accustomed to handling a higher weight-rate that this weepart rate could be rapidly stepped up. In other words it was not part-rate which affected production but weight-rate. This was of considerable importance when, at a later period, the problem of incentives related to part-rate became a *casus belli*. This is not to say that the bonus scheme was not the prime cause of the higher weight production effort. Having learned to handle weights the men were unwilling to lose the bonus increment and would strive to retain it—which was apparently their reason for striking at those times when reduction of longpart manufacture was threatened.

To one accustomed to the rapid effects of incentive schemes in other mass and batch production engineering factories the comparatively slow rise from a 26 to a 55 in two years is not easy to explain. There was no apparent

69

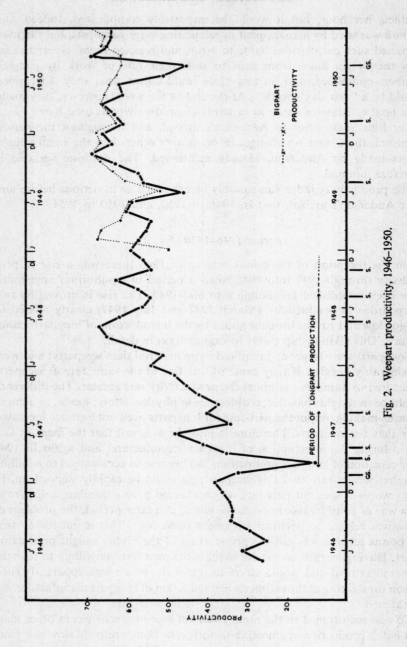

Fig. 2. Weepart productivity, 1946–1950.

'plateau effect' and the breaks in the general upward trend were related to times of dispute. Moreover, bigpart productivity on a line unaffected by longpart manufacture was also rising contemporaneously with the increase in weepart productivity. (Only general, not detailed, figures were available.) This contemporaneity is discussed more fully in Chapter 14.

That the steep fall in productivity in March 1947 was not entirely related to the difficulties in changing over methods on longpart manufacture can be seen in the figures for that period. Table 2.

Table 2. *Weekly Productivity on the Weepart Line on Introduction of Longpart Manufacture*

Month 1947	Jan.	February	March	April
Weekly Prod.	36 39	40 19 29 31	40 18 10 19 4	39 33 29 39
% Longpart	0 0	0 0 0 0	3 38 93 100 100	100 100 100 100

go-slow (↑ under February)   adjustment (under March–April)

The frame of mind induced by the warning that longparts were to be made seems to have led to reduction of weepart productivity for three weeks prior to the commencement of the new production. Whereas in May of that year when the men were again warned that they might have to go on to combined longpart and weepart production, the effects of the short strike were of a totally different character—productivity improved thereafter. Table 3.

Table 3. *Weekly Productivity on the Weepart Line on Decrease of Longpart Manufacture*

Month 1947	May	June	July	August
Weekly Prod.	37 34 41 47	42 54 51 55 43	45 21 30	36 45 49 40
% Longpart	100 100 100 98	99 98 98 98 43	38 36 34	33 22 22 2

Strike (↑ under May)   Holiday (↑ under July)   Strike (↑ under August)

Moreover, in the summer of 1948 when longpart production tailed off, a short strike apparently had little effect, and productivity (on nearly 100 per cent weepart production) actually rose. This suggests that the adjustment to handling an increased weight-rate had been completed. These strike relations will be discussed later.[1]

The period of equilibrium continued until terminated by a sharp fall in midsummer 1949, immediately followed by a short strike in August. But

---

[1] The straddling of the Fair holiday in two successive years, and the occurrence of a strike each August in the years 1947–1950, Fig. 2, suggests a possible relationship to the holiday or season. This possibility was examined by reference to figures over six years: it does not hold.

productivity increased, probably due to some changes at the assembly end of the line, method changes rather than machine. Thereafter productivity remained stable until the summer of 1950 when a tremendous drop to a 45, and as sudden recovery, marked the end of this period prior to Anderson's arrival.

This period can thus be divided into two phases, a two-year phase of increasing productivity and a two-year phase of equilibrium, each broken into subsidiary stages. The first phase showed a sequence of stages thus:

(i) increasing productivity after inception of a bonus scheme;
(ii) seven months of instability following the introduction of longpart manufacture and threat to achievement of bonus;
(iii) eight months of stability and increasing effort as the men adjusted to longpart manufacture.

The second phase showed the following sequence of stages:

(iv) equilibrium at a stable level of bonus earnings, with completed adjustment to longpart manufacture such that the threat of its cessation caused resentment expressed in strikes, but no fall away in productivity;
(v) a short fall-off in productivity in mid-1949 as a result of suspicion about managerial integrity;
(vi) nine months equilibrium at about a 63 culminating in a midsummer dive to a 45 (in a go-slow) and, as shown below in Chapter 9, a great increase in labour turnover. This was the result of a managerial imposition of a change in the bonus scheme with alterations in the use of different units, which the men interpreted as a threat to the comparatively high earnings they were now making—more and lighter parts were coming off the line; and on weight, not numbers, the bonus was calculated.

Period 1950–54 (Fig. 3)

This, the period about which most of the discussion is centred, is readily divisible into two phases each of two stages. The First Phase of low productivity and of industrial war ran from 1950 to autumn 1952: stage 1, from Anderson's arrival until the inception of the incentive schemes in winter 1951–52, a time of violent fluctuations in productivity; stage 2, from the time of the incentive schemes until autumn 1952 when Anderson made his stand after the summer go-slow, a time of fairly stable productivity. The Second Phase of high productivity and industrial peace ran from autumn 1952 onwards: stage 3 from autumn 1952 to about December 1953, when productivity rose steadily, unaffected by the solitary stoppage of spring 1953; stage 4 from the beginning of 1954 onwards, a time of freedom from disputes and of stable productivity.

After the go-slow of summer 1950 and the arrival of Anderson, stage 1 began with remarkably regular productivity for some months, about a 64, but rate of output made a profound plunge in the spring of the following

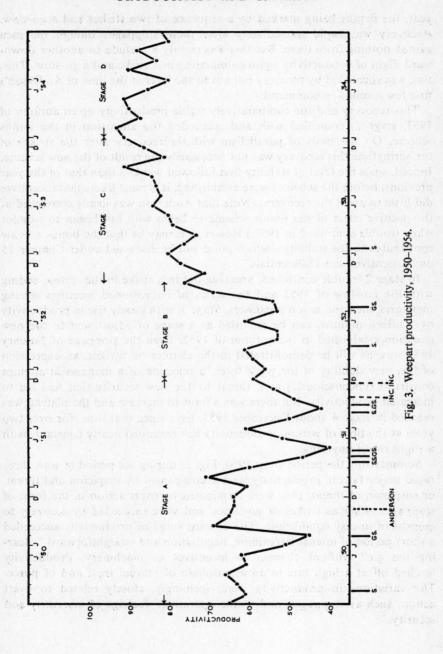

Fig. 3. Weepart productivity, 1950–1954.

year, the depths being marked by a sequence of two strikes and a go-slow. Recovery was rapid immediately after these stoppages though the men gained nothing from them. But this was merely a prelude to another downward flight of productivity again culminating in a strike and a go-slow. This, too, was succeeded by recovery but not to the level at the time of Anderson's first few months in command.

This recovery and the comparatively stable productivity up to autumn of 1952, stage 2, coincided with and succeeded the alteration in the bonus scheme. On the basis of parallelism with the recovery after the strikes of the springtime this recovery was not necessarily the result of the new scheme. Indeed, since the level of stability that followed was less than that of the year previous, before the schemes were established, it is most likely that incentives did little to assist the recovery. (Note that Anderson was firmly convinced of the positive effect of the bonus scheme to begin with but began to wonder when trouble continued in 1952.) However, it may be that the bonus scheme contributed to the stability—which point will be discussed under Chapter 15 on "Incentives and Differentials".

In stage 2 trouble continued, breaking out in a strike in the spring, ending with the go-slow of 1952 and the series of impassioned meetings among managers, men and union organisers. Stage 3, with steady rise in productivity over fifteen months, can be regarded as a stage of adjustment to the new situation established in the autumn of 1952. Even the stoppage of January 1953 was, as will be demonstrated in the chapter on Strikes, an expression of this new stability of the work force, a rejection of a managerial attempt construed (unconsciously) as a threat to the new security that had led to increased productivity. But there was a limit to increase and the plateau was reached in stage 4 about December 1953. Ever since that time, for over two years at the time of writing, productivity has remained nearly constant, with a slight rise if anything.

Summarising the period from 1950, Fig. 2: during the period of war, three rapid major falls in productivity were accompanied by suspicion and threat, or suspicion of threat, they were terminated by overt action in the form of stoppages either as strikes or go-slows, and were succeeded by recovery to months of uneasy equilibrium. The upward surge of productivity succeeded a short period of intense bargaining, negotiation and straightforward "clearing the air" without changes in incentives or machinery. Productivity levelled off at a high rate in an atmosphere of mutual trust and of peace. The variations in productivity were, seemingly, closely related to overt action, such as stoppages, and to the operatives' feelings of insecurity and security.

SPOILAGE

The amount of parts damaged and not up to specification was a measure of efficiency. But it could also be regarded in the same way as accidents. Speaking in loose, but normal terms, spoilage was the result of carelessness during production. Moreover, since the tolerance in specification for wee-parts was very wide, so allowing for non-skilled workmanship, it could be argued again that parts not up to specification were also the result of carelessness; and this carelessness one could expect to be related to changes in the 'frame of mind' of the operatives. That condition or frame of mind known technically as 'anomie', and colloquially as "bloodymindedness", is well known to be related to carelessness. It was thus likely that spoilage would indicate something of operative feelings. This was the case at Glasgow Ltd.

Spoiled parts were discovered on inspection in the finishing-shed, that is, out of sight of the weepart men. Moreover, the inspection took place many hours (occasionally days) after manufacture. Therefore there was no chance of the operatives relating spoilage to their work, or even of knowing the numbers spoiled. They learned this on reading the deduction on the weekly wage bill for the three-shift pool. It was impossible to say who made the mistakes and when. Hence, even though spoilage was measured as a percentage of production, the tonnage handled, it could not, during the process, have any effect on the measurement of productivity; and, vice versa, changes in productivity could not have any direct effect on the measurement of spoilage. The men considered they were paid on what they produced—including spoilage—and only afterwards in their pay packet could extent of spoilage be felt.

Detailed figures for the period prior to 1950 were not available; but in the stage of disequilibrium in late summer 1947 spoilage was of the order of 6 per cent falling to about 2·5 per cent early in 1950. The fluctuations in monthly spoilage rate for 1950 to 1954 are given in Fig. 4.

The spoilage figures can readily be divided into two phases divisible into two stages each.

The First Phase, from 1950 to autumn 1952, was one of violent fluctuations in spoilage, with an average of the order of 2·7 per cent, and upward trend. Stage 1, up to December 1951, was a time of almost continual rapid changes in spoilage. The two most violent upward flights were coincident with two go-slows. A third go-slow was not accompanied by a similar rise. Strikes were preceded by increases in spoilage. Stage 2, from January 1952 to about September 1952, commenced with a fairly smooth but rising trend, the time of "fines" for spoilage, followed by a sharp drop to the go-slow of summer 1952 and slight worsening thereafter. (The peculiarity of the variance of spoilage with go-slows is to be discussed later.)

75

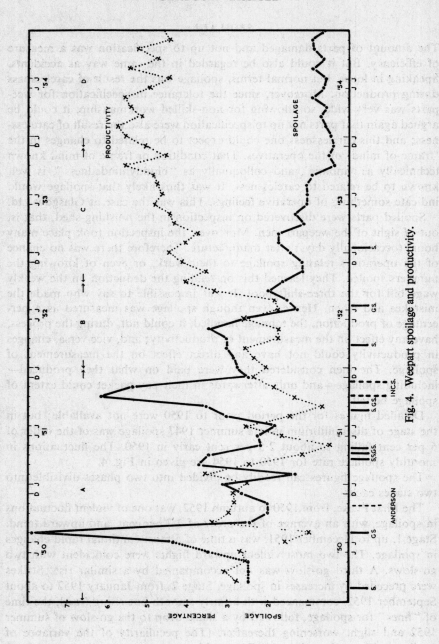

Fig. 4. Weepart spoilage and productivity.

The Second Phase, from autumn 1952 onwards, was remarkable for stability and equilibrium, with an average spoilage of less than 1 per cent, and downward trend. Stage 3, from autumn 1952 to winter 1953, showed a steady trend of improvement downwards, broken only by a slight rise around the time of the only strike in this phase. Stage 4, through 1954 and onwards, was a time of low, and almost constant rate of spoilage; equilibrium.

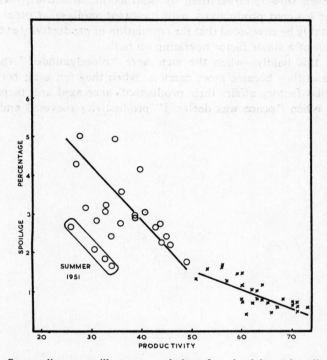

Fig. 5. Scatter diagram to illustrate correlation of productivity and spoilage.

These stages and phases are practically coincident with the phases and stages of the productivity index. Fig. 4 shows this remarkable phenomenon graphically, but Fig. 5 indicates the strength of the correlation, the only "outside" figures being those for the summer months of 1951, the "interval" between the strikes of spring and autumn, when some slight changes in machines were made.

Since deductions for spoilage were small, and since slowing down of production for greater care would have had great effect on productivity, the men were seldom overtly careful in handling the weeparts. On the other hand, it may be said that during those go-slows when spoilage rose to large figures

—and therefore made sizeable cuts in earnings—the men were being deliberately careless, for they had plenty of time to be careful. That would suggest that they were needlessly reducing an already reduced pay packet—which was not part of their attitude to work. The go-slow was deliberate and the wage reduction was a necessary concomitant, hurting the management as well as the men. Further losses could have been more easily achieved by working even slower, rather than by destruction. Moreover, there is correlation of lowered productivity with increased spoilage at other times. It can reasonably be concluded that the correlation of productivity and spoilage is the result of a single factor operating on both.

To put this baldly—when the men were "bloodyminded" their effort dropped and they became more careless; when they felt a bit better about (presumably) factory affairs their productivity increased and their spoilage dropped. When "peace was declared" productivity rocketed and spoilage slumped.

CHAPTER 9

LABOUR TURNOVER

In treatment of labour turnover statistics for a small labour force such as on the weepart line, it seems better to keep to the simplest expressions and to avoid the complexity of other statistical techniques which would add little or nothing to the conclusions. The number leaving each month is a first expression, see Fig. 6.

But since the force changed size on two occasions, from 72 to 54 in November 1951 and from 54 to 63 in July the following year, percentage of force leaving probably gives a more accurate picture of the changes that took place, Fig. 7. The monthly figure is taken as the measure since all other indices are calculated on the same time interval.

Again two phases are apparent, each divisible into two stages, more easily seen in Fig. 7, in which the index is given as a three-month running mean.

The First Phase, from the beginning of 1950 to October 1952, was one of major fluctuations in turnover and a mean of about 14 leaving each month. Stage 1, beginning of 1950 to January 1952, included two big upward surges of turnover separated by a low in the winter of 1950–51. The first rise was contemporaneous with the August go-slow of 1950, and the second, bifid in character, was contemporaneous with the strikes and go-slows of spring and autumn 1950. These fluctuations are statistically significant at a 99·8 per cent confidence limit. Stage 2, from January 1952 to October of the same year, was a stage of rising turnover, culminating in a peak in the last month, statistically significant at a 99·8 per cent confidence limit.

The Second Phase, from November 1952 onwards, was one of downward trend with no major fluctuation. The average was about 4 per month. Stage 3, from November 1952 to December 1953, was one of steadily falling turnover with no significant fluctuations. Stage 4, from December 1954 onwards, was a stage of stabilisation of turnover, consistently low, about 2 per month, rising in 1955 to just over 3, and remaining at that level for another year at least.

The improvement in turnover evident in the difference of these phases is well marked in the annual rates for each successive year.

The average for all these years was about 160 per cent. This did not involve complete replacement of the whole weepart line each year, for a solid semi-permanent core remained, "old stagers". This core increased as labour turnover dropped, a symptom of the bettering work conditions.

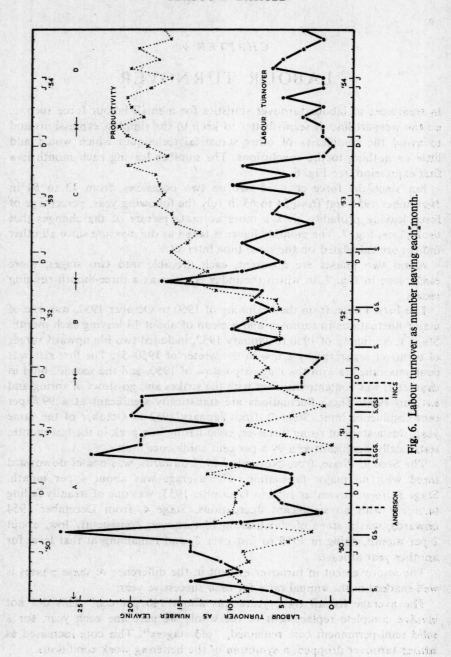

Fig. 6. Labour turnover as number leaving each month.

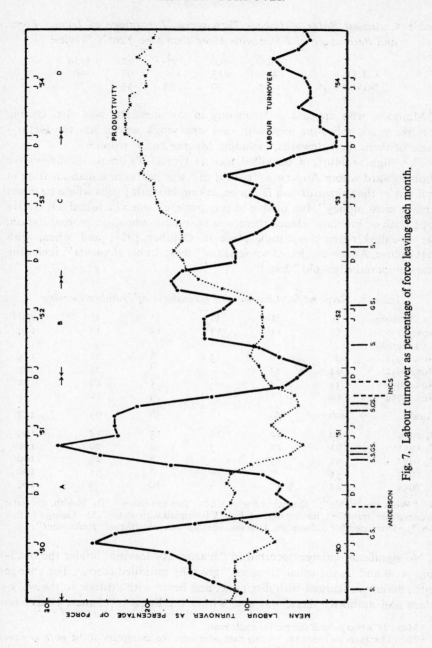

Fig. 7. Labour turnover as percentage of force leaving each month.

Table 4. *Annual Rates of Labour Turnover as Percentage of Labour Force and Percentage of Force with More than One Year's Service*[1]

	1950	1951	1952	1953	1954
L.T.O.	220	215	160	93	49
Service 1 yr.	29	40	54	55	70

Maloney, who appears so frequently in the anecdote, was one. During the five years only four men with over one year's service left the factory, three of them shop stewards, including Macrae and Gordon.[2]

This high mobility of unskilled men is typical. O'Brien, the aggressive shop steward whom Anderson "got rid of" was just such a man, drifting in and out of the shipyards and factories, taking labouring jobs where he could "make most money", but unable to stay put even when he found a lucrative job; restless, insecure. Hence there was no outcry when, on reorganisation, the so-called redundancy took place in October 1951; and when, with that excuse, Anderson ejected some of the "undesirable elements", including one comparatively "old" hand.

Table 5. *Reasons for Leaving as Percentages of Number Leaving*

Reasons	A	B	C	D	E	Totals
Nos. 1950 (9 months)	59	14	13	15	18	119
Nos. 1951	96	16	5	6	32	155
Nos. 1952	44	13	—	7	23	87
Nos. 1953	33	4	—	5	19	61
Nos. 1954	14	3	—	3	11	31
Totals	246	50	18	36	103	453
% 1950	49	12	11	13	15	100
% 1951	61	12	3	4	20	100
% 1952	51	15	—	8	26	100
% 1953	54	7	—	8	31	100
% 1954	45	10	—	10	35	100

A="Work unsuitable", "Dissatisfied with job", "Job too heavy". B=Health, domestic circumstance, travelling, leaving district. C="Dissatisfied with wages". D=Going to other job. E=Dismissed for indiscipline, lateness, absenteeism, unsuitable; "Redundant".

No significant change occurred in "reasons for leaving" under the headings A, B and D, the usual "reasons" given by unskilled labour. The change in E, mainly concerned with discipline, and hence with attitude to the workplace and authority there, was also within the limits of chance. I have no

---

[1] Mean of a two month sample for each year.
[2] The old stagers included the leading men who were the exemplars of the work groups, more stable and less aggressive than the shop stewards.

definite evidence on this continuation of rejection of foreman authority. Only one foreman out of the four was removed (at the beginning of the second phase), but the antagonism expressed against foremen generally was as strong two years after the period discussed as it was during the period. The Bridgeton ethos is definitely anti-authoritarian, and even good working conditions will not alter this.

The only statistically significant change in "reasons for leaving" was in "dissatisfaction with wages". This improvement in attitude to wages began after Anderson's arrival and *before* the inception of the incentive scheme. It is most unlikely that this inception was the whole cause of satisfaction with wages since the improvement in labour turnover started ten months later. The men reacted to Anderson, and the incentive scheme could be regarded as part of Anderson which the men accepted. Unskilled labour always gives reasons such as A, B, and D for moving on, and it would have been surprising to find any big change, even though conditions had apparently altered so much for the better that there was a tendency to stay.

As the anecdotal chapters described, labour turnover seemed to increase at and about the times of strikes and go-slows. There was no relation between "reasons for leaving" and incidence of stoppages and initiation of incentive schemes. In the first stage those months when the rate of leaving was above the average for the whole stage were the months of stoppages.

The relations of length of employment to turnover are to be seen in Table 6.

Table 6. *Numbers and Percentages of Men Leaving According to Weeks Employed*

Weeks Employed	<1	1-1·9	2-3·9	4-5·9	6-9·9	10-19·9	20-52	52+	Totals
Nos. 1950 (9 months)	26	31	20	10	19	12	1	0	119
Nos. 1951	15	56	38	12	13	11	8	2	155
Nos. 1952	14	27	18	12	10	4	2	0	87
Nos. 1953	5	7	13	11	11	5	8	1	61
Nos. 1954	2	9	6	2	5	3	3	1	31
Totals	62	130	95	47	58	35	22	4	453
% 1950	22	26	17	8	16	10	1	0	100
% 1951	10	36	25	8	8	7	5	1	100
% 1952	16	31	21	14	11	5	2	0	100
% 1953	8	12	21	18	18	8	13	2	100
% 1954	6	29	20	6	16	10	10	3	100
Totals	14	28	21	10	13	8	5	1	100

Lengths of service have been broken into eight groups, seven varying from less than one week to between five months and a year, and the last over one year. The fall in numbers leaving was so great that all groups, except the longest service, were affected. But the percentages for each group show that the reduction was greatest for the shortest service group, that is for those staying less than one week, and this was offset by a corresponding increase in the percentage of those staying three or more months. This change is best expressed graphically, see Fig. 8.

Since the break between the two phases took place at the end of October 1952 the annual statistics for this figure have been compiled as from October to October. The statistics for the year 1955 have been added to indicate the condition which held after stabilisation in the second phase.

It would seem that, in the first phase, when men came they either rejected the working conditions after sampling them for a day or so, or managed to hang on for a week to collect a wage packet, and then left. Few lasted more than two months. In the second phase it seems that newcomers found the conditions were not so bad as their predecessors thought, and a greater proportion lasted more than two months, the result being a distribution curve such as that for 1955. If men lasted a fortnight they tended to last more than four or five months, and some even entered the semi-permanent core to become "a Glasgow Ltd man". (See above on the increase of this core, with more than one year's service.)

No relationship was found between length of service and the tendency to leave at the periods of maximum turnover, around stoppages. However, it could be said roughly that the half of the labour force which had been in more than a year were not driven by strike situations to desert the factory, and the half which constituted the "floating population" reacted quickly and fled.

This was the "floating" 50 to 60 per cent which Anderson called "nomadic riff-raff". Such men are typical of the great pool of unskilled labour which figures so largely in the books of Labour Exchanges. They appear as unemployed but are merely passing through the Exchange from job to job— they are really employed, and as "permanently" as they are ever likely to be.

There is also a seasonal effect to be considered. Such unskilled men tend to be more stable during the winter months and more mobile during the summer. The upward movement in spring in the years 1950–52, Fig. 7, might be attributed to this factor; but there was a downward movement in the spring of 1953, and the rise in 1954 was negligible. The "peaks" in autumn of 1950, 1952, 1953 and 1954 may have been due to this factor but their relative importance emphasises the difference between the first and second phases. If the seasonal factor be accepted as in operation it must have been strongly fortified by other factors during the first phase. In the second phase the seasonal fluctuations were not statistically significant.

The changes in size of the labour force also affected the form of turnover. In early winter 1951, when Anderson got rid of many "bad elements", he

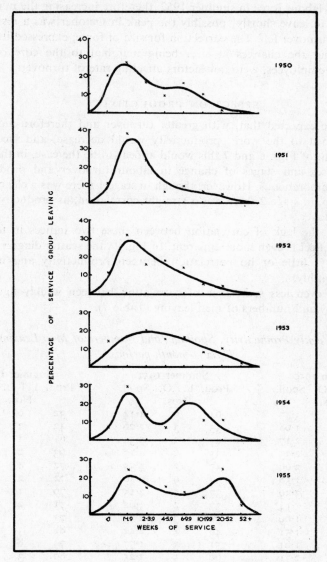

Fig. 8. Time employed of men leaving

was at the same time expelling men who, potentially, were deserters in the coming months. Despite this, turnover rose in the spring of 1952. He increased the labour force in summer 1952, therefore increasing the number of men likely to leave shortly; possibly the peak in October was a result. But thereafter turnover fell. The correction for size of force, expressed in Fig. 7, suggests that the changes in size, being marginal to the core of semi-permanent employees, were not factors affecting rate of turnover.

EFFECT ON PRODUCTIVITY

It might be expected that, with greater turnover and therefore more men unaccustomed to the work, productivity would decrease, and vice versa. At first sight of Figs. 6 and 7 this would appear to be the case, in the broad sense; phases and stages of change in labour turnover and productivity were contemporaneous. However, though in stage 1 there was a clear inverse relationship, in stage 2 there was a straight correlation, as productivity rose so did turnover.

In detail the lack of correlation between these two indices in terms of cause and effect is even more apparent. In Fig. 9A the scatter diagram shows that there is little or no correlation between productivity and numbers leaving monthly.

There is even less semblance of correlation between weekly figures for productivity and numbers of men leaving (Table 7).

Table 7. *Weekly Productivity, Spoilage, and Numbers of Men Leaving during Three 4-month periods*

Autumn 1950			Summer 1951			Summer 1952		
Prod.	L.T.O. Nos.	Spoil. %	Prod.	L.T.O. Nos.	Spoil. %	Prod.	L.T.O. Nos.	Spoil. %
67	4	3·47	64	0	4·14	32	0	1·41
67	2	1·68	55	3	2·26	42	2	1·00
71	2	2·17	47	3	3·54	61	1	1·61
69	1	2·35	35	6	4·13	63	2	1·81
69	2	2·69	47	12	4·55	72	4	1·74
65	1	1·58	36	9	0·76	72	2	2·41
60	0	3·39	37	5	2·15	70	1	1·94
64	0	1·54	37	2	3·02	71	2	1·24
69	0	1·69	51	3	2·73	73	1	2·61
65	2	1·51	48	1	2·42	88	3	1·59
64	0	1·61	51	3	1·77	73	8	1·61
69	0	2·71	60	5	2·25	80	3	1·10
60	2	2·18	49	6	2·61	64	3	2·43
61	1	2·93	55	2	2·36	72	3	1·05
59	1	2·77	61	6	1·99	69	1	1·24
71	1	2·70	62	3	1·71	71	2	1·34

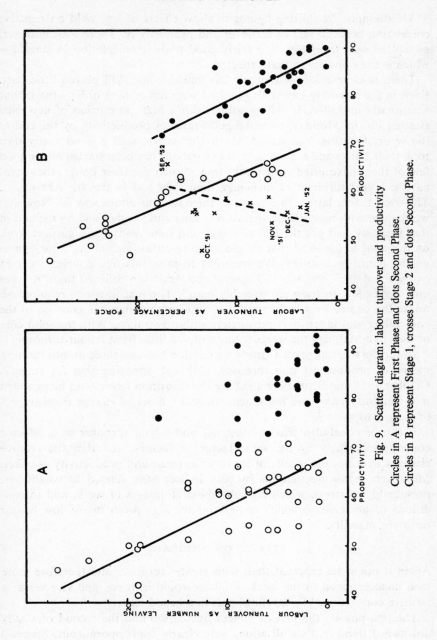

Fig. 9. Scatter diagram: labour turnover and productivity
Circles in A represent First Phase and dots Second Phase.
Circles in B represent Stage 1, crosses Stage 2 and dots Second Phase.

All attempts, by shifting figures to show effects of lag, yield no negative correlation between size of turnover and productivity. There was, however, as will be seen from Fig. 9, a fairly good positive correlation in stage 2—which is the opposite to that expected.

There is clear evidence that on this machine-line skill played little part. Even in the assembly-bay skills required were not of high order—the labour was totally unskilled. It was possible, with a high proportion of new men starting on the Monday, to make good rates of productivity by the end of the week. Quoting Maloney, "About the works, well a good many men took their books and a good deal of new labour has been started and a good few of them have lifted their books too—5 men got their books, they must have a bigger turnover of men here than they had in the 8th Army. . . . The week before last, with 3 gangs of three on, our bonus was 7d. Now that was gained with new labour against one snag and another and by the end of that week we had got the feel of things and were ready for a go next week on the same terms. And that we did in no uncertain manner . . . our figures on the board read an 81. We were out to raise this figure which we very easily could do." The Works Director and Anderson believed that "it takes one day or less to train an assembly man". The machine-men required no more, the controller a little more, but an assembly-man has gone on to the controlling and taken over adequately within two days. With the solid core of men like Maloney the weepart line suffered little from labour turnover.

In Fig. 9B there appears a strong correlation between three-month running means of productivity and turnover, with the opposing sign for stage 2. October 1951 and September 1952 are the transition figures—to be expected in a running mean—and mark accurately the times of change from stage 1 to stage 2 to stage 3.

It can be concluded that productivity and labour turnover were affected contemporaneously by the same factor or factors, and that the relative changes were not the results of turnover as cause and productivity as effect. Moreover, major fluctuations in both indices were related to conditions, presumably of stress, which brought about stoppages of work, and to conditions of homeostasis which brought about high productivity, low labour turnover, stability.

EFFECT ON SPOILAGE

Again it might be expected that, with greater turnover and therefore more men unaccustomed to the work, spoilage would increase, and vice versa; a positive correlation. Fig. 10 shows this in a broad sense.

The two phases, the first of violent fluctuation and the second of steady downward trend and stabilisation, were clearly contemporaneous. Stages 3 and 4 were according to expectation. But stage 2 was one of inverse corre-

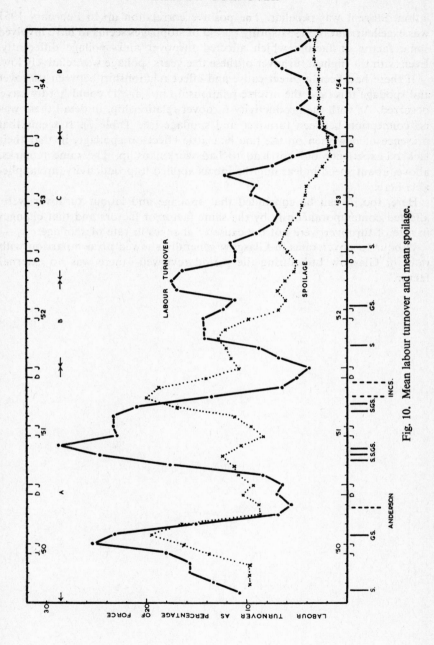

Fig. 10. Mean labour turnover and mean spoilage.

lation. Stage 1 was peculiar. The positive correlation up to February 1951 was excellent, but the 1951 spring period of stoppages seems to have involved some factor or factors which affected turnover and spoilage differently. Even with the highest turnover of these five years spoilage was relatively low.

If there had been a direct cause and effect relationship between turnover and spoilage this (and the inverse relationship in stage 1) could hardly have occurred. As with the productivity-turnover relationship, in detail there was no connection between turnover and spoilage (see Table 7). It seems that presence of new men on the line had little effect on spoilage, in that their lack of experience did not lead to bad workmanship. The same remarks, above, about speed in learning the job as applied to productivity, are applicable here.

Here, too, it can be concluded that spoilage and labour turnover were affected contemporaneously by the same factor or factors and that changes in rate of turnover were not the cause of changes in rate of spoilage.

Labour turnover rates in Glasgow generally showed no comparison with rates in Glasgow Ltd during the period reviewed—there was no external factor.

CHAPTER 10

ACCIDENTS

An accident, as used here, is defined as 'any injury incurred at work and requiring treatment in the ambulance room'. This includes cuts, lacerations, burns, bruises, sprains and strains as described in the ambulance room records. At Glasgow Ltd the men were exposed to materials which affected the skin—those are regarded not as injuries but come under the heading 'skin dysfunctions', in the next chapter. Injuries received while not actually at work in the factory, for example, while playing football during the meal-break, were not considered as accidents. There has been no attempt to differentiate between accidents so defined and those which specifically led to loss of at least a shift of working time, or which led to compensation.

The factory was not dangerous in the sense that life was frequently at risk as in mines or explosive factories, but, comparatively speaking, it was more dangerous than the majority of engineering factories. Two men have been killed in the factory in a period of six years known to me and the rate for the weepart line over the five years discussed was more than 150 accidents per 100,000 man-hours worked.

The accidents treated at the ambulance room were always injuries that definitely required treatment. Cuts were cuts proper and not scratches. A bruise was always visibly a bruise, and sprains were definitely oedematous. These men were brought up in the atmosphere where treatment of a "scratch" was regarded as the sign of a "softie", not a reputation to have in a neighbourhood culture which laid stress on being "tough" and able "to take it". It may be thought that treatment in the ambulance room might have been used as an excuse to escape from work, but to escape without "proper" cause from work on a pool-bonus system of incentive was frowned upon. The fluctuations in accident rate and, as will be seen, their correlation with other indices, suggest that accident rate is an index upon which some reliance can be placed. There was one small difficulty which, however, does not affect the general conclusion. The recording of accidents in the early part of 1950 was not so full nor so accurate as in all later periods owing to a change in ambulance room personnel and method of recording. All subsequent records were made by the same people. It is very likely that the low rates in early 1950 were not a true picture.

The variation in rates as number of accidents per month is illustrated in Fig. 11, and as accidents per man per month (three-month running mean), in Fig. 14. The latter shows more clearly that, again, there were two phases,

91

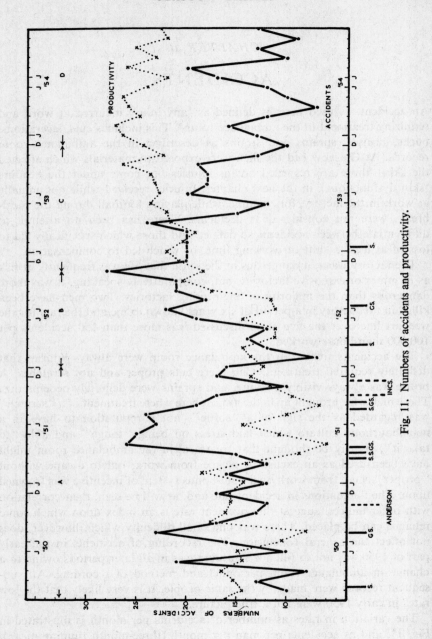

Fig. 11. Numbers of accidents and productivity.

one before October 1952 and the other following, and these can also be sub-divided into two stages.[1]

The First Phase was one of trend upwards to the maximum at the end of the phase, this maximum, and one peak in the summer of 1951, being statistically significant at the 99·8 per cent confidence limit. Stage 1 is not easy to delimit. There were clearly marked upward surges at times of stress as marked by stoppages, especially significant in spring to autumn of 1951. The fall that succeeded could be taken as finishing this stage in November 1951, or, after a quick rise over December and January, in February 1952. The interval may have had some relation to the inception of the incentive scheme in October 1951, and the attendant reduction in size of labour force; but since, as Fig. 14 shows, there is a close relationship with labour turnover, the stage is taken to end in February 1952. Stage 2, from February 1952 to October of that year, was one of constantly increasing accident rate culminating in the maximum of the October peak.

The Second Phase was one of constantly falling trend with a levelling-off at a rate lower than the average of the lowest rates in the First Phase, winters 1950–51 and 1951–52. There were no statistically significant fluctuations, though a prominent rise occurred in the summer of 1954. Stage 3, from October 1952 to December 1953, showed a fairly regular trend downwards interrupted only by an upward bulge in the late summer of 1953. Stage 4, from the beginning of 1954 onwards and for 1955 as well, was a stage of consistently low accident rate, with the already mentioned rise in the summer.

Seasonal fluctuations are discussed below in the section on correlation of labour turnover and accidents.

ACCIDENTS AND PRODUCTIVITY

There is clearly evident some relationship between these two indices, as shown in Fig. 11. The two phases were contemporaneous, stage 2 in both were positively related, and stages 3 and 4 inversely correlated. Stage 1 shows inverse correlation, and the doubtful passage between that stage and stage 2 in productivity is emphasised in accidents. The general upward trend in accidents in the First Phase was not accompanied by corresponding lower productivity, but the inverse relationship was fairly constant in the Second Phase.

These relationships are evident in broad inspection of Fig. 11. In detail there appears to be only poor correlation between numbers of accidents per month and productivity per month, Fig. 12A.[2]

If, however, trends seen in three-month running means are measured against each other, Fig. 12B, a highly significant correlation appears, inverse for stage 1 and the Second Phase, and positive for stage 2. This suggests

[1] Corrections have been made for lessened exposure to accidents during holiday periods.
[2] Weekly productivity rates and accident figures show no correlation whatsoever.

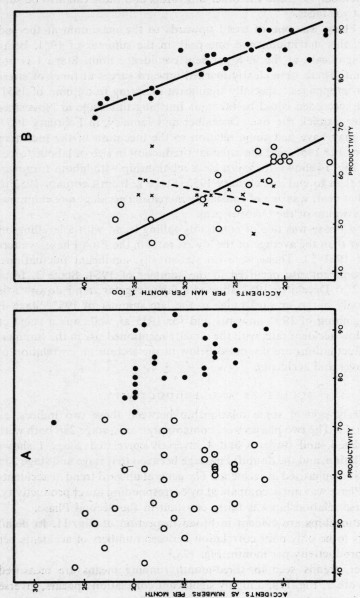

Fig. 12. Scatter diagrams: accidents and productivity.

A. Productivity and accident rate as numbers per month: circles, First Phase; dots, Second Phase.

B. Three-month running mean of productivity, and three-month running mean of accident rate as accidents per man per month.

Circles, Stage 1; crosses, Stage 2; dots, Second Phase.

that during stages 1, 3 and 4, as the men worked harder they had fewer accidents; otherwise it would have been expected that the relationship in stage 2 should hold. Because there is no clear direct relationship between productivity and accidents in detail, Fig. 12A, but only in larger periodic changes, Fig. 12B, it would seem to follow that the real relationship between accidents and productivity was not directly causal. That is to say, pace of work had no effect on the chances of a man's having an accident. These chances, and the effort made in work, were governed by a factor or factors affecting both contemporaneously; as was found with labour turnover and productivity.

ACCIDENTS AND SPOILAGE

Spoilage may be regarded as injuries to the weeparts as a result of carelessness or mistakes by the men, just as accidents are injuries resulting from

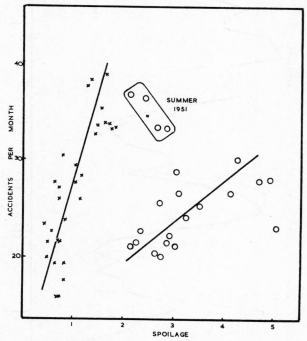

Fig. 13. Spoilage and accidents as numbers per month.
Circles, First Phase; crosses, Second Phase.

carelessness or mistakes by the men. If increase in accidents were symptomatic of carelessness then it could well be expected that the carelessness would spread over to the work. In this case it did (see Fig. 13). There was a

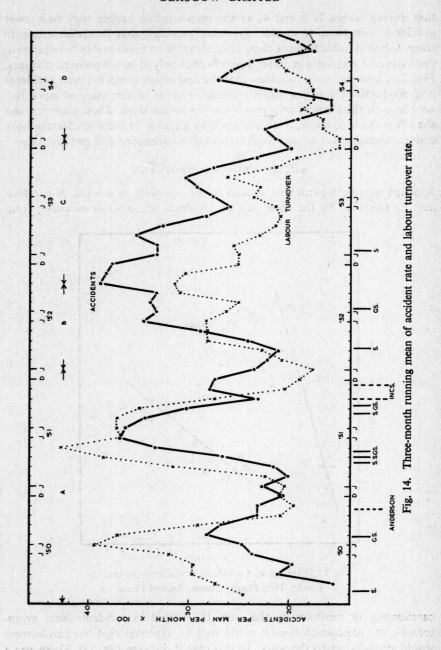

Fig. 14. Three-month running mean of accident rate and labour turnover rate.

fair degree of correlation between these two indices especially in the Second Phase. The correlation in the First Phase is fairly high if the abnormal four summer months of 1951 are excepted. The exceptional character of spoilage of these months has already been remarked upon in the comparison with labour turnover. Leaving them apart it seems justifiable to assume that the causes of accidents and the causes of spoilage (as accidents) were the same, or, if different, were acting contemporaneously in the same direction.

ACCIDENTS AND LABOUR TURNOVER

These two indices were closely related (see Fig. 14). The accidents mounted during the same spring seasons, and fell in winter-time. But, as with labour turnover, there was a downward movement in the spring of 1953, and the peaks of 1950, 1953 and 1954 were not statistically significant—the peaks of 1951 and 1952 were significant.

These fluctuations were much greater in the First Phase, up to October 1952 and, like labour turnover, the Second Phase is comparatively steady in its downward trend. The upward trend in accidents during the First Phase was not accompanied by a similar trend in labour turnover. Again it is deduced that, though a seasonal factor may have been in operation, it was not consistent throughout and was likely fortified by some other factor or factors.

The correlation of these two indices was good for the Second Phase but not so good for the First (see Fig. 15A). In particular, during the five months over the winter of 1950–51 these indices bore a relationship quite distinct from that of other months during the First Phase, and closely similar to the relationship in the Second Phase. (These were the months immediately succeeding Anderson's arrival and recorders and methods of recording were different.) The relationship during stage 2 was also of the same kind as that during the Second Phase.

Fig. 14 does show, however, that there is a close connection between the indices if the figures for accident rate are advanced one month so as to compare with the figures for labour turnover of preceding months. Fig. 15B shows how close this correlation is in both phases. Again the figures for the winter 1950–51 and for stage 2 are of the same kind as those for the Second Phase.

These findings immediately suggested that: (1) The newcomers to the factory were those sustaining the large majority of accidents, being less skilled, and (2) they were more careful during their first month in the factory and became careless as they became accustomed to the work after about a month's time.[1]

---

[1] This was put forward as an explanation by a successor to Anderson.

8   97   G.L.

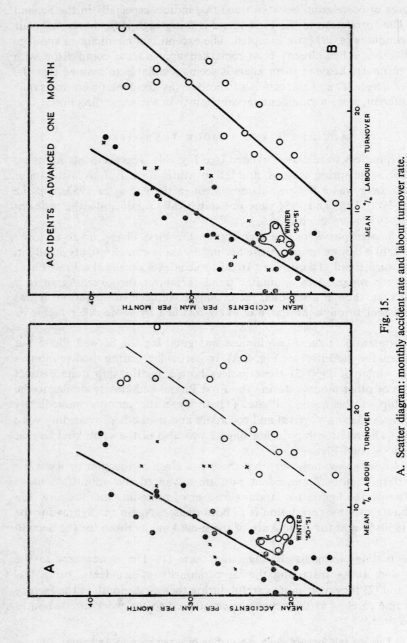

Fig. 15.

A. Scatter diagram: monthly accident rate and labour turnover rate.

B. Similar to A, but correlation of three-month running mean of accident rate with mean turnover rate for month preceding.

Circles, Stage 1; crosses, Stage 2; dots, Second Phase.

This suggestion was tested by sampling the same two months of each year, breaking down the accident figures in terms of length of service of each man sustaining an accident. The cohort with less than one month's service was compared with the rest; less than two months with the rest; and more than one year's service with the rest. Each cohort was calculated as a percentage of the total force, and the corresponding percentage of accidents sustained was compared.

Table 8. *Comparison of Length of Service with Proportion of Accidents Sustained*

		1950 Apr.	Aug.	1951 Apr.	Aug.	1952 Apr.	Aug.	1953 Apr.	Aug.	1954 Apr.	Aug.
Up to 1 month's service	% Force	20	25	14	28	15	13	10	16	5	10*
	% Accdts.	22	45	8	10	7	0	17	0	0	36
Up to 2 months' service	% Force	28	88	20	43	17	22	24	21	6	11
	% Accdts.	22	60	17	40	14	18	21	8	0	36
More than 1 year's service	% Force	39	20	53	27	54	53	55	55	60	80
	% Accdts.	33	18	58	25	43	59	37	46	43	62

* The figure for August 1954 is abnormal since one newcomer, who stayed only one month, had four injuries; he was accident-prone.

It was at once apparent that (1) newcomers, with up to one month's service, did not sustain as many accidents as would be expected by chance, and assuming they were as skilled as the rest; (2) in general, newcomers with up to two months' service sustained slightly fewer accidents than would be expected by chance, and assuming they were as skilled as the rest; (3) in general those men with over one year's service also sustained slightly fewer accidents than would be expected.

Therefore those men with over two months' and less than one year's service were injured slightly more often than would be expected. But the variations from expectation for all four service categories were not statistically significant—they could have occurred by chance; there was no relationship between length of service and accident liability.[1] Therefore it seems that experience or lack of experience played little or no part as factors in accident causation. If anything, the newcomers were more careful when they arrived, but after one month's service they had apparently so adjusted to conditions that they incurred injuries as often as, but no more often than, any others.

[1] For a definition of accident liability see Paterson, T. T., "The Theory of the Social Threshold, The Social Aspect of Accident Causation". *Soc. Rev.*, 1950, p. 53.

Therefore it must be assumed that the strong correlation between accidents and labour turnover was not a function of skill. The factor causing fluctuations in both indices was the same, but the reaction of the men to this factor was different. Some men left, and those who remained incurred injuries on the average about one month after their mates had decided to leave; or the more mobile of the population reacted by leaving, the more stable reacted finally by incurring injury.

CHAPTER 11

HEALTH

The index of health usually taken is the time lost through illness, and called 'involuntary absenteeism' to distinguish it from 'voluntary absenteeism' as time lost wilfully. In this case neither statistic for weeparts was available, as explained in Chapter 1. Moreover, it was felt that voluntary absenteeism as time lost was not a good index since ill health was so variant in its incapacitating effects; in this factory a certain kind of skin complaint was liable to keep a man off work for months, while another sickness could be cured quickly by modern medical treatment.

It seemed better to consider ill health in terms of incidence rather than of duration. An incident was defined as a report to the ambulance room of a case of sickness (other than due to an accident) occurring at the work-place. This, then, did not include all cases of sickness which kept men off work, 'involuntary absenteeism', for which a "doctor's line" (certificate) was necessary, especially if health insurance compensation was likely to be involved; though it did include some cases which led to absence, and then a "doctor's line".

The records, kept by a trained nurse, showed three categories of cases:

Nervous system: 'headaches' (791),[1] 'dizziness' (780.7), 'neuralgia' (366), 'lassitude and lassitude with sweating and no temperature or pulse' (318.2–4).
Digestive system: 'indigestion', 'gastric pain', 'acid stomach', 'nausea', 'sickness and vomiting', 'dyspepsia' (316.2–3, 544.2).
Skin: occupational dermatitis (702.4).

The disorders so recorded could all be regarded as psychosomatic, either in origin, or as being exacerbated by stress. Thus it seemed within the bounds of possibility that the stresses of the work situation could be reflected in the statistics. This was apparently the case (see Fig. 16).

The incidence was not high, so the small figure statistics had to be treated with caution. In only one month, March 1951, as the first of that year's strikes was about to explode, was the total statistically significant, 16. In each of two other months, August 1950—a strike month—and November 1952, when stress was highlighted, 13 cases were recorded. However, it was mainly in trends and major fluctuations that there appeared some conformity

---

[1] The numbers in parentheses refer to class in 'The International Statistical Classification of Diseases', *W.H.O. Bulletin*, 1948.

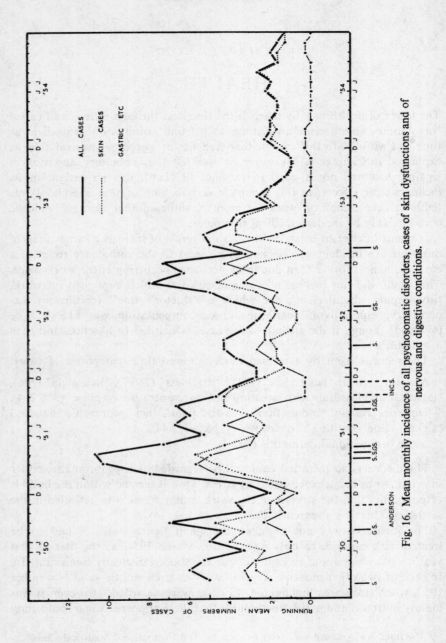

Fig. 16. Mean monthly incidence of all psychosomatic disorders, cases of skin dysfunctions and of nervous and digestive conditions.

with the phenomena described in preceding chapters. There was no seasonal fluctuation.[1]

First there was again a clear separation into phases on either side of early winter 1952.

The First Phase showed wide fluctuations, about an average of five cases per month with upward movements at every stoppage, and terminating in an upward movement. It is difficult to recognise the division into stage 1, up to winter 1951–52, but the character of the fluctuations is of the same kind as already observed, the troubles of summer 1950 followed by a "low" after the arrival of Anderson, the large upward sweep in the troublesome spring–autumn of 1951, the "low" followed by the rise in 1952 of stage 2.

The Second Phase was almost exactly parallel to that of every other index, continuous improvement to winter 1953–54, stage 3, and then a steadying out at an unprecedented low level, stage 4, the average for the phase being just half of that for the first.

The 'Nervous' and 'Digestive' cases together about equalled those for occupational dermatitis. These two groups, conveniently called 'psychosomatic' and 'skin dysfunctions' were analysed separately. Fig. 16 shows that the two groups conformed in fluctuation to a considerable extent. The 'disconformities' were in the 'lows' of the first group in late summer 1950 and in autumn–early winter 1951. During the Second Phase the improvement of the first group of disorders was statistically significant. After February of 1953 only three cases were recorded. This was not due in any way to changes at the ambulance room, either in methods of recording or of treatment. The nurse was quite astounded when the statistics were placed before her—she could offer no explanation other than to suggest that "perhaps the men had started carrying bottles of aspirins". They hadn't.

The skin dysfunctions require fuller treatment as presenting a specific disorder. In this factory the men on both lines were exposed to a chemical, used in treatment of the parts, which appeared to cause skin irritations leading occasionally to certifiable occupational dermatitis.[2] During the period discussed there were no changes in the metals and other materials used, and only in the last few months was a change made in the kind of barrier-cream issued. (The stabilisation of the dermatitis incidence—especially among operatives in other parts of the factory—was complete by that time.)

The three-month running mean of incidence is given in Fig. 17, with the curve for productivity superimposed.

[1] Dr Horne, Medical Officer of Health for Glasgow, very kindly supplied figures on the health of Bridgeton district during the period examined here. Two other factories also gave health statistics. There was no indication of similarity, either in fluctuations or trends, between Glasgow Ltd statistics and any or all of these three.

[2] For reasons of anonymity no more can be divulged as to the nature of the materials involved.

103

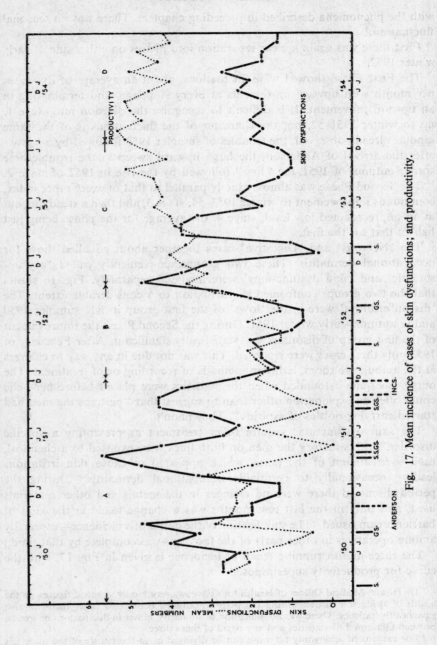

Fig. 17. Mean incidence of cases of skin dysfunctions; and productivity.

Apart from the peculiar, and significant, drop in the early part of 1953[1] there was, again, a remarkably good inverse correlation. A positive correlation with labour turnover is also to be seen in Fig. 18.

A 15 per cent sample of cases was examined in detail for length of employment and speed of reaction to materials. (*a*) 10 per cent reported skin dysfunctions within one month of their coming to the factory; of these half left within the month, the rest remained in the factory for several years; (*b*) 50 per cent reported within one year of their being hired, of these 65 per cent remained in the factory for three years and more; (*c*) 40 per cent reported after having been with the firm more than a year, and they all remained more than three years with the firm; (*d*) 20 per cent of those reporting left within one year of hiring; 35 per cent reported within one year but stayed several years; 45 per cent reported after a year and stayed several years.

It seems that the great majority of those who reported skin dysfunctions were men who were liable to stay put in the factory. In contrast over 90 per cent of those reporting to the ambulance room for treatment of nervous and digestive upsets were men who remained less than one year with the firm; mobile operatives. Hence, when stability was established in 1953–54 the incidence of these cases was reduced nearly to zero. In other words mobile men tended to get nervous and digestive symptoms in conditions of stress, and stable men tended to react by having skin dysfunctions. The steady incidence of skin cases in 1953–54 was to be expected as an irreducible minimum reaction of stable operatives to the materials causing trouble, but in a constant and favourable social environment of minimum stress.

These operatives were of a distinct category in their functions on the weepart line. Most of them were machine-controllers and shop stewards; few were leading men. (It has been from the controllers and shop stewards that foremen have been promoted.) They were aggressive in their relations with those in positions of authority, that is to say, relatively aggressive when compared with the leading men who, in general, were more quiet and more amenable to managerial authority; though even these leading men, drawn from Bridgeton as they were, would be regarded as aggressive in any other situation.

This difference was evident in the incidence of long-term compensatable occupational dermatitis. In a period of twelve years, out of a 'population' of six controllers, there have been nine cases of compensatable absence compared with one from the assemblers, an average 'population' of thirty-six; and among processing and preparatory men (twenty-four), handling much more of the material than the controllers, there has been no case.

[1] The nurse believed that the lack of record of any case in January and February of 1953 was due to her absences on sick leave during these months, when her replacement did not consider treatment of 'skins' as "reportable". It might be added that these were the nurse's only absences during the five-year period under review, during which she made no change in recording procedure.

105

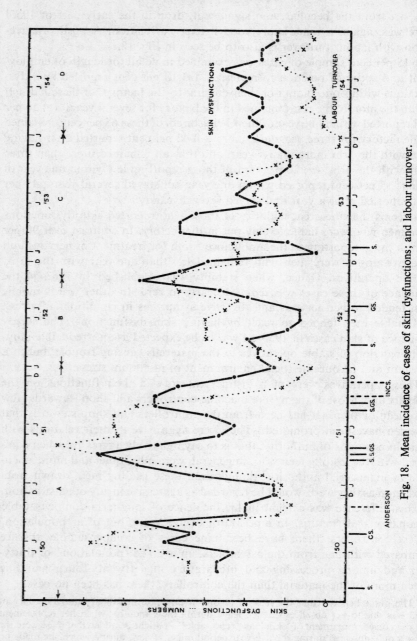

Fig. 18. Mean incidence of cases of skin dysfunctions; and labour turnover.

In the ten-month sample taken to establish the relations between length of service and liability to accident not one of the twenty men recorded as reporting a skin dysfunction for treatment during these ten months suffered an accident. It seems likely, therefore, that the stable, aggressive operatives had less tendency to accident than the stable, less aggressive operatives such as leading men.

This broad finding may be summarised thus: during the First Phase, up to winter 1953–54, the mobile element of the weepart population tended to react to stress by leaving the factory or by nervous and digestive upsets. The comparatively aggressive members of the stable population, controllers and shop stewards, tended to react to stress by showing skin dysfunctions. From these, too, came the only men with more than one year's service who left during the period under examination. During the Second Phase, even though there was still a fairly high mobile population (see Fig. 8) it did not appear to require treatment for nervous and digestive conditions. Therefore it must be assumed that the situation was no longer one of stress. For the same reason, presumably, these mobile men tended to stay longer in the Second Phase than they did in the First.

Since the stable, but aggressive, men who tended to have skin dysfunctions survived from the First Phase into the Second, and since they were still exposed to the material which was mainly contributory to their skin dysfunctions, the incidence of that disorder could not be expected to fall to zero. But it fell from an average of 34 cases per annum to 24 per annum and, more important, the rate remained steady. Therefore it can be assumed that stress, as perhaps a precipitating factor in causing fluctuations, was reduced and that the difference in these rates was, to some extent, a measure, though in themselves the figures are not statistically significant.

The relationship between changes in incidence of dermatitis and in spoilage and accident rates was not so well marked as for productivity and labour turnover. Leaving apart the peculiar (and suspect) 'low' in skin cases in the early part of 1953, there seems to be some agreement in trends and fluctuations for that disorder and spoilage, Fig. 19A. Stage 1, up to winter 1951–52, showed upward surges at about the time of the three stoppages in August 1950, and spring and autumn 1951. But spoilage rise during the spring of 1951 was not of the same order as that of dermatitis rate. This peculiarity in spoilage fluctuation has been noticed before; and a second peculiarity, the continued decrease during stage 2, was also not to be found in the dermatitis rate. Thereafter the fall and levelling out in stages 3 and 4 are comparable.

The parallelism of skin cases and accident rates in these two last stages can be seen in Fig. 19B (again neglecting the suspect figures). But in the First Phase accidents and dermatitis did not follow each other closely. What could

107

be said is that the autumn 1950 period of stress was reflected in both indices nearly contemporaneously, and the peak in autumn of 1952 showed in both

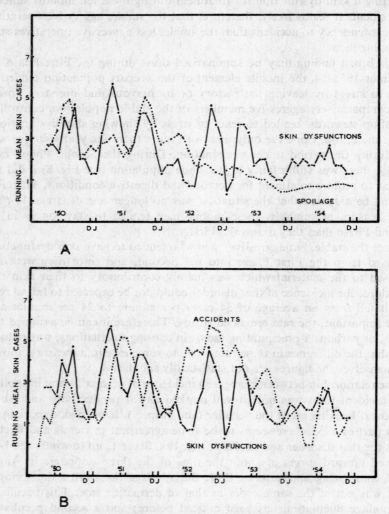

Fig. 19. Mean skin dysfunctions, mean spoilage and mean accident rates.

statistics. Otherwise the bifid character of the 1951 troubles, so well marked in the skin figures, is apparent only as one restricted wave in the accident figures. Stage 2 shows no correlation whatsoever.

108

CHAPTER 12

TRENDS IN WEEPART STATISTICS

A general picture of the changes that took place on the weepart line can be obtained by gathering together the trends in the five indices.

The break between the two phases of war and peace is particularly marked in labour turnover, accidents and skin dysfunctions, and is clear in productivity in the rapid increase at the same time, October 1952. The exact time of change in spoilage is less clear, but the commencement of the steadiness in rates of spoilage dates from autumn 1952. It can be assumed therefore that the autumn of 1952 (and particularly October) was the point at which the weepart men, the manager and the union organiser found a *modus vivendi* for peace. The strike at the end of January 1953 was of a character quite different from that of previous stoppages (to be discussed in the chapter on strikes) and had no effect whatsoever—as far as the indices show—upon the frame of mind, general feeling, *esprit de corps*, morale, whatever it may be called, engendered in the autumn of the previous year.

Another universal break is that between stages 3 and 4 of the Second Phase. But here the contemporaneity is not limited to a span of one month but is spread over the period December 1953 to February 1954. Since stage 4 can be interpreted (without much need for theoretical analysis) as a levelling-off in the adjustment which started in stage 3, it is to be expected that the break be 'wider'. Stabilisation of accidents and productivity appears to have lagged a little.

The break between stages 1 and 2 is not so clear. Nevertheless, the worsening trend of stage 1 is, in all the indices, replaced by a sudden improvement about December 1951 and January 1952. The improvement is short in labour turnover and accidents but is continuous in productivity and spoilage.

Stage 1 shows a worsening trend in all indices, broken, except for spoilage, by two major fluctuations. The exception in the spoilage figures lies in the improvement in the summer of 1951 which may have been the result of Anderson's mechanical improvements at the assembly end of the machine-line. (This merely retarded the deterioration which is evident in other indices and shows itself in the final peak of autumn 1951.) The first major deterioration in indices is that for the late summer of 1950, when the go-slow marked the men's disapproval of Bulgin. The improvement thereafter may be ascribed to his enforced retiral from the scene of battle and/or to the arrival

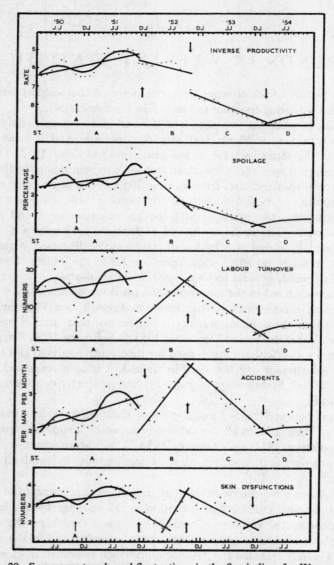

Fig. 20. Summary: trends and fluctuations in the five indices for Weeparts.

110

of Anderson (marked by arrow A). This recovery was of short duration. The second major deterioration in indices extends over the period of spring to autumn of 1951, the period of four strikes and two go-slows.

The end of stage 1, and its developing state of war, coincides with the introduction of the new incentive scheme, not Anderson's but its modification by Head Office, coming into action at the beginning of December 1951. Here commences stage 2 with its abnormalities in conformity and non-conformity of indices. These abnormalities are in striking contrast to the conformity in all three other stages. Productivity does not improve but remains fairly constant. Spoilage improves. (Was this the result of Anderson's fining procedure which, though ill-conceived, brought the need for attention to quality more firmly to the notice of the weepart men?) Labour turnover, dropping at once to a low level, rises rapidly. Accidents also drop at once, then rise rapidly; and skin dysfunctions, dropping more slowly, also rise towards the end of stage 2.

It may be that the sudden drop in labour turnover at the beginning of stage 2 could be ascribed to redundancy removals on inception of the new incentive scheme, but this would not explain the contemporaneous and congruent movements of the accident and psychosomatic indices. It is likely that all three were affected in the same way because of some other common factor operating on them at the same time.

The non-conformity of the productivity-spoilage indices with the others suggests that different factors were in operation during that critical year. Since deterioration of labour turnover, accident, and psychosomatic rates succeed the first sudden improvement the suggestion may be hazarded that this is a continuation of the process in action during stage 1; whereas productivity and spoilage rates change completely in trend. Therefore it can be assumed that a new factor was introduced with inception of the incentive scheme and that, although this affected all five indices at once, it was not sufficiently powerful to nullify the effect of the factor or factors in operation during stage 1—and still in operation in stage 2—which continued to affect adversely the labour turnover, accident and psychosomatic indices. But in the case of productivity it reduced and, in the case of spoilage, nullified the effects of the factor or factors then operating.

Since the incentive scheme is economic we may assume, therefore, that an economic factor was the most powerful (during stage 2) in affecting productivity and spoilage, and the factor or factors affecting the other indices were not economic. Since productivity and spoilage are the bases upon which earnings are calculated it may be said, somewhat tritely it must be admitted, that it is 'natural' they should be affected by an economic factor. But, it may be asked, why should all other indices be affected at once as well, and what were the factors operating in stage 1, and continuing to operate so

111

strongly during stage 2, that they could partly counteract the effect of the economic factor in productivity and not at all in spoilage[1]?

It has already been seen that all five indices are correlatable, not in terms of cause and effect but in association. They are, apart from the discrepancies in stage 2, associated as symptomatic of reaction to the same factor or factors in the same way and contemporaneously. In the first phase the reaction is one of deterioration (in general) and in the second phase the reaction is one of improvement. The introduction of a specific economic factor, the incentive scheme, seems to have led to an immediate but not continuing change in all of them. But at the passage from phase to phase there was no change in economic factors in the same way, that is, no change in the incentive scheme.

It must be assumed therefore that the factors operating about autumn 1952 during this passage from phase to phase were akin, not necessarily similar, to those operating in stage 1, and continuing during stage 2 when they counteracted the economic motive; for the change again brought into being congruity of indices—they were all moving in the same direction. This passage was marked by changes in the relations among the men, and between the men (plus union official) and the manager. Those changes in environment may be called 'sociological' and 'managerial'. Until the relative effect of each factor is estimated they can be referred to together as 'social'.

There is now the proposition that during stage 1 social and economic factors were in operation, during stage 2 the economic factor was altered, and at the passage between phases the social factors were altered, adjusting during stage 3 and adjusted, in balance, during the 'plateau' of stage 4. Because of the congruity of indices during stages 1, 3 and 4 and the immediate reaction of all indices at the beginning of stage 2 it can be said that the economic and social factors affect all indices, though not necessarily equally—as stage 2 shows.

The kinship of factors may be propounded as lying in differences of positive and negative character. Thus it may be said that the economic factor in operation during stage 1 was negative, and during subsequent stages was positive, in that the motives generated led to deterioration and improvement of the indices respectively. The same can be said of the social factors—they were negative in the first phase and positive during the second.[2]

---

[1] The word 'factor' is used here as distinct from 'motive', or 'motivation'. It has an active, a 'doing', root and therefore implies action; but this is upon the man, who then reacts by generating motive. In other words, factor is an environmental constituent. An economic motive is not the same as the economic factor which brings it about; e.g. supply is an economic factor, demand is descriptive of a motive. Motive is quite distinct, and is the subject of later discussion in the part given over to analysis.

[2] I am not implying that the words positive and negative have any moral value such as good and bad.

The broad picture provided by Fig. 20 can be set out as follows:

Stage 1=situation of negative influence: —economic —social;
Stage 2=situation of confused influence: +economic—social;
Stage 3=situation of positive influence: +economic+social; adjusting;
Stage 4=situation of positive influence: +economic+social; adjusted.

The key points are therefore the winter of 1951–52 (stages 1 to 2), and the autumn of 1952 (stages 2 to 3), if we are to unravel the interrelations of the various social and economic factors; crudely, men, management and money.

While still considering Fig. 20 it seems worth while introducing a concept which will be used in a later part of the analysis. The word 'efficiency' is generally used by students of ergonomics to refer to relative rates or speeds of work. One who produces more than another (with the same techniques) is considered to be more efficient; efficiency equals production per unit time worked. But this efficiency is measured over comparatively short periods, say a week, sometimes even less. Such rates are usually then employed to set standards or norms as bases for calculating bonus rates, such as that used in Glasgow Ltd, so many parts (or so much weight of parts) produced per hour as measured over a 44-hour working week. In some operations the norm may be set up as a result of camera or stop-watch studies lasting even minutes.

In a stable condition productivity equals production since production is usually measured over a one-year (financial) period. Efficiency may also be stable (as shown by the six-week period analysis during stage 4 of the three-shift crew in Table 1, p. 68). In a non-stable condition, such as in stage 1, variation may be very wide. The period of *attendance* may be the full 44 hours, but the period *worked* may be reduced—hence efficiency is high but appears to be lower. This happened especially on night-shift working at Glasgow Ltd.

The ideal condition both for men and management is a steady rate of work or efficiency, but this ideal is seldom attained. Quite apart from mechanical difficulties there are all the difficulties engendered by social and economic factors, such as those operating in Glasgow Ltd. The ideal of a continuous uniform rate of work, uninterrupted by strikes, accidents, sickness and labour turnover, can only be attained by introduction of positive social and economic factors. If this ideal be taken as the desideratum, then it is not efficiency as understood by the "work study merchants" that becomes the criterion of what is positive and negative, but the result of all social and economic factors acting upon efficiency. This general measure I propose to call 'performance' as distinct from efficiency, since I can then refer to the effect of all factors at once.

For example, during stage 2, although productivity remained constant and spoilage decreased, an improvement of efficiency, the performance was not necessarily improving since other indices were deteriorating. One finds this kind of thing quite clearly evident in coal mines. Mechanisation has so assisted the miner in producing more coal per shift that his efficiency has risen enormously. But his performance, as measured by production per annum, loss by strikes and go-slows, increasing accident rates and the "silent strike" of inadequate recruitment,[1] is decreasing. In other words the social and economic factors in coal production have considerably reduced the advantages of the mechanical. The integration of mechanical, social and economic factors in bettering of performance is to be discussed more fully.

[1] A large proportion of men recruited to the mines is composed of men who have been in the mines before.

CHAPTER 13

THE BIGPART LINE

Although as important and almost as prominent as the weepart line in production, the bigpart line was, apparently, no powerful element in the factory politics of the period under discussion. This difference in itself will merit analysis at the appropriate place.

The records, and the memories of men, carry little information about the line in the time previous to 1949, again symptomatic of the relatively "backseat" position. The bonus scheme of 1946 was applied to the bigpart line as well as to weepart, and productivity was then about a 26. The figures available do not cover that period, earlier records having been consigned to the furnace room. The earliest figures come from 1949 (see Fig. 2), and show that bigpart productivity, about a 65, closely followed that of weepart. In July of that year, Bulgin, then manager, had threatened to alter the scheme as it applied to bigparts, and demanded higher output, even though the men said it was impossible—just as the weepart men said increase was impossible. The bigpart line did not join the weepart in the strike of that August but they were also complaining about their earnings, despite the fact that they were greater than those of the weepart owing to the method of measurement of productivity. Bulgin proposed taking them off the three-shift pool bonus system and on to an individual shift system, in reply to their complaint that the bonus was not so great as that for similar work in other factories. He met them, and the weepart men, in the canteen during the third week of December, and argued the point—this was when he threatened closure of the works. He specifically addressed the bigpart men in saying that he could not guarantee that their earnings continue greater than those of the weepart, but intended to keep them on the pool bonus scheme. At no time did Macdonald take up the bigpart differential in other factories; the bigpart men were not "pushing" him.

During 1950, Fig. 21, productivity kept in line with that of the weepart to begin with, but whereas the weepart productivity declined towards the strike of August that year, the bigpart productivity remained uniform. The bigpart men were not "inveigled into" the two weepart strikes of that year despite attempts to do so. The coming of Anderson seemed to bring about a slight improvement, though this is not statistically significant in the figures.

The differential between bigpart and weepart earnings remained, and in early 1951 this amounted to about 9 shillings per week. The weepart men commenced to point this out to Macdonald, as well as continuing their

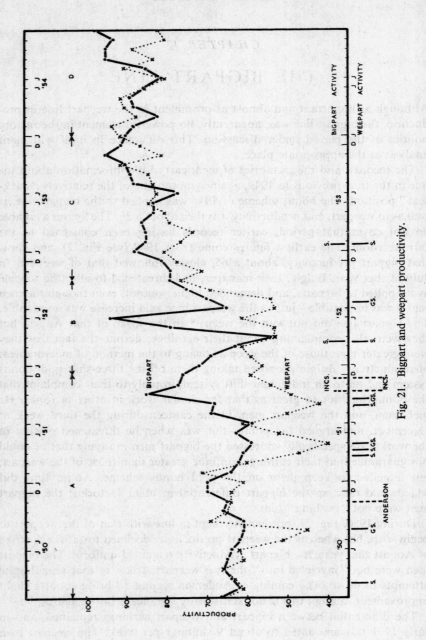

Fig. 21. Bigpart and weepart productivity.

complaint about greater earnings elsewhere. With the lowering weepart productivity in spring this differential rose to as much as 14 shillings a week. The bigpart men were making no complaints, but were certainly making no attempt to respond to Anderson's repeated demonstrations that higher productivity was "within comfortable attainment". They continued stolidly to make their bonus and were apparently unperturbed by the strikes and go-slows and general warring of their colleagues on the neighbouring line.

But when Anderson introduced the new incentive scheme (his own one prior to Head Office ratification) in October 1951, they reacted at once, and productivity shot up to as high as a 90 in the first week. This Anderson-pleasing reaction did not continue long. First there was the disappointment of the Head Office cheese-paring cut of $\frac{1}{4}$d. from the shilling target bonus. This led to growing suspicion of his motives, exacerbated by weepart recalci-trance and the spoilage fines; for on bigpart production the men were having difficulty in reducing spoilage, which was a little above normal. The suspicion grew to such an extent that the grumbles came to Anderson's notice. He not only explained the system of calculation of bonus to the stewards and leading men but issued a clearly worded statement to the foremen which they could quote if queried by the operatives. Productivity steadily declined as spring advanced.

Then came a most extraordinary chain of happenings. In March the wee-part men came out on strike protesting against running of their machine-line during meal-time breaks; and the bigpart men came out in sympathy. The weepart men got some satisfaction from their protest but remained unconvinced of Anderson's motives. Apparently the bigpart men felt the same way, for the week following they reached only a 41 in productivity. Thereafter their effort steadily and rapidly increased, but whereas the wee-part swore that never again would their machine-line run during meal-times, the bigpart men began skimping their meal-times so as to have their line running longer. (It is worth while recalling here that the weepart line pro-ducts could be readily piled up for the assemblers to deal with, and the foremen, with stand-in help, could do this piling up. But it was much more difficult to do so on the bigpart line, for the products were heavy, not easily moved, and not so readily piled up.) They reached a 101 in June. The reason for the bigpart change in attitude at this precise juncture I could not discover by questions. Anderson himself believed that "at last they decided that I was a 'straight guy' and, as I had repeatedly told them, I would not tamper with the bonus scheme whatever level their production efficiencies reached". An additional explanation is hazarded in the chapter on strikes.

The bigpart men "broke through the sound barrier" as they put it. Their bonuses were now over one shilling an hour, and they were in a "seventh heaven", according to the weepart men. But just then the weepart men were becoming more obstreperous about the pressure by foremen (and Anderson) to keep their machines working during meal-times, and the bigpart example was too much for them. They were against "eating their meal on the job" as one put it. The weepart stewards—not discouraged by Macdonald—approached the bigpart men and pointed out that Anderson could use their bad example as a weapon against the weepart men. This pressure from their comrades forced the bigpart men to cut the flat-out effort. Then, as fortune would have it, the production manager slipped up in organizing the flow of parts from the assembly bay into the finishing-shed, parts began to pile up, bogies and mobile cranes were not available at the right time, there was general chaos. So productivity again dropped. And, on top of this, machine faults developed, and one week productivity barely exceeded a 60. Anderson preserved his good name with them by granting special allowances, a source of some dissatisfaction, or rather envy, on the part of the weepart men who had just returned from the Fair holiday and were in the throes of their last big struggle with management, culminating in their August go-slow.

This weepart battle seemed to affect the bigpart men, though they were not participating in the go-slow, for absenteeism was rife and much overtime had to be worked. But productivity began to rise steadily and continued to do so, until well into 1953, apart from a short sharp drop to a 63 during the week of the January strike in which they joined the weepart men protesting against their being temporarily transferred to N.A.P. There was a slight brush with Anderson during the summer of 1953 on a question of arrears of overtime payments, but Macdonald solved this satisfactorily, without productivity or any other indices being affected.

During this spring the weepart men, as in the year before, interfered in bigpart working. A new holiday-with-pay scheme had been introduced, the holiday pay to be calculated on the earnings of the twelve weeks prior to the summer holiday. The bigpart men, inspired by their shop steward, decided to increase their output for these twelve weeks by doing maintenance work during running-time, instead of stopping early (or starting late) to do so. They estimated they could get another penny an hour.

No one in management knew of this but it became known to the weepart crew, and, before the bigpart men could start their scheme (which was to run only for the twelve weeks), a weepart steward came over and castigated the bigpart men for taking "a patent bait from management and changing their traditional practice for so little extra reward". The scheme was abandoned without further argument.

At the end of 1954 Anderson carried out a change he had long contemplated. The three-shift pool bonus was broken down into individual shift working. He suggested to the crew that two men from each shift act as watch-dogs upon the other shift, but this was not followed. "We'll see to it" was the answer, "We've got used to our mates", implying that there would be "an understanding" of how much ought to be done. The following week the combined productivity had gone up by five units and, by the end of 1954, over 100 was reached in one week.[1]

This history of bigpart changes, and the comparison with weepart activity are apparent in Fig. 27. Stage 1, as in weepart history, terminates about the same time, the bigpart line reacting to the first incentive. Stage 2, from December 1951 to October 1952, is one of confusion as in the weepart history. Stage 3 is again a period of rise to consistent effort, followed by a period of adjustment, terminating in autumn 1954 by the inception on the bigpart line of the individual shift bonus system and re-adjustment.

SPOILAGE

The changes in this index are quite different from those for the weepart line, Fig. 22. There is no correlation of spoilage with productivity, as there is in the weepart statistics, nor is there correlation with weepart spoilage. Throughout the whole of the period surveyed the spoilage rate remains nearly constant. The only similarity to other indices that can be observed is that, after spring 1953, the rate is remarkably constant, contrasting with fluctuations in the first phase. These fluctuations are not significant though a sharp peak in the summer of 1951 is noteworthy. There is nothing in the office records, or in memory, to account for this sudden rise, which was entirely due to an extraordinary jump to nearly 10 per cent spoilage in the week preceding the Fair holiday. After the holiday, spoilage was again 'normal'. The cause may have been mechanical faults, corrected by holiday maintenance.

The reason for the consistent rate in spoilage is not far to seek. As distinct from weeparts, the bigparts required less handling in the assembly-bay, and their construction was such as to render them less liable to damage by bad manipulation. Nevertheless, some parts could not help but be faulty because of inadequate maintenance of the line in a continuous three-shift cycle. That is to say, the bigpart spoilage was not far from a nearly irreducible minimum. Perhaps Anderson took this into account in his comparative neglect of it. Nevertheless, when, in 1952, Head Office forced a drive against spoilage, he had of necessity to do something about bigparts as well as weeparts, which may account for the 'low' during that year.

---

[1] In 1955 this levelled off to just over 100 but 110 was made occasionally, this on the same machines by men who once thought it was impossible to make more than 65. Anderson could not get the weepart men to go on to this system.

119

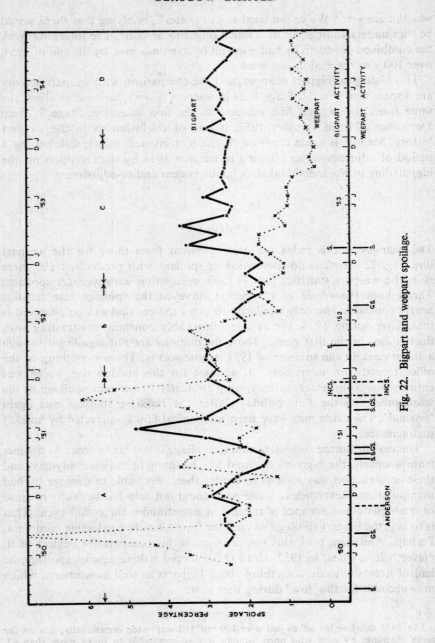

Fig. 22. Bigpart and weepart spoilage.

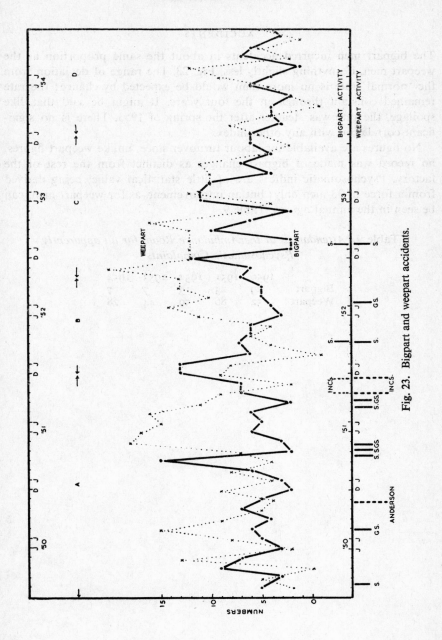

Fig. 23. Bigpart and weepart accidents.

121

ACCIDENTS

The bigpart men incurred accidents in about the same proportion as the weepart men, if anything slightly less, Fig. 23. The range of deviation from the 'normal' rate is no more than would be expected by chance; the rate remained constant throughout the four years. It might be said that, like spoilage, the rate was steadier after the spring of 1953. There is no significant correlation with any other index.

No figures are available for labour turnover since, unlike weepart figures, no record was made of bigpart changes as distinct from the rest of the factory. Psychosomatic indices are of little statistical value, being derived from a force of 33 men only; but an improvement, as for weepart men, can be seen in the annual figures, Table 9.

Table 9. *Attendances at the Ambulance Room for all apparently Psychosomatic Complaints*

	1950	1951	1952	1953	1954
Bigpart	29	23	13	7	7
Weepart	52	86	59	44	28

CHAPTER 14

THE REST OF THE FACTORY

So far the description has been confined to two units comprising a little over a third of the complement of the factory. The rest of the factory consisted of the N.A.P. unit and all the ancillary people, receivers, preparatory men, packers, despatchers, finishers, inspectors, transport men, maintenance engineers, laboratory and canteen workers, office staff. Compared with the weepart line, the history of these people, 'the rest' as they might be called, was singularly uneventful, even less exciting than that of the bigpart unit. They undoubtedly reacted to the weepart struggles, but overtly only in a negative fashion. The union became a "weepart union" in their eyes, and the weepart troubles became identified with the union, even though the union organiser did negotiate on physical conditions of work for truckers and N.A.P. during these five years.

Since my personal contacts with them were of the most meagre kind—I was concentrating on the production lines—I have no notes of attitude apart from those appearing in the records or transmitted by my weepart acquaintances. The office and union files, too, are somewhat bare of recorded incidents. The statistics made available to me are also lacking in the detail I should have liked. Nevertheless, these statistics have some value for the analysis that is to follow.

PRODUCTIVITY

The only other production unit was N.A.P., of an average strength of 56, all women, working under the eye of Ackroyd, the senior foreman. For three reasons the figures on productivity changes in N.A.P. are of little value, even if they had been available—which they were not. First, since their raw materials came off the weepart line, which was governed by weepart rate of effort, the N.A.P. rate had to be geared into the weepart to some extent. Secondly, and most importantly, the range of products, or rather kinds of adjustment to semi-finished parts, was wide, and the sales' demands varied almost from week to week. Since piece-rates were not uniformly standardised (work study techniques were minimal at Glasgow Ltd), there was no consistent rate, or norm, against which all work could be measured, as on the two main lines. Thirdly, the women were on an individual bonus scheme, not a pool.

The productivity or, more accurately, change in effort in the other parts of the factory could not be measured. Everyone was on a time-rate, and those who handled finished parts, truckers, finishers and the like, were given additional payments dependent entirely upon the output of the two production lines. A bonus scheme for all but weepart, bigpart and N.A.P. personnel was instituted on the second week of April 1951. It was based on "actual weight handled" by the various groups and would be "reduced by weight of any breakage".

SPOILAGE

There was no possibility of measuring quality of work in the rest of the factory except in N.A.P. for which figures are available. The N.A.P. history was fairly free from overt controversy. During the reign of Bulgin there were frequent complaints about working conditions—which may have been rationalisations on general dislike of the man. For two years, from the time of Anderson's coming, they did not seem to have required to make any trouble whatsoever, until in autumn 1952 a spate of petty grievances was aired, such as complaints about the quality of materials off the line, and the quality of the barrier cream being issued to them.[1] There was a rush of visits to the ambulance room for treatment of skin rashes (see Fig. 27), and absenteeism was rife. Labour turnover increased. And just then Anderson was required by Head Office to increase the production from N.A.P. It was to satisfy this that he proposed shifting weepart men into N.A.P., a proposal that led to the strike of late January 1953. In November 1953 a new variety of N.A.P. products was introduced.

In a way the spoilage index reflects some of these occurences. Before 1950, spoilage oscillated between 1·5 and 2 per cent but increased in the summer of 1950 to above 2 per cent, reaching a peak of 3·2 per cent during the autumn troubles, prior to Bulgin's final breakdown and removal. It plummeted at once on Anderson's arrival, but rose to about 2 per cent until January of 1951 when it started to fall to below 1·5 per cent. This fall was fairly continuous until winter of 1952–53, broken only by two upward oscillations during the weepart 'troubles' of spring and autumn of 1951. The smoothly dropping rate characteristic of 1952 commences in December 1951, the time of the weepart change from stage 1 to stage 2. This upward oscillation of early 1953 is coincident with the introduction of weepart men into N.A.P. and is to be expected; there was rapid recovery to the 0·4 per cent rate. The rapid rise in the winter of 1953 was coincident with the introduction of the new product, and it too was followed by recovery.

The comparison with weepart spoilage, Fig. 24, shows contemporaneity of fluctuations and changes of trend except for the natural difference during stage 4. The trends in stage 1 are opposite in sign, but similar in stage 2, and

---

[1] The cause of the spate of petty grievances I do not know, but it was something about working conditions.

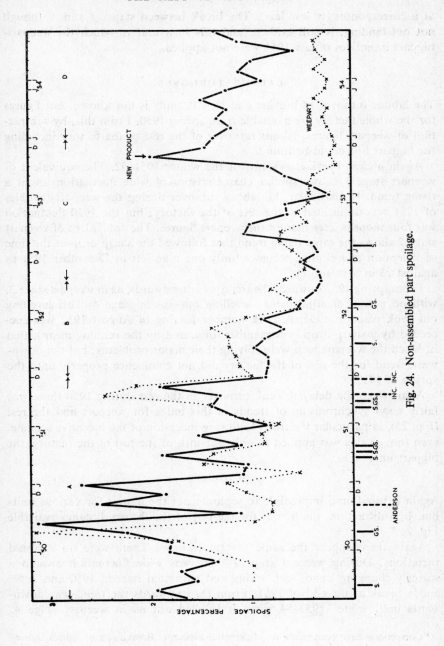

Fig. 24. Non-assembled part spoilage.

125

at a correspondingly low level. The break between stages 1 and 2, though not outstanding, is still evident, and this in a unit to which the weepart-bigpart incentives of late 1951 were not applied.

LABOUR TURNOVER

The labour turnover of bigpart and N.A.P. units is not known, but figures for the whole factory are available from spring 1950. From this, by subtraction of weepart figures, labour turnover of the rest of the factory including the bigpart line could be found.

Again a clear break is evident for the winter 1951–52. The equivalent of weepart stage 1 shows similar characteristics of wide fluctuation about a rising trend. In particular the labour turnover during the weepart troubles of 1951 was duplicated in the rest of the factory; but the 1950 fluctuation was four months later than in the weepart figures. The equivalent of weepart stage 2 shows the same rising trend that followed the sharp drop at the time of inception of incentive schemes (only one man left in December 1951 as against 23 in September).

From spring 1953 onwards the trend was downwards, as in weepart stage 3, with no period of adjustment—levelling out—as in stage 4. This levelling out took place in 1955. A peak number leaving in August 1952 was succeeded by a sharp drop in September (obscured by the running mean), that is, when the weepart men were solving their major problems; but the downward trend for the rest of the factory did not commence properly until the spring of 1953.

Apart from the delay in peak turnover in the rest during 1950 there was fairly good synchronising of trends in this index for weepart and the rest (Fig. 25), in particular the trend following inception of the incentive scheme, even though this was applied to only one-fifth of the rest of the factory, the bigpart line.

ACCIDENTS

Again it was found impossible to separate out the figures for various units but, by subtraction, the figures for the rest of the factory became available Fig. 26.[1]

Again there appear the same general features. There were no seasonal variations. During weepart stage 1 there was wide fluctuation around a scarcely changing trend, with spring and autumnal rises in 1950 and 1951, and a break at the end of 1951. From then onwards the trend was downwards until winter 1953–54 when it levelled out as in weepart stage 4.

---

[1] Corrections have been made for differential exposure. Breakdown of figures showed no significant changes in type and place of accident.

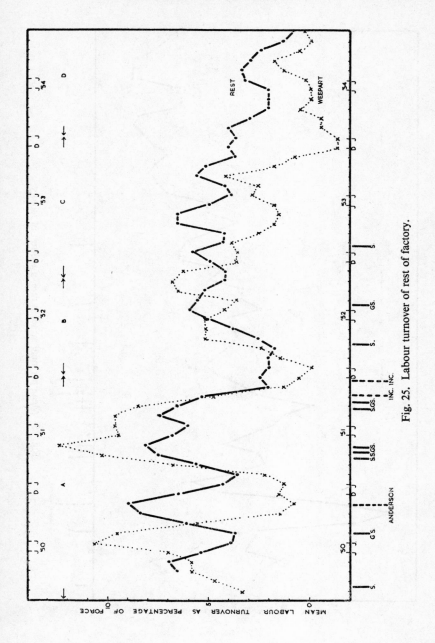

Fig. 25. Labour turnover of rest of factory.

127

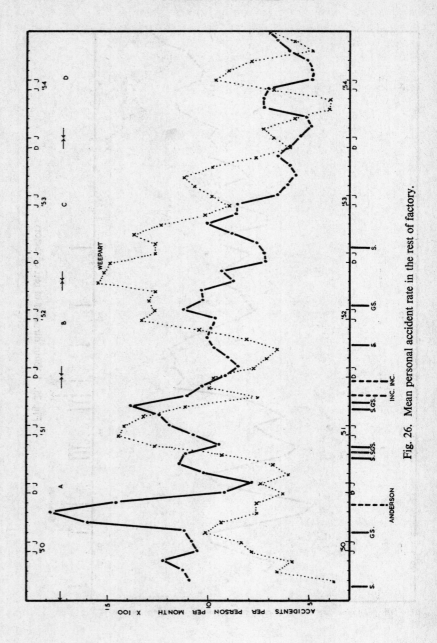

Fig. 26. Mean personal accident rate in the rest of factory.

128

However, this downward trend can be broken up into parts. A sharp peak in August 1952, obscured by the averaging process, marks the real beginning of the downward trend interrupted by a rise in spring of 1953. The similarity with the rates for weeparts is also shown in Fig. 26, the major difference lying in the greater improvement in the second phase for the rest of the factory.

PSYCHOSOMATIC DISORDERS

Since the figures for the bigpart line are small they have not been separated out from those of the remainder, but annual totals for the two-year periods preceding and succeeding the initial year show the same improvement (see later in Table 10). Fig. 27 shows the changes in incidence, and the breakdown into skin dysfunctions and gastric and other groups.

The two most outstanding features are the enormous fluctuations in autumn 1952 and the low and consistent rate in 1953 and 1954. The 1952 fluctuation was the result mainly of an extraordinary series of attendances at the ambulance room of N.A.P. women who, at that time, were giving vent to a series of grievances, including the danger of working with the materials sent into them from the weepart line. Since the weepart men and others handling these same materials showed no corresponding marked reaction of the same kind, it cannot have been the result of change in materials. My impression was that the women were making, as part of their grievances, the most of small skin troubles that otherwise would not have brought them in for treatment. The barrier cream being issued was "no good" they said. This would account for the low contemporaneous figure for other psychosomatic complaints.

The total rates (for all complaints) again show the difference between the marked fluctuations around a nearly level trend in the years 1950 and 1951, and the low and uniform level trend during the two years succeeding the weepart crisis. The introduction of a new barrier cream in the summer of 1953, and hailed with satisfaction, does not seem to have made any difference to the incidence of skin troubles. But it was "nicer" than the previous one! I suppose it was because it smelled better.

ABSENTEEISM

Although figures for weepart line absenteeism itself are not available there are some figures on factory absenteeism; and subdivided into male and female. The female absenteeism applies almost wholly to the N.A.P. since the only other women workers are canteen staff of negligible number. Monthly absenteeism is here expressed as lost percentage of working hours possible.

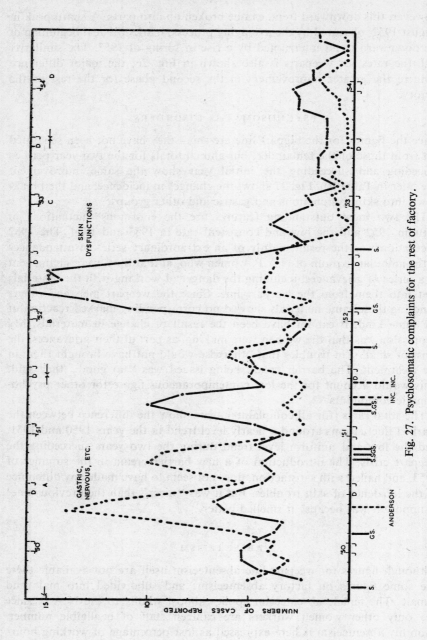

Fig. 27. Psychosomatic complaints for the rest of factory.

'Voluntary absenteeism' was absence for which no reasons were given, usually of short duration, and due to a variety of ostensible causes, mid-week football matches, failure to come on night-shift after a 'party in a pub', getting up late for the early morning start and not being "bothered" to go, just a "dose of the can't be bothereds" itself—"you know, there are times when you feel you just can't face another day on that line". And the like.

Involuntary absence was almost wholly due to sickness for which a "doctor's line" had been submitted. Undoubtedly some voluntary absence was the result of sickness but not severe enough (in the eyes of these 'tough characters') to merit obtaining a medical certificate—"You're not going to cry in the doctor because your nose is running, are you?"

Total voluntary absenteeism, Fig. 28, again shows the general characteristic of all other indices, a higher fluctuating rate in 1950–51, a break in late autumn 1951, and a low uniform rate in the years 1953–54. The male rate was much more uniform than the female, perhaps because there were five times as many men as women, and the improvement was more marked. The fluctuations in stage 1 were not contemporaneous, and the fluctuations in the female rate for the last three years were not duplicated in the male. There were three peaks in the female figure, the autumn of 1952, early spring of 1953 and November 1953, all times when N.A.P. was having trouble. The rise in 1952 was the equivalent of the weepart stage 2 sequence, but this did not appear in the figures for men.

Some data on numbers of persons and amount of time off were collected from April 1951 onwards, and expressed as numbers absent per week, and the average absence per week each month. About 23 people were off each week during the period prior to the break at the end of stage 1, and they were absent about 1·42 shifts each. Whereas, during the second phase, the numbers absent averaged nearly 7 per week and they were off about 1·15 shifts each. That is, both numbers staying off and the length of time away decreased appreciably. During the three peaks of autumn 1952, early spring 1953, and November 1953, the numbers staying off did not increase, but the number of days off were markedly and significantly greater.[1]

Involuntary absenteeism, or sickness, Fig. 29, shows the same general form as voluntary absenteeism in trends and fluctuations, a first fluctuating stage with a sharp break[2] in autumn 1951, and the two-year period 1953–54 much lower and much more uniform. The female rate rose during the critical year of 1952 to the sharp peak in early autumn at the time of the N.A.P. grievances. The male rate, having risen a little in the spring of 1952, fell in

---

[1] It is a pity that the names of those absent were not available since a comparison might then have been made with those showing other forms of 'deviant' behaviour.

[2] This sharp drop in late 1951 is not due to change in methods of recording or of calculation.

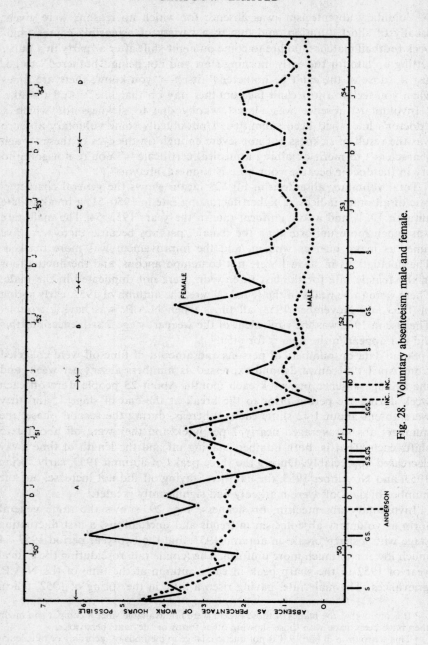

Fig. 28. Voluntary absenteeism, male and female.

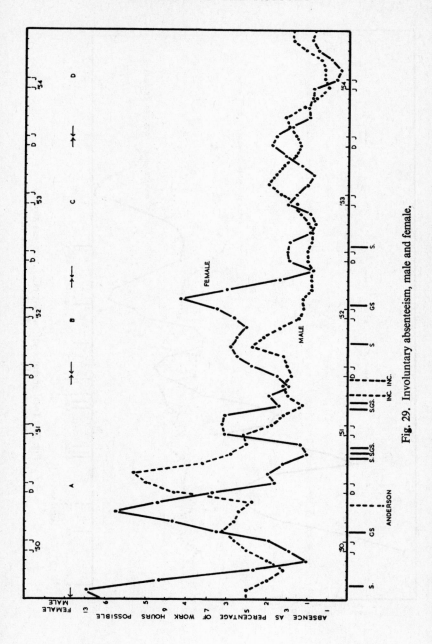

Fig. 29. Involuntary absenteeism, male and female.

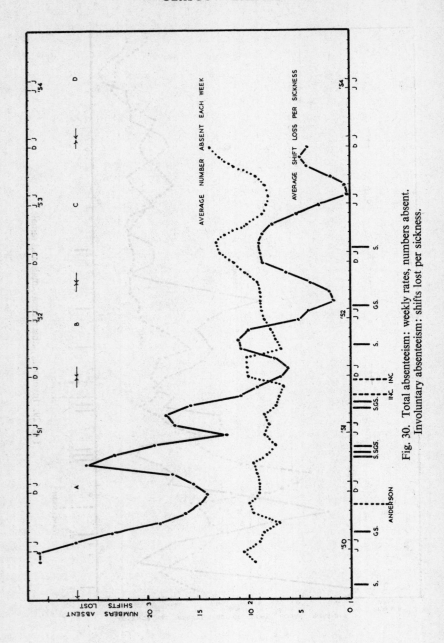

Fig. 30. Total absenteeism: weekly rates, numbers absent.
Involuntary absenteeism: shifts lost per sickness.

134

summer and thereafter remained consistently low. Again there seems to be no clear-cut seasonal variation in peak rates and, since the male and female peaks did not coincide in time, it is likely that these peaks were not wholly the result of changes in the clinical ecology.

The data on weekly sickness, again starting in April 1951, show a marked difference from those for voluntary absenteeism, Fig. 30.

The numbers of shifts lost show a downward trend with no seasonal peaks. But the numbers of those going sick, fairly consistent up to the winter of 1952–53, rose during the second phase. In other words, during the peace and prosperity of the years 1953 and 1954, more persons stayed off work on account of certifiable sickness, but they recovered much more quickly than did persons going sick during the first phase. It seems logical to assume that either they were healthier, or else they did not take advantage of mild disorders and stay off longer than necessary—which is, broadly speaking, a form of better health.

Total absenteeism shows the same characteristics as for its constituents; stage 2 seems to disappear as a distinct stage. Since male absenteeism, especially voluntary, stabilised on passage from stage 1 to stage 2, weepart absenteeism almost certainly stabilised like that for the rest of the factory.

LATENESS

Some records of lateness were made available to me. They were compiled in terms of average number of late-comers per week and average numbers of minutes late per person per week, Fig. 31. The statistics unfortunately were not gathered before April 1951, but there is enough to show that, prior to the stage 1–stage 2 break, both numbers and average time late were high compared to those after. The improvement remained fairly uniform through weepart stages 2 and 3, their rapid deterioration set in at the beginning of stage 4. Both numbers and time late rose in unison. This levelled out in 1955. During this rise Anderson was not worried by lateness (nor by the slight contemporaneous increase in absenteeism). His production and costs were satisfactory and he did not trouble his men, as he did (and Bulgin before him) when fines for lateness were a source of discontent. During the period discussed there was no change in the fining system.

SUMMARY

These statistical data concerning the factory and 'rest of the factory' may be summarised in the same way as those for the weepart line, Fig. 32.

The well-marked break between the two weepart phases is apparent in half the number of indices and is missing entirely in male absenteeism and

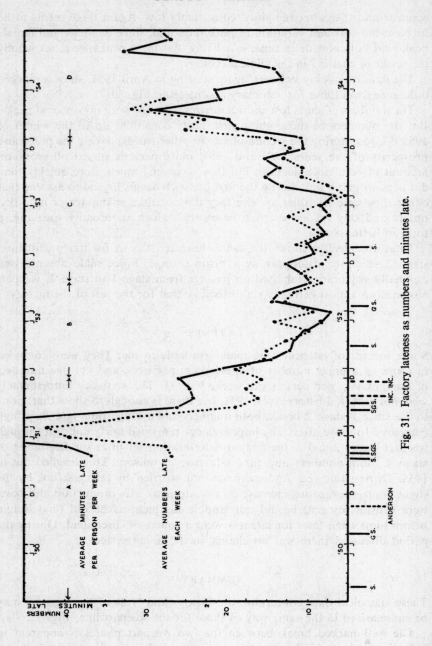

Fig. 31. Factory lateness as numbers and minutes late.

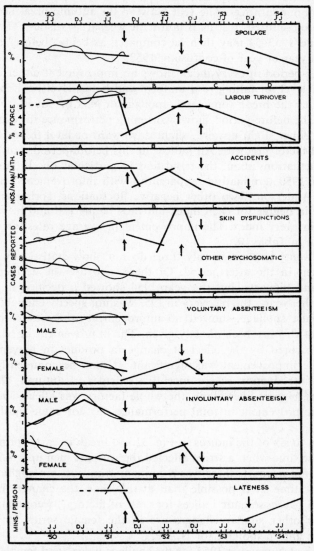

Fig. 32. Summary: trends and fluctuations in indices for the
factory and rest of factory.

lateness. But the break between the weepart stages 1 and 2 (time of incentives) is clear in all but N.A.P. spoilage, and particularly clear in absenteeism, lateness and labour turnover. The year between the autumn breaks of 1951 and 1952 is here confused, just as it is for the weepart statistics. The two years 1950–51 and 1953–54 may then be compared as being 'before' and 'after' the critical year or year of confusion, 1952.

The after-period in every index shows an improvement either continuous to a better level, or falling to a uniform and better level or, if broken, improving after the break (one case—spoilage in N.A.P.—due to a change in product). The before-period shows worsening performance for every weepart index, but either slight upward, slight downward or level trends for bigpart and rest-of-factory indices. All indices in this before-period, however, show marked fluctuations about the trend line, in particular one in late-summer–autumn of 1950 terminating (apparently) with improvements, or with the arrival of Anderson. Two other negative fluctuations, spring and autumn 1951, vary in degree for each index but may be merged and be regarded as occurring in every index. The improvement in average rates for each index is presented in Table 10.

Of the twenty-two series only three do not show statistically significant improvement in the after-period. Of these, two are the accident rates in weeparts and bigparts, but the year 1954 showed a decided improvement over any other year—the recovery in 1953 was not speedy enough. The other series, bigpart spoilage, showed no improvement whatsoever—but an explanation of this has been already given. The improvement in N.A.P. spoilage was obscured by the effect of change in product in November 1953. Even so the improvement was significant. It may be confidently assumed that, after introduction of the incentive schemes of autumn 1951 for the weepart and bigpart lines alone, the whole factory was affected in performance, but improvement in total performance did not come until 1953 and 1954.

Common to six of the indices in Fig. 32 is a break in early spring of 1953. This was the time when a strike affected the weepart men and N.A.P. In all the indices for weeparts there was a contemporaneous, but slight worsening at this same time. It is possible that, at this time, the changes in accident rate, and in psychosomatic indices for 'rest of factory', were mainly due to N.A.P., for other similar changes are in the female series for voluntary absenteeism and in spoilage for N.A.P.

The break at November 1953 for the spoilage index (and female voluntary absenteeism) was probably due to the change in product in N.A.P., but contemporaneous with that was the change in lateness, the fluctuation in male sickness and lateness; and with this there was flattening of all the weepart indices.

138

The contemporaneity of changes and the character of these changes lend themselves to the same kind of analysis as that of the weepart series in Chapter 12. All the indices show a reaction after the introduction of the incentive schemes for the production lines, even though these incentives were not applicable to the rest of the factory directly. Certainly some men such as truckers, finishers and despatchers would have had the possibility

Table 10. *Comparison of Indices for the Periods Before and After the Critical Year*

			1950–1	1953–4
Weepart Line	Productivity, rate		57	84
	Spoilage, % production		3·03	0·88
	Labour turnover, % of force monthly		15·6	6·5
	Accidents, for the period		370	351
	Skin trouble cases reported	ca.	71	44
	Psychosomatic cases reported	ca.	70	28
Bigpart Line	Productivity, rate		66	88
	Spoilage, % production	ca.	2·63	2·70
	Accidents, for the period		132	120
	Skin trouble cases reported	ca.	25	9
	Psychosomatic cases reported	ca.	29	5
N.A.P.	Spoilage, % production		1·65	0·98[1]
	Involuntary absenteeism, %		6·1	2·2
	Voluntary absenteeism, %		3·3	1·4
Rest	Labour turnover, % of force monthly		6·2	3·6
	[2]Accidents for the period		666	377
	[2]Skin trouble cases reported		93	39
	[2]Psychosomatic cases reported		110	14
Factory	[3]Involuntary absenteeism, %		2·7	1·2
	[3]Voluntary absenteeism, %		2·8	0·6
	Total absenteeism, %		6·0	1·9
	Lateness, minutes lost per person per week		3·4	1·5

[1] Change in product. [2] Less bigpart figures. [3] Less N.A.P. figures.

of earning more than before because higher production from the lines would mean a bonus for handling greater quantities of materials. But the lines did not produce more (the increase of bigpart production was short-lived); and yet the indices show continued reaction. Moreover, N.A.P., as well as other personnel, was not affected by the incentive scheme, or the possibility of gaining from it, and yet that department seems to have reacted.

The same kind of comment can be made about the changes that took place a year later, in autumn 1952. No group other than weeparts was changed—

though N.A.P. did get some slight improvement in physical working conditions—and yet, apart from some absentee and the lateness indices, a break occurred then. Weepart indices (but apparently not bigpart productivity) and all other indices, excepting absenteeism and lateness, were affected[1] by a change in early spring 1953, and the only common experience then was Anderson's address to the whole factory—certainly not a change in economic factors.

For the whole factory it seems possible to postulate the same series of situations as for weepart:

Stage 1 situation of negative influence: —economic—social;
Stage 2 situation of confused influence: +economic—social;
Stage 3 situation of positive influence: +economic+social; adjusting;
Stage 4 situation of positive influence: +economic+social; adjusted.

But there are some differences in the situation of confused influence, stage 2. Considering Figs. 20 and 32—the reactions at the beginning of this stage were of three kinds:

(i) Immediate deterioration continuing—labour turnover and accidents in weeparts and the rest, and female absenteeism, voluntary and involuntary;
(ii) Immediate improvement, then deterioration—psychosomatic complaints;
(iii) Continuing improvement—productivity, spoilage, male absenteeism (including weepart presumably) and lateness for the whole factory.[2]

It would seem to follow from this, and the analysis of environmental changes in the preceding paragraph, that:

(i) Labour turnover, accidents and female absenteeism were strongly affected by social factors to the extent of damping down the effect of the economic;
(ii) Psychosomatic complaints were not so strongly affected, and the social factors gained sway only after a short delay;
(iii) Productivity, spoilage, male absenteeism and lateness were strongly affected by the economic factors to the extent of damping down the effect of the social.

Moreover, since all these last indices throughout the factory improved, even though the economic change was limited in application to the two production lines, it follows that *the economic factor was not money itself* since money was not earned (and in N.A.P. could not be earned) by reason of the change. Therefore the factor involved must lie in the content of the

---

[1] The changes in the weepart and bigpart series are not statistically significant or even outstanding.
[2] From the beginning of 1952 very few women indeed were late, and this continued until November 1953 when they began to 'fall behind'.

incentive scheme. It should also be noted that the inception in August 1951 of the bonus scheme for all but bigpart, weepart and N.A.P. personnel appears to have had no effect on the indices discussed.

Furthermore, the social factors involved in the changes in autumn of 1952 were not universal throughout the factory. The sociological and managerial changes that were made concerned only the weepart line. In the change of spring 1953 a change in the managerial factor affected all the factory contemporaneously and directly—the address to the factory. In some way or another the motives engendered by the social changes of autumn 1952, involving the weepart line alone, were transmitted to the rest of the factory and became universally effective.

PART IV. ANALYTICAL

INTRODUCTION

Immersed as they were in the daily routine of factory life neither men nor manager at Glasgow Ltd found it easy to see their affairs other than as a sequence of incidents requiring 'on the spot' treatment. This is not unusual—managers tend to work on that basis—but men, and especially trade union officials, tend to work according to precedent or "tradition". That tendency among the men becomes evident only when the historical method of analysis is applied. Their behaviour throughout these five years seems to have been governed by judgments of the kind that are expressed as 'fair' or 'unfair', 'reasonable' or 'unreasonable'. Indeed, as the last expression suggests, these judgments have an essentially moral basis, much as our 'traditional' common law has a moral basis and frequently requires interpretation of what is reasonable.

But just as we so often find difficulty in explaining 'reasonable', just as we 'feel' rather than work it out logically, so the men at Glasgow Ltd felt, and were nearly inarticulate about their feelings; and being so became vociferous. It was hard for the manager to understand the men in this condition, not only because they were inarticulate and expressed their feelings in all manner of rationalisations, but because, being a manager, his own frames of reference, the standards upon which he made his judgments, were different. This is what happens daily when we, outside the battlefield of industry, pass judgment on the behaviour of both men and managers. Our frames of reference are again different.

It is therefore essential, in trying to understand Anderson and his men, to remember this, to avoid colouring the understanding of their behaviour by making judgments of it the while; though it is not easy to be thus objective in dealing with problems that arise out of situations so highly charged with emotion as are these modern industrial dilemmas.

CHAPTER 15

INCENTIVES AND DIFFERENTIALS

Anderson, and his production managers, always talked to me about the "bonus scheme" as an incentive towards greater productivity. But it was not always an incentive of that nature. When the first bonus-scheme was instituted in 1946 it was not intended primarily and purely as means of gaining greater productivity. It was also intended as an attraction to recruit men. "When the bonus scheme was introduced it was for weepart men only as an inducement to keep them on the job" (Maloney, p. 35). "It would be impossible for the employers to find weepart assembly-men if the present basic wages being paid weren't boosted by the bonus earnings, and I repeat that weepart assembly-men without skill would make it quite impossible for any of the team on the weepart line to earn more than basic wages" (Macdonald, p. 42). The original bonus scheme was therefore not an incentive. It seems advisable, before proceeding, that the terms incentive and differential be defined, for confusion existed in the minds of Bulgin and Anderson, or at least they did not recognise that they were thinking of the bonus scheme in a confused fashion.

A monetary *incentive*,[1] as I comprehend it, is a money reward for bettering of some aspects of performance: efficiency (manipulative skills), stability of output, labour turnover, absenteeism, accidents, better industrial relations. The incentive provides an end and hence a motive, which is the desire to achieve that end. The money reward itself is usually the end (or rather what money can obtain), but the end may be the achievement of better performance—for some operatives thus find satisfaction—which achievement is symbolised by the financial reward.

A *differential* payment, or shortly a differential, is a money payment for special capacities or needs, *without* necessarily any connotation of *bettering* performance. It may be given for

(a) Content of the work

(i) Because the work requires manipulative skill.
(ii) Because the work requires technological skill, specialised knowledge.

---

[1] Henceforward the use of the words incentive and differential will imply that they are monetary. There are non-monetary incentives and differentials which do not concern this discussion.

11   145   G.L.

(iii) Because the work requires dependability, for example, care of expensive machinery or consistent accuracy in any form.

(iv) Because the work requires a high rate of output (this over and above an incentive to high productivity).

(b) Recruitment

(i) For recruitment into the firm—attracting labour when alternative vacancies are available.

(ii) For recruitment into an occupation—attracting labour into new kinds of job.

(c) Social Needs

(i) For status[1] within the firm—reflecting standing without any reference to skills or recruitment.

(ii) For status outside the firm—reflecting domestic needs, size of family, married or single, etc.

(d) Moral Considerations

Because of what is considered "fair" or "just", without explicit reference to the foregoing.[2]

The incentive and differential are intimately related. A differential payment for skill can be comprehended by an operative as a reward to be gained for bettering his skill. Once he has bettered his skill then the payment is no longer an incentive but remains a differential. Similarly an incentive can become a differential—as happened in Glasgow Ltd. The bonus scheme of 1946, a payment by results (P.B.R.) scheme, allowed the unskilled worker to make more money by working harder, more precisely, at a faster rate, that is by increasing his manipulative skill. Two things were the result.

Since unskilled men do not make their wage by reason of special skill, they tend to work on a time-rate, and make extra earnings by over-time working. By getting the chance to make more money without over-time the potentiality of greater earnings is increased, and this is an attraction, a differential for recruitment. But since the P.B.R. implies an increase in skill the unskilled man becomes, to some extent, semi-skilled, hence his status rises, and again this becomes a differential for recruitment. This went so far at Glasgow Ltd that the weepart men demanded in effect a skill differential—see Macdonald quotation above—despite the fact that the job required no extra skills that could not be learned in a day, and certainly in

---

[1] I shall use the word 'status' in the loose sense, meaning a combination of rank and prestige; but see p. 168.

[2] To my colleague, Mr D. J. Robertson, I am much indebted for the clarity of his discussion of these differences and categories.

less than a week, as the weekly productivity with new labour showed. To quote Maloney again (p. 38) "a good deal of new labour has started and a good few of them have lifted their books too . . . they must have a bigger turnover of men here than they had in the Eighth Army . . . (a big bonus) was gained with new labour against one snag or another and by the end of that week we had got the feel of things and were ready for a go next week on the same terms. And that we did in no uncertain manner . . . our figures on the board reached an 81".

Once the bonus had become a differential in 1947 the incentive to increased productivity was reduced. This would account for the flattening out of productivity in 1947 and 1948, confused of course, by the vagaries of long-part manufacture. Certainly the weepart men were capable of greater effort, as later figures demonstrate, but they claimed they could not do better—because the machine-line was incapable of the higher speeds. This claim seems to be a rationalisation on some other and deeper-seated cause.

Towards the beginning of 1949 the weepart men, and the bigpart men too, began to wonder about their bonus in relation to that of similar workers in England. In other words, the bonus was still very much a differential. (It seems clear that the compilers of the original bonus scheme had not taken into consideration the differential aspect and that, with strengthening of the union hold in the factory, this aspect was bound to become at least a 'bone of contention' if not a *casus belli*, as it did.)

At the same time another process was in operation affecting the differential evaluation of the bonus. Just after the war negotiation at national level for related industries had given assembly-men a 1½d. per hour basic wage differential over men in non-production occupations, truckers, despatchers, loaders, finishers and such like. These non-production men had also been put on a P.B.R. scheme, the 1½d. differential remaining. National negotiation in 1949 increased basic wage-rates of non-production men by 1½d. so wiping out this basic work content differential. In other factories (in England), mechanisation had allowed the assembly-men to make greater P.B.R. bonus earnings than those on ancillary occupations, hence the removal of the basic differential could be accepted by national representatives of the assembly-men—the bonus differential was comparatively big compared with the basic wage differential. But this was not the case in Glasgow Ltd. So the assembly-men on both lines discovered that an internal differential had been wiped out and, at the level of productivity at that time, their earnings were sometimes less than those of the ancillary workers. The bonus was maybe a recruitment differential as over and against unskilled occupations elsewhere in Glasgow district, but it was not a work content differential as over and against similar (and partly skilled) occupations in England and non-skilled occupations in the factory itself.

Bulgin was apparently incapable of seeing that the bonus scheme was no incentive but essentially a differential payment, and a badly designed one at that. He could not understand the demands of the production men. All he could see was that they could make greater earnings if they worked harder because, on the surface, the scheme was P.B.R. That the men saw the scheme in terms of comparison with schemes for similar and ancillary work had no meaning for him. In effect he was saying, "If you would work harder and make as much as others, you need not bother about whether workers elsewhere have a different bonus scheme."

Anderson, however, immediately he arrived, saw the inequity of the situation. But, instead of regarding the scheme as a bad differential payment, he saw it only as a bad incentive payment, and tried to alter it in terms of an incentive, by new ways of calculating and by re-distribution of personnel. His first sympathetic approach improved performance, but his action restored the feelings of differential discrimination. The external differential remained and the whole factory, if the indices be read at their face value, felt the production-lines had due cause for complaint, and sympathised. That the weepart line alone took strong action in strikes and go-slows in the spring and autumn of 1951 was the result of other circumstances as well.

Anderson, trying to get a better incentive scheme in July 1951, actually proposed an increase in bonus payments to act as a recruitment differential— "to attract a better class of labour instead of nomadic riff-raff". He then also saw the payment as an internal work-content differential—"the weepart men have to work very hard indeed . . . their rate of pay should be, if anything, at the higher level among the factory workers as a whole". The bigpart men were not making too much fuss, for their particular bonus now gave them earnings with a positive differential over the ancillary workers, and over the weepart men.

The new bonus scheme that Anderson brought into being in autumn 1951 was a copy of one employed at an English factory. It was accepted and the external differential disappeared. Strangely enough Anderson still did not see that what he had done was to remove the external differential; he talked of it as a better incentive, "at least some recognition of the manual work put in". From that time neither the external nor the internal differential was mentioned. And from that time, for *all* the factory, those indices which were intimately related to earnings, productivity, spoilage, absenteeism (not N.A.P.) and lateness improved.

Yet the non-production workers, including N.A.P., were not directly and financially affected by this new scheme; nor was there a question of an external differential for them. If anything the internal differential between production and ancillary workers widened to the detriment of the latter—

and they reacted with better performance. They had been comparatively peaceful throughout the previous four years, presumably because both external and internal differentials were favourable, and they had little to complain about. Moreover, when they had been granted a new bonus-rate in the early part of the same year, increasing the chances of greater earnings (provided the parts to be handled were coming off the production lines in large enough quantities), they showed no sign of improving their performance. Their behaviour was therefore quite anomalous at first sight or, at least, quite unexpected. Why should they not better performance when given a greater incentive, and why should they better performance in response to a change that had no relation to their own bonus scheme? It must be assumed that something about the new bonus scheme was not only acceptable to the production lines but to the ancillary workers.

For the production men the scheme became a pure incentive scheme—which is evident in the remarkable and immediate rise in bigpart productivity, a typical reaction to a good incentive scheme. (It was a rise that suffered later from social factors just as weepart increase suffered, only more so.) But since the rest of the factory reacted positively as well, it must be assumed that it was not the incentive aspect of the scheme that recommended it but the change in the differential aspect. It was not a question of a change in attitude to content of the work, nor of a change in recruitment differential; nor was it a recognition of status outside the factory, reflecting domestic needs. It might have been a recognition of status within the factory, that the line ought to be given higher status. But the bigpart men did not require this higher status, already having got it, and the differential between the two lines remained; and the differential between weepart and ancillary workers (who reacted positively) was narrowed, even reversed. It seems most likely that what appealed to everybody in the change was the moral consideration. The change was "fair". Said Maloney, "It was a' richt—but!"

The substance of this is that it seems a bonus scheme cannot be effective as an incentive until the rightness or fairness of its differential content is established. What establishes the sense of rightness or fairness is a matter for deeper analysis.

It is to this essential difference between the differential and incentive character of the 1946 bonus scheme that I attribute the slow rise in productivity after the scheme's inception, this in contrast to the rapid rise in productivity in autumn 1952 after the social factors had become positive and permitted the 1951 scheme to operate. The 1946 scheme was a differential, the 1951 scheme was an incentive. The slow rise in 1946–47 I have already commented upon as being unlike the usual effects of an incentive scheme elsewhere. The rise in 1952 was typical of the proper reaction to an incentive scheme. But just as longpart production confused the effect of the

1946 differential so did the social factors confuse the effect of the 1951 incentive to the extent of almost nullifying its value as an incentive.

The next question that follows automatically is what was inherent in the "—but!" of Maloney's remark. In this lies the failure of the bonus scheme, now a pure incentive, to inspire the weepart men to a rapid increase in productivity during 1952. Since it was effective at once with the bigpart line then, for that line, the scheme had no faults. The fall of bigpart productivity in the spring and summer of 1952, after this first reaction to the incentive, was due, as the narrative shows, to the character of bigpart relations with the other production line and with the manager, and not to a fault in the incentive. (These relations are not relevant to this chapter.) Presumably the scheme had faults as an incentive in its application to the weepart line; and since the complaints that accompanied the weepart troubles of 1952 were mainly concerned with methods of calculating how much bonus was earned, including methods of work, these methods require examination.[1]

There were three variables in methods of bonus calculation, the speed of the machine-line (machine productivity), the rate of output on assembly (man productivity), and the numbers of men employed on the assembly. Each of these variables at one time or another, singly or in consort, was a source of complaint.

SPEED OF THE MACHINE-LINE

While the resentment against the external differential was building up in 1949 (p. 29+), a proposal by Bulgin to run the machine-line during meal-hours, because continuous running was mechanically more efficient, was strenuously resisted. A suggestion of this kind at any later date (as Anderson learned to his cost) brought this resistance to the surface at once—it became a traditional bone of contention, a *cause célèbre*. By 1950 the men became convinced, or at least seemed to become convinced, that the line could not run fast enough to give them the chance of achieving a maximum bonus.[2] Anderson believed this was a symptom "of the deep feeling of injustice and sense of exploitation which at that time permeated the minds of the weepart personnel" (p. 35). But, shortly afterwards, even he apparently became convinced as well. He wrote his directorate that "it is not possible to run constantly at much more than a 76" (p. 36), and he, like Bulgin, attempted to make up for this by trying to get the men to accept meal-time running, and by staggering of gang breaks. Nevertheless, during 1949, the line was certainly capable of running for several hours at an 83

---

[1] There was, in addition, the matter of fines for spoilage.

[2] The real trouble here, not recognised even by the men, was the complication induced by drawing off part-finished materials to N.A.P.

(p. 30), but, as Bulgin discovered, not even by increasing the number of men at the assembly end could an increased line speed be maintained. Anderson spent much time during 1951 trying to make mechanical changes in the line that would speed it up, still believing that it was mechanical inefficiency that kept speeds down. What he apparently did not see was that the assembly men could force the controller to cut down speeds, in fact that if the assembly-men didn't feel like, or didn't seem to feel like working beyond a certain rate, then the line had to slow down. It was only when he and Ackroyd, in April 1952, tried it out personally that he found it could be done.[1] They were controlling and the men could not force them to slow the line. So he could finally say to his foremen in late August 1952, "the time has come to maintain and improve the technique of line-control so that we become accustomed to weekly productivities of the order of at least a 77" (p. 59). And this did not require meal-time running!

NUMBERS EMPLOYED ON ASSEMBLY

There were several changes in the constitution of the crew employed on assembly. Before 1946 and longpart manufacture there were three gangs of four. From 1947 to 1949 there were two gangs of five men each per shift. In trying to speed up assembly Bulgin put more men on assembly, first by going back to having three gangs of four, then three gangs of five. Though he obtained greater production he did not increase productivity and the bonus earned did not rise. On Anderson's first attempt to mend matters after he arrived he reduced the gang to four each, but this had no effect. With shortage of special alloys and such like in spring 1951 he cut the gang to three apiece, adding two spare men at intervals up to March 1952. In June 1952 the gang was back to four, three gangs to each shift. These changes required different techniques of assembly organisation—to be described in the next chapter— and changes in line speeds. Changes in line speeds, measured against a norm of running-time for a given size of crew, meant complicated calculations not only on the office desks but on scraps of canteen paper on Fridays and Saturdays. These calculations frequently did not coincide.

MACHINE LINE AND MAN PRODUCTIVITY CALCULATIONS

The men measured their effort by the number of parts produced. The office measured productivity by the tonnage of materials that passed through the line. But the office computation was complicated by the varying "draw-off" of partly finished materials to the N.A.P. From experience the men would know fairly accurately how many parts they assembled related to the

---

[1] The night-shift never seemed to have trouble, that is, when N.A.P. materials were not drawn off—and when Anderson was not present!

machine-rate. It is not to be wondered that the office calculations gave frequent cause for suspicion in the minds of the assembly-men. Anderson did two things to sort out this muddle. First, in the bonus scheme of 1951 he admitted the number of parts assembled to be a criterion of productivity. This apparently made little change in the attitude of the men. What pleased them more in the system of working he introduced in July 1952 was the standardisation of "draw-off" to N.A.P. so that the assembly-men on the day-shifts "knew better where they stood". The night-shift men always "knew where they stood", and could run the line so fast that they would finish their decided quota an hour before stopping time. What amazes me was that Anderson never got to know of this, or that the night-shift foreman did not see it and report it.

But the major muddle in the period after inception of Anderson's bonus scheme was in the calculation of the bonus in terms of machine and man productivity—which is described in the narrative (p. 41+), and need not be repeated here. By returning to the assembly crew of three gangs of four per shift this difficulty was automatically cut out, for the norm of machine productivity was measured in tonnage in standard time running with such a crew. (Bulgin at one time had had such an assembly crew but his troubles then arose out of the question of differentials.)

With these points in mind three occurrences become significant as giving a clue to what elements of the situation were important during that critical year of 1952. In April Anderson personally demonstrated that the machine-line could provide all that was necessary for the men to achieve the bonus level he had prophesied. The crew was of three gangs of three per shift. In June and July, with new organisation of N.A.P. draw-off, and a crew of three gangs of four per shift, productivity did not increase as expected. Anderson was away most of that six weeks trial period. During August Anderson again personally demonstrated that the line could give all that the new crew, three gangs of four, would require. This brought about immediate reaction in a rapid rise in productivity. It seems, therefore, that it was the combination of change in crew size and personal approach of Anderson which was necessary before the incentive took effect in the weepart line.[1]

This finding can be arrived at by a comparative argument. The bigpart line reacted at once to the new incentive scheme, with an immediate rapid rise in productivity. But this tailed off in approach to the strike of spring 1952, in which the bigpart men took a hand, expressing dissatisfaction with the manager, and with meal-time line running—the cause of the weepart men going on strike. Yet immediately afterwards the bigpart men began meal-time working. There had been no change in size of crew or method of

[1] There were no contemporaneous external economic factors, such as sudden rise in cost of living.

calculating bonus. The strike did not ostensibly answer any bigpart grievance. All that seemed to alter for the bigpart men, as far as I could find out, was the attitude to the manager. They discovered he was a "straight guy" and would not alter bonus-rates however much their bonus earnings increased. This bigpart change could therefore be ascribed only to a managerial factor. There was apparently no contemporaneous change for the weepart men. It apparently required an alteration in weepart crew size before the managerial factor became operative; and then the incentive could act on weepart men as it did on bigpart. "After August", said Maloney, "Mr Anderson just needed to ask us and we'd do it." He was no longer "the manager", he was "Mr".

It seems, therefore, that (1) in the case of the bigpart line the sociological conditions were appropriate at the time of inception of the bonus scheme, but it required a change in the managerial factor to bring about a permanent positive reaction to the scheme; (2) in the case of the weepart line the sociological conditions (the constitution of the crew) and the relations to the manager required attention before the incentive took effect.

It would seem that, in situations of this kind, an incentive scheme is not likely to be fully effective until the appropriate social conditions (sociological and managerial) are established.

Even though these changes in the bigpart and weepart lines apparently affected the rest of the factory contemporaneously, it was not until spring of 1953 that the rest of the factory showed a general bettering of performance. This took place after the short strike about N.A.P. manning in January 1953, when Anderson addressed the whole factory at one time. It seems reasonable to suggest that here the managerial element was effective alone. During the remaining part of the weepart second phase the economic (incentive), the sociological, and the managerial factors appear to have reached an effective balance. In what way the sociological and managerial factors acted upon the attitudes of the men in reaction to the incentive requires separate treatment.

CHAPTER 16

MANAGEMENT AND AUTHORITY

The two managers who appear in the narrative were dissimilar in many ways, as their behaviour shows. I had little to do with Bulgin, meeting him by chance on only three occasions, but Anderson I came to know better, not only as a manager but as a student. Some time after he had left Glasgow Ltd, he wrote me on several occasions on his opinions about the way a manager should look upon his job, and how he himself acted.

Looking back it is manifestly clear to me that I am by nature a bit of a dictator, but a benevolent one; I do like to get my own way and will fight all and sundry to get it. I believe in my job to which I am irrefutably dedicated and that my actions will affect many more than my employees (most of them have families). Therefore justice, equity and fair dealing must dominate my every act, but courage, strength of character and determination are essential if one is to succeed as a manager in the industrial conditions of today.[1] Men like a strong manager who knows his own mind and acts quickly and fairly when the occasion demands it, even though such action may be 'unpopular'. A good manager gradually proves to his employees that in the long run his actions and decisions have been sound and to their advantage. Naturally a good manager follows up his actions and if the results are not as successful as they ought to be he should do something about it without delay, even to letting it be known that such and such an action instituted by him was wrong. Of course if a manager makes too many mistakes he will lose the respect of his men, but I am quite certain that men have no time for the type of manager whose vanity is such that he will never admit to making a mistake. This is most important. I myself made several mistakes but because I was only too ready to admit and correct them, I gained the affection of the men—'he is only human like us', you know.

About the crisis of summer and August 1952 he wrote:

Even protracted periods of performance demonstration in the mid-summer of 1952 by Ackroyd (the General Foreman) met with only partial success and so I reached the conclusion that certain elements (close to the men) were not working with me and I did something about it after returning from holiday at the end of August 1952. An unsatisfactory Shift Foreman was replaced by a more progressive one and a certain Shop Steward was virtually sacked—actually he 'left'.[2] These actions shook the whole section quite somewhat and demonstrated that I 'meant business'. To sum up this phase, therefore (having previously introduced over a period of

[1] This sounds in part if he had had been reading one of the many texts on 'what makes a good manager', but he spoke like that before he took classes in management.
[2] The foreman was Simpson, sacked for blustering, aggressive behaviour towards the men. The steward was Macrae, who 'left' not because Anderson got rid of him, but because he "did a bunk" after mishandling union matters.

about eighteen months better working conditions plus a much more equitable bonus scheme, designed to encourage high productivity with every incentive to do so) the two salient features inducing greater efficiency and improved morale were: (1) positive and irrefutable demonstrations by the Management as to what could be achieved in the way of production and quality. In this context the Manager himself helped with the demonstration and put himself in the position of the workmen, so to speak, taking them into full confidence: in fact being thoroughly 'matey' and behaving and talking to a certain number of them as though he clearly wanted them to earn good bonuses without sweating the guts out of them, showing them how it could be done, and
(2) eliminating incompetent supervision plus certain alien or undesirable characters among the rank and file. This action (especially the removal of the incompetent foreman) clearly showed the men (and the floor supervision!) that the Manager was really getting tough and as such had better be treated with a little more consideration or else. . . .

He described the result of his meeting the factory during the last strike in January 1953 in these words:

The men realised that I really was honest, intended to treat them fairly and equitably and that I was not in the least afraid of them and could treat their 'spokesman' with open contempt[1] when the situation required such treatment. I am quite certain that workmen do *not* like weak managers. That vital meeting with all the men in January 1953 set the seal on any further distrust or suspicion by the men of the Manager. They finally realised that although I could be tough and certainly talk tough, I was in fact intensely human and possessed of a fanatic belief in justice and fair play. I am convinced of this conclusion because afterwards we went from strength to strength and one was greeted with smiling faces when entering the factory instead of the previous dour look of resentment and of suspicion. When I left Glasgow Ltd in the autumn of 1955 the productivity on the weepart line had risen 82 per cent since 1951. All of which goes to show what can be done in a factory by employing a satisfactory production bonus scheme and developing implicit trust and esteem in the men for the Manager who, while he must know the technique of producing his material, must above all be imbued with human understanding, tolerance, sympathy and justice. If he has not these things he will never be supremely successful at his job . . . but I am not an Olympian.

The last strike at Glasgow Ltd is a classic for future students. I deliberately set about the problem 'according to the book' with liberal and free consultation, presentation of production data and so on—all in a most friendly manner. Yet despite all this the weepart men's spokesman announced at the last consultation: 'We agree that you have a case but we're just bloody well *not* going on N.A.P.' So never let any student of yours, Sir, go away with the idea that he only has to act with punctilious constitutional correctness in order to solve all industrial problems!

His attitude to trade unions was summarised thus:

I consider them to be essential in the industrial conditions of today and that they can be of great value so long as (1) the T.U. leaders and officials enjoy the con-

[1] Referring to O'Brien.

fidence and esteem of the rank and file; and (2) there is mutual respect and understanding between the local T.U. representative and the Manager.

It is indispensable that the Convener of Shop Stewards, i.e. the leader of all shop stewards in a factory, should be a 'good man'. By this I mean sensible, intelligent, respectful, tactful, honest and straightforward. He will then earn the respect of and gain easy access to the Manager. That was where Mr Macdonald blundered in the early Glasgow Ltd days and only by bitter experience did he learn that negotiation with me was virtually impossible unless his Convener was acceptable to me. Finally, I think that Trade Unions should never become so powerful that they can dictate to employers and thus render them impotent to govern according to the best interests of industry and the nation generally. Managers *must* be able to manage. As I see the situation today the function of the Trade Unions is to safeguard the workers' interests and to protect them against the rapacity and stupidity of employers (the capitalist class). It is one of the functions of Works Management to hold the balance between these two opposing interests.

Admittedly these expressions of opinion and belief, and statements of what Anderson did in the light of these expressions, are *a posteriori*, but they come from the figure central to what is being discussed, and therefore must be taken into consideration. And what he states as having occurred agrees with the evidence of men and union organiser. These beliefs are also valuable if they give a clue to the managerial factors particularly important during 1952, the year of crisis. But it is unlikely that Anderson behaved strictly according to those beliefs for he was certainly no "Olympian", and as likely as anyone to stray from an idealist path of managerial rectitude. Even so his errant wanderings may be as important for analysis as his more conformable steps.

His beliefs may be put into five categories:

(*a*) *Belief in the authority vested in the manager.* This authority is what Anderson implies when he talks of a strong manager, with courage, strength of character, determination and such like. It is also what he implies when he uses the expression "getting tough", and that "workmen do not like weak managers. He should be empowered to act quickly and firmly when the occasion demands it." He does not mean autocratic power of an arbitrary nature wielded without a sanctioned right to command and to enforce obedience (i.e. authoritarian), for he talks as well of justice, fair play, equity, humanity and such-like characteristics which are not normally outstanding in the use of authoritarian methods of control. He means that a manager who gives a proper order should exercise, and *must* be able to exercise, power to see that it is obeyed, for the propriety of the order involves sanctioned use of power. His authority to so govern must not be trammelled by trade union power.

This form of authority is the right (stemming from the legal character of the enterprise and of the contractual system of hiring labour—law of master and servant, for example), vested in a position in the enterprise to order and co-ordinate functions, and to expect obedience in the ordering and co-ordinating. Depending upon the purpose of the enterprise and upon the position, the person so vested with this authority may have the right not only to expect obedience but to require it, meaning that he has the legal power to enforce it. This form of authority I call STRUCTURAL AUTHORITY since it is inherent in the hierarchic structure of an enterprise. It is often called "line authority".

(b) *Belief that a manager should be "human"*. The manager "must above all be imbued with human understanding, tolerance, sympathy". In situations such as those during summer 1952, he should be able to become "thoroughly matey, behaving and talking to a certain number of them as though he clearly wanted them to earn good bonuses, etc." Able to admit mistakes and to correct them—"he is human like us"—Anderson "gained affection". The manager must be "easy of access". Talking of another manager who was not easy of access Maloney said to me, "It's a bad thing when you can't get to see the head of the house". Other remarks from the men about Anderson were that "you can always see him", "he's always down among the men", and "he could get his jacket off to it". It seems that the men's feelings justified this belief of Anderson. Since this form of behaviour, and its acceptance by the operatives, depends upon the personalities of the manager and the men, and since its acceptance is conducive to what is known loosely as 'informal leadership', I propose to regard it as a form of authority, distinct from structural and sapiential (below), and to call it PERSONAL AUTHORITY. I define it as the entitlement to command and/or direct by reason of the fittingness of the personality with the purpose of the enterprise and with the personalities of the members of the enterprise.

(c) *Belief that a manager must be competent*. This does not necessarily mean that a manager of an engineering works should be a skilled engineer, but he should "know the technique of producing his material", he should know what he is doing, he must not make too many mistakes, his actions and decisions in the long run must be sound. In Anderson's case he could not only "get his jacket off", but he could do things on the machine-line himself and he knew how, and showed the men how, to run the line at higher speeds. He should also know enough to "eliminate" the incompetent such as bad foremen. He must know enough to govern according to the best economic interest of the firm and to hold the balance between the two opposing interests of employer and trade union. His competence involves authority of the kind that is meant when talking of expertness.

This is not the same as structural authority. It is the entitlement to be heard by reason of knowledge and expertness, for which reason I call it SAPIENTIAL AUTHORITY. Such knowledge is personal and therefore the authority is vested in a person and is not in the position occupied by the person.

Sometimes this authority is loosely called "staff authority" to distinguish it from "line authority", but the fact that a man is in a staff position does not mean that he has staff authority. When a person takes up a position he is automatically vested with structural authority, he is not necessarily vested with sapiential authority.

(d) *Belief that a manager must be moral.* Anderson implies morality in his use of such words as "justice", "equity", and "fair play". These are necessary to develop implicit trust and esteem. He must not be dishonest— "only a fool and a knave would even contemplate such a thing" for "any manager worth his salt knows that his men can't be fooled". They must trust each other. He must have integrity. His actions and decisions in being sound (competent) must also be moral in that they are to the advantage of the employees as well as of the employers. His holding the balance between the employers and the trade unions involves making moral decisions. A manager regarded as a moral man in these senses may be said to exercise MORAL AUTHORITY which I define as the entitlement to control and direct by reason of goodness and rightness in action according to beliefs of the members of the enterprise.

(e) *Belief that management and men should work together as a team.* This was a belief Anderson expounded in addressing the whole factory in January 1953; giving them his aims for the men themselves and the factory as a whole. He was quite prepared to sack the lot and start over again to build up a team. As one of the men said afterwards, "we're all in this together". Though he was never quite clear on this matter Anderson, in writing of "improved morale" is implying, as I know, team-work and general air of contentment— "smiling faces".

By morale I mean "obedience to an internal personal authority (obedience to a sense of duty, it is sometimes called), which arises out of an ideal or value common to the group (enterprise)". "Action in obedience to the sense of duty is essentially one of service in a rôle for furtherance of the aim of the group (enterprise) in achieving its goal." By team-spirit I mean "common appreciation by members of the team of the unity of purpose in their service drive; that is, an appreciation of the common obedience to internal authority, which is morale. If each member of the team knows that every other member is filling his rôle solely for the purpose of achieving the goal of the team (enterprise), then team-spirit is high. If it is believed that members are activated by purposes other than those of achievement of the goal of the group (enterprise), then team-spirit is low."[1]

It is difficult for an observer to decide when a manager is using autocratic power as distinct from the power of structural authority. Indeed, it is difficult for many conscientious managers to decide that themselves. It seems that

[1] Paterson, T. T., *Morale in War and Work*, Max Parrish, London, 1955, p. 99.

the essence of the distinction is whether the man wielding the power is also a moral man as far as the enterprise is concerned, that he is considering the total good of the enterprise which includes shareholders and employees alike. For the employees it does not matter whether the manager is a church-going, teetotal 'do-gooder', or a hard-swearing, heavy-drinking iconoclast, what matters to them is whether the manager is making just, equitable and fair decisions as far as their affairs are concerned.[1] Given this recognition the manager can wield structural authority, for it is sanctioned. If he does not have this recognition, then the power he wields is only that vested in him by the laws of property, being thus of origin external to the enterprise; it is autocratic power.

Bulgin was a manager who did not recognise this difference, and appeared to depend upon autocratic power. He threatened closure of the factory because the men would not work harder. He failed to realise the inequity of penalising the men for mechanical faults. He persisted in forcing upon the men a scheme they did not like, leading up to the February strike of 1950. The operatives considered him to be more interested in money than in men—immoral behaviour in their eyes. He "gave promises without doing anything about them"; "he was not a man to be trusted". And even when he deputised for Anderson in 1952 at a time when a moral scheme had been inaugurated—"the best scheme yet" the men and Macdonald thought—he was apparently incapable of wielding sanctioned power for "the men put the fear of God into him". Over and above that he seldom came near the men, giving his orders through Ackroyd, and, being no engineer, could not "take his jacket off"—he was not considered competent. In short he was an authoritarian (in an anti-authoritarian community); he seemed incapable of using structural authority to the full; he had little sapiential authority, no personal authority, and he was regarded as having no moral authority. (Yet, according to Chalmers, he "wasn't a bad bloke at heart".) It is to be little wondered that he failed as a manager and finally "had a nervous breakdown".

Whereas Anderson's behaviour was most erratic, at least up to the autumn of 1952, right from his arrival he was regarded by the men as competent. He was an engineer, had worked in similar factories in England, could "take his jacket off and get down to it", was always trying out ideas to increase mechanical efficiency; "he knew his stuff". In this he was granted sapiential authority. His manipulation of bonus schemes and calculations was also recognised as masterly even though they were questioned. He was also accepted as a person in his own right—he had personal authority. He seldom gave orders through the foreman if he could avoid that, and he "came down" among the men. He was always available to the stewards and leading

---

[1] This is a matter which requires extensive treatment and is to be discussed in a later volume.

men. His language was 'colourful' to use that euphemistic expression, but it was language his men were accustomed to from childhood. (It was merely outward form which meant nothing compared to its content.) What the men sensed on his arrival was his sympathy towards their troubles; he listened. The fact that at times the men considered throwing Anderson into the canal, or wanted to "bash 'im", was not necessarily a rejection of his personal authority. They would never have dreamed of doing this to Bulgin (I asked about this). Anderson was more of a man than a manager at these times. Maybe they were angry with him, but it was like being angry with someone close, and not unreachable and protected by law and social distance. More than he wot of, Anderson was not an Olympian!

In my opinion the all-round bettering of factory performance immediately on his arrival was probably due to the contrast between his sapiential and personal authority and the lack of it in Bulgin. But to have these two was not enough.

Anderson was not competent enough to see "what was biting his men", the matter of differentials unsolved. He could see their behaviour only as a lack of effort in taking advantage of an incentive scheme, though sympathising with them to the extent of trying to get Head Office to agree to a change in the scheme, and making efforts to improve the mechanical efficiency which he thought was impeding the making of good bonus earnings. Therefore, since he did not make a change in the differential payments, however "matey" or sympathetic he might be, however often he "took his jacket off", he would still be suspect of being unjust or unfair—lack of moral authority. This was the suspicion that troubled him throughout the greater part of 1951.

Nor was his position strengthened by Head Office conceptions of his rights and duties as a manager. At the time of the April 1951 strike he "wanted to give the men a penny" but he had "no authority" to do so from Head Office. The directorate was making decisions on a matter upon which he alone could judge, and which would require action by him. The men were holding him responsible for that which he could not control; and Head Office were holding him responsible for good industrial relations while denying him the means for bettering them. It must have been most difficult for him; and this accounts for the presentation of an ultimatum to Head Office—either he get a new incentive scheme or he resign.

Putting this new scheme into operation "off his own bat" was symptomatic of his having taken full responsibility and therefore being vested with complete structural authority. Hence the incentive scheme of 1951 was not merely an economic change but one of managerial status. Because of his assumption of complete structural authority it was he who was blamed for the Head Office cut of bonus earnings by $\frac{1}{4}$d. "Anderson's let us down. As soon as he gets us going he cuts us down". Thenceforward there was growing suspicion of his methods of calculating the bonus as already mentioned, a suspicion that he was making an unfair misuse of the difference between machine productivity and man productivity. The men could not know that this was forced upon him by Head Office pressure. All they could know or sense was that he seemed to have an approach which was more concerned with production than with the effects of the production on the men. The bonus only went up if machine productivity (production) increased was Anderson's attitude, according to the men. Because of the smaller crew, the men had to work harder to produce the same amount, but didn't get an adequate and proportional allowance for the difference in numbers. Anderson, they believed, could not see this was unfair; therefore he lost moral authority. The same suspicion spread to the bigpart line, and Anderson found it necessary to issue a note to his foreman on how to explain the scheme to the men.

Apparently the bigpart men became convinced of Anderson's good faith shortly after he dealt with the March 1952 strike, and they proceeded to "break the sound barrier" in productivity. Exactly how this conviction came about I do not know. It seems to stem from the week following the strike when he went on to the work floor and became more "matey" with the men, talking to them about the scheme, and taking over the controlling on the weepart line to show that the men could get all they wanted from the machines, which they blamed for the difficulty in making a good bonus.

Talk with the bigpart men may have been sufficient but it was not so with the weepart operatives. There was suspicion about the "spoilage fines" procedure, and about office figures. Anderson's apparent willingness to add to the crews was believed to be an indication of previous "jiggery-pokery". The March strike stopped or slowed down production during meal-times, and his demonstration of possible increased speeds was merely "a stunt" to get the machine-line running again during meal-times. That was why it was rejected despite Anderson's "mateyness". As Macdonald regarded the position, it was typical "monkey business" of Glasgow Ltd.

This breakdown, or loss of moral authority had, correspondingly, an effect on structural authority, since sanctioning of structural authority depends to a great extent on the belief in the morality of actions of the man in command. Anderson's April threat to dismiss men for bad workmanship passed completely unheeded—he was losing the power in his authority. The exposure of what the men thought duplicity in the fining procedure did not help any. Poor Anderson! Pressed by Head Office to reduce spoilage, he tried an arbitrary, autocratic procedure but, being sympathetic to the men, made up for the fines in better allowances; then he was caught by the men 'on the hip'. He was again between two millstones.

June 1952 came. The weepart operatives' suggestion that they work in gangs of four was seized upon by Anderson, searching for a light in the gloom of such tense industrial relations. That is to say the initiative came from below not from on top. His scheme to suit the change seemed still to offer too little (the bonus hadn't altered), but the shop stewards could not resist Anderson's claim to show that the line could produce enough at the right time, for the basis of their claim was that the line was inadequate—an excuse for their deeper feelings of unfairness, because they knew the line could run faster (all of them had worked on night-shift at high speeds). Having demonstrated the fallacy of the stewards' claim Anderson then put forward his proposal in the most conciliatory terms. "It is evident, then, that the Management is asking too much of the weepart men", but salting this with, "the decline in output clearly reflects the results of shutting the machine-line down during the meal-breaks" and "they cannot accept all the parts the line could give them". Then back again to the velvet touch, with "always bearing in mind one of the over-riding considerations in this business—the maintenance of a contented labour force", he proposed to do what the men had suggested be done, which was no demonstration of power in structural authority.

It was a good scheme of working, and Macdonald commended it. It was an example of Anderson's sapiential authority the men felt, should be listened to and tried out, but his moral authority was still in question and they remained suspicious. Was he still production minded or man-productivity minded? They were not long kept in doubt of his attitude (so they thought) for his minions, the foremen, began piling up the parts during meal-breaks, forcing the pace. Right from the time of Bulgin, the foremen had been "manager's men" and their meal-time pressure had become associated with all that Bulgin stood for. Here it was again. So Anderson's moral authority sank, and his structural authority weakened. As a result, when he posted the list of men selected to clean down the machine at the beginning of the Fair holiday week he got a blank refusal, and an alternative backed by a threat of strike action.

Into this atmosphere Head Office pitched Bulgin during Anderson's leave— it was throwing him to the lions. For the men, here was the complete symbol of immorality and autocracy. And he proceeded to act as he had done in the past. He would not (could not) take upon himself to act firmly, he had to get Head Office direction. Even Brown, his production manager, thought it better to telephone Anderson for advice. It is no wonder that the men decided to wait for the return of Anderson and Macdonald.

Anderson returned from his holiday in a new frame of mind. He told Macdonald in effect that he was "having no more of this nonsense", he told the foreman that the line was going to be run at the proper speeds (without their meal-time pressure), he sacked a foreman he thought a trouble-maker and incompetent, and he told the shop stewards and leading men that, whatever they said about the incapacity of the line, it could be done and he was going to show them how it could be done. Here was a man exercising structural and sapiential authority in no uncertain terms. The fact that the plan was good was known at its inception. Why was it not then accepted as moral and was now accepted as moral? For now it must have been, since the power was sanctioned by the men; and subsequently weepart performance improved.

The sequence from April to August can be summarised thus:

April—Anderson exercises personal and sapiential authority but not structural. He has little moral authority.

May—His moral standing is lessened still further.

June—He exercises personal and sapiential authority in putting forward a scheme which becomes acceptable, the change of crew being suggested from below. His moral authority is still low and is not helped by foreman behaviour. As a result his structural authority is weakened.

July—The symbol of immorality and autocracy appears on the scene in Anderson's absence; confusion worse confounded.

August—Anderson, returning, finds he can exercise strong structural authority, for the men sanction it. He also exercises sapiential and personal authority. Presumably the men invest him with moral authority.

If the unfortunate Head Office intervention of Bulgin be omitted as having no relevance to men-Anderson relations,[1] it becomes apparent that personal and sapiential authority alone could not carry Anderson through his industrial morass as long as his moral authority was low, and hence the sanctioning of his structural authority. On change of crew the suspicion of immorality remained because of the activities of the foremen, but when these activities were curbed the suspicion of immorality disappeared and structural authority could be wielded. But before the change was made (from April to June) the foremen's activities had been curtailed and yet suspicion had remained. Therefore it seems that, given the removal of the foremen activities, the change of crew was intimately related to the vesting of Anderson with moral authority and hence sanctioning of his structural authority. This is to be analysed further.

The final stage of this vesting of Anderson with complete authority came at the meeting with O'Brien and the other stewards a week after Anderson's return from leave. Anderson talked in a fashion to which the men were well accustomed (personal authority), but used structural authority as well in his

---

[1] It might be said, of course, that the men were so glad to see Anderson back after suffering Bulgin's rule that they were prepared to go in with him. However, the trouble had begun before Bulgin arrived.

treatment of O'Brien. By not sacking O'Brien Anderson "did not make him a martyr", said Maloney. The opposite happened—Anderson made himself a saint, a moral man in the eyes of his men. He became their 'leader' in all senses of that word, exercising all four forms of authority.

Macdonald's part in this metamorphosis is fairly clear. Before the holiday he too had felt, and voiced, the suspicion of the weepart men. He too attended the big meeting immediately after the holiday when Anderson made his *démarche* and, like the men he represented, he was convinced of Anderson's morality. He was a 'true-blue' trade union official, reacting as his members reacted, fighting for what they wanted.

But even though the weepart men's relations with Anderson were now on a much better footing, it seems that it was not until January of 1953 that the whole factory was finally and effectively brought to see Anderson as the weepart men did. The change dates from Anderson's address to the assembled factory personnel. First he stressed what *his* aims for the factory were, that is, not the employers' aims but the manager's. And what that implied was 'the manager together with his men', and he was going to get such men even if it meant sacking everybody and starting over again. Here he showed structural and sapiential authority allied to the recognition of team spirit. But he also exercised moral authority in promising no tampering with the bonus scheme, and recognising it would be foolish of him to try anything dishonest with them. Undoubtedly affected, as always, by weepart feelings towards Anderson, emphatically represented by Macdonald, the rest of the factory found here this final justification for accepting him as the production men had done. He was now 'the compleat manager' as far as the operatives (and, in part, the Head Office[1]) were concerned. But he was not so to his foremen.

THE FOREMEN

Only Ackroyd, the General Foreman, was known to me personally, and not very well. The attitudes of the others I gathered from two sources—the men, admittedly very biased, and one of the production managers. The latter also mentioned some characteristics of the foremen which may be significant from a wider sociological point of view. Most of them were Protestants and Freemasons—in this Roman Catholic community! Apart from Ackroyd, who was "imported" from England, the foremen had all been drawn from the labour in the factory and were therefore unskilled and semi-skilled men.

---

[1] He was getting quality production, and that was their main concern.

(The maintenance engineers were insignificant in the general picture.) These foremen had 'risen from the ranks' on the production-line, via the job of controller; and the controllers all appeared to be aggressive in personality, much like the shop stewards. Indeed, controllers were referred to by Anderson as being men "who could easily be shop stewards". These controllers showed an extraordinary attitude of antagonism towards their colleagues on the line and, it would seem, this attitude had expression in behaviour when elevated to foremen.

The foremen were all decidedly antagonistic towards their former mates. Some of their remarks have been quoted. The spring 1952 strike was ostensibly (at least to Anderson) the result of one of the foremen "being brutally rude to the weepart men on account of their eternal grumblings". Simpson's attitude was "you'll bloody well do this whether you like it or not". Ackroyd himself who, according to the production manager, set the example for the other foremen, was a "Management's man" and "a polished type who'd promise you the world, at the same time putting a knife into you behind your back"—according to the men. Anderson could say, "the trouble with Ackroyd is that . . . he doesn't know the men". He had no sympathy for them. Talking to me about the 1953 strike Ackroyd said "they weren't losing anything (by going on N.A.P.), they just didn't want to work". He was always against trade unionism in the factory. And he it was who instigated the meal-time running of the line, and the piling up of parts for the weepart men to sweat over on their return from eating. (This was exactly what controllers tried to do—small wonder that the foremen, ex-controllers, seized the chance to do what they could not do as controllers.)

During the Bulgin régime the manager always gave his commands through the foremen but seldom went near the men. This gave Ackroyd and his henchmen great scope on the shop floor to exercise their feelings of aggression, copying Bulgin's autocratic behaviour. Bulgin gained his knowledge of the production line through the foremen, not by personal investigation. The foremen were the tools of the manager, and were disturbed as he was. They were up to "jiggery-pokery" like Bulgin and the Head Office. They had no moral authority and all, except Ackroyd, had no greater competence than their former mates.

Anderson did little or nothing to change this rôle of foreman. He certainly made the change of obtaining his information by personal contacts on the line. Otherwise he issued his commands through the foremen in the proper formal manner. But he did not consult them other than to instruct them on the changes he proposed, and also how to explain the bonus system to the men. Their competence in this was derived from him and was not their own. On occasion he hectored the foremen much as he hectored the men. He had a low opinion of them generally and kept his distance. Their behaviour towards the men did not alter with his coming nor during his stay, and as far as I know, to this day the relations of men and foreman are unaltered.[1]

---

[1] In coal-mines I have seen the same kind of metamorphosis in attitude in translation of miners to semi-managerial posts. The process is slower, however, and seems to take a few months. A miner studies for his manager's certificate and becomes a junior official. He voices sympathy with the men he leaves, about their troubles which he has shared. Then somehow he adopts an attitude which he regards as traditional in mine management—so I believe—and he starts to scorn the men for complaining about those very same conditions he had deplored. My impression is, to put it in naval language, that he switches from a 'lower deck' to an 'upper deck' mentality. On the other hand there are some men who, promoted, never seem to lose the 'lower deck' mentality, and appear to be afraid to command their former mates. Such foremen, oft-times, are more trouble than the new-fledged autocrat.

CHAPTER 17

WORK-GROUP METHECTICS

Several problems arise from the analysis as it has proceeded so far:

(1) How was the change in constitution of the weepart work-group related to Anderson's final assumption of structural and moral authority? Was the constitution of the work-group related to a decision on the morality of Anderson's action?

(2) Why did the bigpart men make their decision on Anderson's behaviour before the weepart men? Was this related to a difference in the make-up of the two work-groups?

(3) How did the weepart group affect the bigpart in making decisions? Was this also related to a difference in make-up of the two work-groups?

(4) How did changes in the weepart line affect the rest of the factory? Was this a relationship in the character of the work-groups?

(5) How did the weepart and bigpart men make their decision on their different rates of productivity at various times (rate-fixing)?[1]

The reference to work-groups in each of these questions implies a study of those social groups in which structural authority is not an element—non-power groups they are called, as over against the formal power groups wherein managerial authority is an integral part of the structure. The relationships involved will be those stemming from exercise of sapiential, personal and moral authority alone, demanding the use of such terms as group, rôle, function, and operation, which will require definition for their use here and in succeeding chapters.[2]

'Group' has for me this meaning. It is a collection of people having a common purpose, a symbol of their commonality, functions for achieving the purpose and a structure of functions. A football team is a collection of men having a common purpose of winning; a symbol of their commonality in their name, jersey and colours; a set of functions, attacking, supporting, defending; organised in a structure, all designed to win games. What a man does in performing his function might be called *operation*. His *function* is the contribution he makes towards achieving the purpose of the group. His *rôle* is the part he plays in relation to all the others in their performance of function.

Thus, in a football team a man operates, 'does', by catching, kicking and

---

[1] The relationships of work groups to labour turnover and accident rates, health and strike action are to be discussed in the next chapter.

[2] Paterson, T. T., *Morale in War and Work*, Max Parrish, London, 1955, pp. 75–6.

bouncing a ball in performance of his function which is goal-keeping. He operates to keep goal, his function is goal-keeping, his rôle is goal-keeper. Goal-keeping is one of several functions which include attack, support and defence, and can be talked of without reference to the persons who perform the functions. But immediately the person performing the function is considered, implied in the '-er' ending, then human relations enter into the situation and rôle is involved.

The various functions in a group may have different values ascribed to them—a high value if the function is considered to be of major service in the attainment of the group desires, and a low value if of minor service. So functions tend to be judged on a superiority-inferiority scale, and position on this scale is social rank, or simply, *rank*[1] Thus in a football team an attacking function may be considered to be higher in rank than a supporting or defending, centre-forward(-ing) superior to half-back(-ing) and goal-keeping. In other teams supporting may have higher value than attacking, much depending upon tradition and techniques. The persons given these functions to perform will be granted the ranking of their functions.

Accordingly as a person fulfils a function and so fills his rôle, well or badly, as judged in terms of service to the group, so he will be given high prestige or low. For example, in a football team a centre-forward might have higher rank than the goal-keeper, but the goal-keeper, in brilliant performance of his function, serves the team better than the centre-forward who does not shine. In such a case the goal-keeper will have higher prestige than the forward. Esteem and admiration of the person filling the rôle enters into prestige, quite apart from judgment of the value of his function to the group. Frequently prestige is given a person merely because his rank is high, and not because he performs his function well. Thus a crowd, giving an attacking function high rank (probably because the attacker is the goal-scorer and goals are what most of the crowd want), will give a particular forward their adulation (external prestige). Whereas the other members of the team, knowing that one of the half-backs engineers the majority of movements leading to goal-scoring, will grant that man prestige (internal prestige), for they know he fills his rôle to the benefit of the team more admirably.

THE WEEPART ASSEMBLY GANG

The three assembly gangs formed the core of the weepart line crew. The line men, as described in Chapter 3, moved up and down the line watching the machines and keeping in touch with the controller. They were comparatively distant from each other, seldom able to converse and could meet to talk

---

[1] The word 'status' usually implies rank and prestige. To be more precise I use 'rank' here and later, so as to avoid confusion.

only when the line slowed or stopped, or at meal-times; whereas the assembly gangs, working in the less noisy assembly-bay, and close to each other, could talk and "josh each other" with comparative ease. The rate of the line production was governed by the speed of assembly, and so the line men depended to a great extent upon the assembly-men for their bonus earnings.

But this dependence worked to a slight extent in the reverse way, for quality of finish of the parts coming off the line, and hence ease or difficulty of assembly, was governed by the care of the line men. The controller was the medium, and his function and operation is described in detail below.

The sociological implication of change in gang size can best be illustrated by describing the operations carried out, and considering first the difference between gangs of three and four. There were nine groups of operations, seven of them performed by two men in unison. (In the interests of anonymity, the operations cannot be exactly described, but in any case, their description would not add to the value of the analysis.) The men were grouped around the assembly table thus:

Three-man gang   *Four-man gang*

X ▭ Y   A ▭ B
     Z   C   D

and the operations were carried out by the various men in the following sequence:

Operation	Three-man gang	Four-man gang
1	XZ	AC
2	XZ	DC
3	XZ	DC
4	YZ	AC
5	XZ	AC
6	XZ/YZ	BD/AC
7	XZ/YZ	BD/AC
8	YZ	BD
9	YZ	BD

In two major operations, 6 and 7, there were two subsidiary operations which, with a four-man gang, could be carried out simultaneously, but with the three-man gang, had to be carried out consecutively. In the three-man gang spells at position Z were taken turn about by all three since it entailed the heaviest labour. In the four-man gang the men remained in their same positions. Hence in the second case there was a certain amount of 'specialisation' of work, if it can be called that, compared with the non-specialisation

169

of the three-man gang. It also meant that, since the four-man gang had fixed relations in space, orientation and operation, their co-ordination could be built up to a maximum by habituation. At the same time the loss, or absence of any one member of the four could deal a serious blow, since the others would not be so readily adaptable as those in the three-man gang, less specialised. There was, therefore, an economic pressure of interdependence to preserve the four-man gang intact, quite apart from its sociological significance.

The four-man gang could produce at a much faster rate than the three-man gang mainly because of the speeding up in operations 6 and 7 which were the lengthiest. It also meant that the four-man gang had more leeway in speeding up or retarding their pace of production according to their whims and needs. They could afford to take time off to rest, and to work at high speeds in between such spells (the other gangs also seeing to it that they didn't "lie off" too much!). The three-man gang could have fewer spells, for which reason Anderson increased the crew by two men to help out in taking the place of any men who couldn't keep up the tempo.[1] In the four-man gang crew such men were unnecessary, and all the crew men were fully occupied in production; whereas the extra men in the three-man gang crew were often being 'carried' by the others. It was therefore better, from a work study point of view, to have four-man gangs despite the increase in number to share out the bonus. It should be noted that the assembly-men made their own decision on how to do the work—and in June 1952 it was their own suggestion that the four-man gang be brought into being.

Another operation performed by each gang was the transfer of the part from the conveyor belt to the assembly table, usually carried out by two of each crew. In the three-man gang men on X and Y position usually did this, but in the four-man gang A and C did it while B and D finished off the assembly, operation 9 being completed by lifting the part on to the adjoining bogie to be taken to the inspection and finishing-sheds. Here too was a gain in time.

Originally the crew size was two gangs of five each, and the two men extra to the four carried out the feeding of the tables from the conveyor belt. Then Bulgin increased the number of men by introducing the crew of three four-man gangs and finally three five-man gangs. How this worked I do not know, unless he used the extra three men as "stand-ins" during the high absenteeism and labour turnover then prevalent. It must have been wasteful of effort. Anderson at once reduced them to four each. (I can only assume that the sociological and operational value of the four-man gang at this period was offset by the economic and managerial factors already described.)

Each gang had a leading man. Ostensibly these leading men were appointed

[1] Spare men for both kinds of crew were always available in case of absenteeism.

by the manager, but they were informally elected by the gang members whose suggestions were passed by the foremen to the manager, who then appointed. The manager retained the nominal right to appoint, by virtue of the fact that the leading men were paid one penny per hour for their function of presenting to the gangs those requirements of the manager which were not passed down through the foremen. The foremen also gave orders through the leading men, if the orders concerned gang activity and not individual operation.

Each shift of weepart men had a shop steward, and he was always one of the assembly-men. This is indicative of the importance, in more ways than mere number, of the assembly-men. The election of shop stewards was by the usual formal union ballot system. Seldom was a leading man a shop steward, though there have been exceptions. Maloney was one. The function of the shop steward was the usual trade union one. He was representative of the men who elected him in their dealings with management and union. But he seldom, if ever, could take action without either being instructed in the first place by a leading man or asking a leading man. For example, a production manager by chance glanced at his watch while in the assembly-bay. He saw that at once one of the leading men approached the other two and all three went to the shop steward who, in turn, came to the production manager and protested against any timing of operations. For the greater part of the description of these people in action I am indebted to that particular production manager, Chalmers, formerly one of my students. He also supplied the following information on methectic rôles. These rôles are described in *Morale in War and Work* (op. cit.). It may be useful to summarise them roughly here.

(1) The *Exemplar* rôle is concerned with representation of the group norm of opinion; the holder of the rôle exemplifies the group. In our society he is usually relatively non-vociferous and non-bellicose, the 'good man on a committee', say, whose opinion 'sets the tone' of the group, whose opinion is usually paid great attention by the others.

(2) The *Exdominus* rôle is concerned with external relations between the group and other groups. The holder, relatively vociferous and bellicose, is often regarded as 'the spokesman', and is the apparent 'leader' when it comes to group action consequent upon the statement of group norm of opinion from the exemplar.

(3) The *Indominus* rôle is concerned with internal relations, among members of the group itself. The holder, relatively vociferous and non-bellicose, is one who sees to it that the group conforms to its norms, that the group holds together. He is the one who, at the appropriate moment, quietens him who becomes too truculent, encourages him who holds back in fulfilling his duties to the group, and intercedes in members' disagreements, a 'good committee man', for example.

(4) The *Eccentric* rôle is concerned with the expounding of belief and with behaviour which is beyond the norms of the group, yet acceptable when performed by the rôle holder. The beliefs expounded by the eccentric are not, therefore, representative, but they may become so since, in this rôle, the eccentric is expected to point out views that are worthy of group consideration; just as the eccentric may quote from *The Times* to a group whose reading is the *Daily Worker* and the sports page of the *Daily Express*. Other eccentrics are the clowns, jokers, and such-like of the group.

(5) The *Mimetic* rôle is that taken up by all who follow the exemplar and domini rôles. The exemplar is mimetic when he follows the exdominus, the exdominus is mimetic when he agrees with the exemplar. Some members of a group may do nothing else but fill a mimetic rôle.

(6) The *Isolate* is not a group rôle since he is one who is not a member of the group proper; but it is a rôle in that the holder is one who does not conform to the norms of the group, and so must have no part in it.

The controllers (and all controllers seemed to be alike) were aggressive persons. Few had been leading men, and those who had been returned to assembly work. Controllers seemed to feel that they had to dominate the assemblers. "They even dream about it—dream that they have got to be on top of the assemblers", was a description. They constantly tried to force the pace of production but could not in the face of assembly resistance. If they adjusted the machine speeds (in conjunction with other line men) beyond what the assemblers regarded as a satisfactory or reasonable speed, then the parts would begin to pile up on the conveyor belt until the line either had to slow down or stop. Even though the parts were removed from the belt and stacked the assemblers would work at their own pace, and the stacked parts would then become part of the production quota of the next shift. Since there was intershift competition (see below), the controller tried to avoid stacking.

Shop stewards and controllers seemed to have something in common. Controllers were described to me as "could easily be shop stewards". And both have been the source of recruitment of foremen. But, as far as I know, no leading man has become foreman, with one exception. This leading man had the aggressiveness that seemed characteristic of shop stewards and controllers, and it was noteworthy that of all the gangs on weepart assembly his was the one with "no discipline"; and he took his troubles to a foreman. The other leading men had no trouble with their gangs, and would have scorned the idea that they should consult the foreman. Nevertheless, their attitude to managerial and foreman authority was noticeably much less aggressive than that of the shop stewards, who required much tact in handling, that is to say if foremen were tactful, which was infrequent.

The leading men took the exemplar and indominus rôles within their gangs. They expounded the gang feeling, as for instance in the reaction to ostensible timing just described. Timing involved a matter of principle, and the exemplar represented the attitude towards it. But it was the shop steward, filling the exdominus rôle for the whole shift, who took action on that principle and approached the production manager. The shop steward's aggressiveness was the necessary concomitant of his rôle.

Just as the shop steward was the shift exdominus, so one of the leading men became the shift exemplar. He appeared to have several functions. He, as shift representative, accompanied the shop steward in approaching the manager. (It is traditional practice in engineering factories that two men at least interview the manager.) The steward might do the aggressive talking, but it was the leading man who did the arguing on principle. Here was a rôle in which Maloney, expert on figures, excelled. Another function was to pass on to the oncoming shift exemplar the word about production targets and other intershift matters. He also had to make clear to other groups what his group regarded as its point of view. When it came to forcing others outside his group to conform he took little part. This was again the function of the aggressive shop stewards. For example, it was the weepart shop stewards who restrained the bigpart men from working too hard during meal-times, and stopped them working too hard (as it was thought) to make bigger holiday pay in 1953—even though the plan to make bigger pay had been inspired by a bigpart steward!

THE BIGPART ASSEMBLY GANG

Unlike the weepart gang this suffered no change in constitution. The machine-line was somewhat more simple than the weepart, requiring four attendants including a controller. The assembly process was a continuous flow kind of operation, and required more men. The part coming off the conveyor belt was lifted straight on to a ten-foot-wide table and two men, one on each side of the table, removed templates and jigs. The part was then passed along the table to two more men in similar positions who carried out a second operation of a like nature. The part was then lifted on to another large table (more than one could be used) and two more operations were performed on it by two more pairs of men, making eight in all. The second lot of four men worked sometimes as much as fifty feet away from their colleagues at the end of the line.

Each pair worked in unison only in lifting and passing the part over. Otherwise each man performed his operation as he liked, but generally at a speed to suit his 'partner'. However, on the first table the two pairs had to work in some kind of adjusted speed since the parts had to be taken off the belt as soon as they arrived at the table end. If parts were not removed the pile-up on the table would stop the work, for the parts were clumsy to manœuvre as well as being heavy. So that, on this table, the men were under pressure from their mates behind them to pass them material to work on, and from the controller who could govern the rate at which the parts came off. He could "make them sweat", "work them until they drop".

The contrast with the weepart line lies in the fact that the weepart gang was working together at one time on the one part, and therefore there was

173

no pressure upon them from mates farther down the assembly-line. Close together and with movements in unison, they could regulate their speed and defy the controller. It could be said that the weepart gang was a tightly built little group, its members in close proximity to each other, very much inter-dependent in operations, and able to communicate readily. Whereas the bigpart gang was loosely knit, its members were widely separate, working almost independently in terms of operation (though not function), and in constant communication. The three gangs of the weepart line formed a group in itself with one exemplar (one of the leading men). They were closely knit and able to communicate freely, but each gang was independent. They were interdependent in terms of function since their rest periods, and hence productivity, were governed by joint appreciation of each others' needs. Each produced the same or nearly the same number of parts. It seems that the most important factor contributing to the difference between the lines was the facility for communication while working; and the second factor was interdependence.

The difference between bigpart and weepart group cohesion[1] can be seen in two other ways. When the weepart men finished a shift they would talk of production, "we have done so many parts and that's enough" (all being in agreement on that), and seldom mention bonus. That was mentioned only when the bonus was "posted", and then the talk was of its correctness or not. The bigpart men at the end of a shift could be seen, some singly, to start counting what their bonus would be as a result of that shift's work. Describing this, Chalmers put it, "The bigpart men seem to have an attitude that is individualist". The second instance was in the reaction to Anderson's attempt to change from the three-shift pool bonus scheme to single-shift bonus. The bigpart men assented without any difficulties being raised, even though they replied (to Anderson's query) that they would have an "under-standing" on the rates of work for each shift. The weepart men immediately and unequivocally refused to move from the three-shift pool bonus.

The three-shift pool bonus scheme required of each shift some kind of agreement on rates of working. It would be contrary to most experience, certainly that of industry, to expect that any one shift would knowingly work at a much harder rate than another for the same reward—it was in effect the question of differentials on the factory floor and within the same work-group. Only here the matter was settled by the men themselves without outside and power-centred interference. As Table 1 (p. 68) shows, each weepart shift somehow managed, despite all the deviating effects of mechanical breakdown, spoilage, and changes in personnel, to work at the same rate

[1] By 'cohesion' I mean the tendency for individual members of the group to feel and behave as if they are aware of their being a group, to show a sense of 'we-ness' rather than 'I-ness', i.e. group awareness.

over weeks. To a lesser limit the same held for bigpart shift working. How the three shifts came to agreement can be judged only by records of output, and by Maloney's meagre description.

In June 1952 at the inception of the new scheme of working, the shifts seemed to vary in their reaction to its difficulty. The morning shift of 13 June found they were "rushed"; the afternoon found it "easy", and "sat waiting for parts" to come off the line. Yet by the end of the week, and up to the holiday when they started to go slow, the productivity remained fairly constant. Immediately after the meeting with Anderson on his return, the productivity leapt about ten points and remained like that, varying only two points either way. According to Maloney, the men of each shift talked among themselves, and "somehow" they decided on what was "all right". Then the leading man exemplar for the shift met his opposite number of the shift coming on and told him what his shift thought. These three exemplars thus conveyed the opinions of their shifts, and among them the decision was made. But of the three, one man seemed to have the greatest say. There was no question of deciding exactly what number of parts was going to be handled. It was more a statement of what the shift was doing, and thought reasonable or "fair", and this was passed on, each shift influencing the other, but one shift exercising most influence; and in that shift one gang exercising most influence, the gang whose leading man was the shift exemplar. In Maloney's shift he seemed to have been the exemplar. I could not gather from him what rôle he played *vis-à-vis* the other shift exemplars—perhaps that was his modesty, for he was a modest man—but he was always the man who accompanied the shop stewards to interview the manager. "You can depend on it", a secretary of the stewards wrote Macdonald, "that whenever we meet him (Anderson) to talk bonus we will not be without Maloney the only man who can match our friend Anderson at figures on weeparts."

Maloney had competence, sapiential authority, for he was a repository of information and of tradition, as well as being a long-term employee. I can only add that Anderson and Macdonald had a very high opinion of Maloney as well.[1] He was not the aggressive type, he was a leading man; as exemplar he represented the group's belief in what was fair; he was, for them, a moral man. He had sapiential, personal and moral authority.

The shop stewards played no outstanding part in these decisions on what was "fair"; they had the same say as the others taking the mimetic rôles. They only came actively into the picture during the negotiation resulting from disagreement between manager and men as to what was "fair"; and they did so as acting in two roles. First, they were the local officials of the

---

[1] It was my good fortune to have the confidence of Maloney for, in effect, I was obtaining from him, the exemplar, the general feelings or the norm of the attitude of the weepart men.

union with whom the manager (according to agreement with the union) had
to negotiate. Secondly, they had the informal rôle of exdominus, that is,
representing the informal groups in their dealings with external agents. They
had therefore structural authority to negotiate, and personal authority in
being exdomini. Their moral authority was derived from the leading man
exemplar who accompanied them, and who, as in the case of Maloney, was
also vested with sapiential authority.

The behaviour of the weepart controllers was related to the inter-shift
agreement on what was "fair" production. The machines were automatic for
the most part, and there were few indicators of machine-rate. The controller
learned (and very quickly because of the simplicity of automatic operation)
the 'feel' of the line. He could adjust rates according to his own particular,
almost idiosyncratic, settings of some of the controls, reflecting this feel.
According to Chalmers, who surreptitiously watched their 'unofficial'
practices, the controllers felt they had status; and this was reflected by their
penny an hour differential payment. But they seemed to desire acknowledg-
ment of this status in two other ways. First they tried to "drive" the
assembly-men, who resisted this. It seems to have been a need that was
almost a compulsion, as described already. But, secondly, they competed
with the controllers of the other shifts. A controller would know that his
shift had produced so much, and thus set a target for the next shift, which
target was well within the capabilities of that shift, as the 'committee' of
the exemplars knew. The controller, on leaving his post at the end of his
tour, would "de-set" his controls, as the line was coming to a standstill for
between-shift maintenance, so making re-adjustment difficult for the oncoming controller, and hence cutting the time for the next assembly-crew to
make their 'quota'. A good controller and the line men would earn the
praise of their shift colleagues (internal prestige) if they could get the line
running quickly, and efficiently as well. But withal, the controller would not
make it impossible for the next shift to make their 'quota'. He only made
it difficult for them and, in particular, for his opposite number on that shift.
There was no inter-shift competition in the sense of numbers of parts produced, but there was competition in efficiency in the sense of being able to
make their target with ease or with difficulty (as was the case among the
gangs of a shift crew). The controller, in his peculiar position (and with his
aggressive personality) was taking part in such a competition.

One finds this in industry generally. An efficient worker will not use his
efficiency to make more than his work-group consider "reasonable" or
"fair", but he might use it to gain time to "play about", help others (as in
the classic Hawthorne case of the bank-wiring assembly room), or sharpen
and prepare his tools, looking for and accepting recognition that he is more
efficient. He seeks prestige. A section of miners, having finished their stint

176

in short time, will make friendly jeering remarks to another section that reaches the pit bottom after them, having taken a little longer to finish off. But the efficient section would never dream of using their extra time to tackle more work than is regarded as a "fair" stint.

It would seem, therefore, that the decision on group rate of work came about through communication of what each gang considered to be "fair" or "reasonable", that a particular gang on each shift had the most influence on the decision, and that a particular man, the shift exemplar, had the most personal influence. Since this "reasonableness" or "fairness" of rate of work was essentially a moral for the group and for the gangs, for the decision was normative, it is most likely that a comparable moral decision, on the morality of the bonus scheme which was intimately related to the rate of work, was arrived at in similar fashion. And so would a decision on the morality of Anderson's actions connected with rates of work. It would seem, therefore, that it is within the gang work-group that the key to the final acceptance of Anderson's moral authority can be found; and the key lies in the change from the three-man to the four-man gang.

But first, it must be remembered that change in size did not have effect upon the rate-of-work decision, just because the new grouping provided a more efficient operational technique. Even though the change from three-man to four-man gang might seem efficient, it might not produce greater individual productivity. Indeed, since the four-man gang had already been in existence, and the rate of work had not changed appreciably on its inception, it can be assumed that the operational technique in itself was not the cause of the change in the autumn of 1952. *The cause lay in a change of function not of operaton.* Rate-decision was concerned almost wholly with function. The decision was not 'how' the rate could be achieved but 'how much' would be achieved.

Therefore it is not in the actual differences of operation in the two sizes of gang that the key lies, but in the functional relations of the individual members. First, the three-man gang had no 'specialisation', the relations of each man were fixed neither in space, orientation nor operation, but they were all so fixed in the four-man gang. The absence of one man in the non-specialised gang meant little to the others in terms of their fulfilling their function of a particular output, since that man could be replaced at once by another non-specialist. It meant that, in the three-man gang, the man absent (and any one of them might have been) could have no sense of being indispensable or important, or rather of his being of individual worth-whileness in the fulfilling of the function of the gang. He could see himself only as a nondescript member of a larger group, the assembly-crew, relating their effort to earnings in terms of the effort-earnings relationship of a non-existent crew (three four-man gangs), and through a mathematical process almost incomprehensible to him.[1] He had no recognisable function that was his in the eyes of his fellow workers, and, even if he had, he could not relate that function to an abstraction that had no cognisance of him in his function.

Whereas in the four-man gang the opposite situation held. The gang relations were fixed in space, orientation and operation. There was inter-dependence of 'specialisation' and each man was important, worthwhile in fulfilling the function of the gang. He could see himself as a distinct member of a group, distinguished by his performing a specific and interdependent operation, and whose absence was of consequence in the fulfilling of the gang function. And secondly, he could with ease connect his work to the effort-earnings relationship, for the bonus was calculated basically upon the four-man gang. He was of consequence in terms of operation, function and rank; and in the stability of the four-man gang his idiosyncratic personality could have expression in methectic rôle-taking. In such a *milieu*, therefore, it became easier for the men to make a normative decision on the morality of Anderson's scheme—i.e. question 1.

The same reasoning could be applied to the bigpart line. There too the gang members were interdependent in function, though nearly independent in operation (except for pairs). There too the gang relations were fixed in space (maybe widely separate), orientation and operation. Each man could see himself as distinguished by his performing a specific though independent operation, and his absence also was of consequence in the fulfilling of the gang function. And for this gang, too, the effort-earnings relationship was clearly to be seen, though only after the bonus scheme had been thoroughly expounded by Anderson and the foremen in the spring of 1952. Hence they could then decide readily upon the morality of the scheme; and so, while the weepart three-man gang was still undecided, the bigpart men could sweep ahead and "break the sound barrier". They "knew where they stood" in every sense of that expression—i.e. question 2.

What has emerged from this analysis can be summed up in the platitude, "an incentive scheme doesn't work very well if the men don't like it". For Glasgow Ltd, at least, this platitude can be enlarged. Further analysis is needed before the main clause can be fully expounded, but the conditional clause can be stated fairly concisely in detail as follows.

An incentive is not likely to better performance if
(1) the rightness or fairness of its differential content has not been established, q.v. above;
(2) the morality of the manager has not been established,

---

[1] Said Macdonald, "The men don't appreciate these calculations to three decimals or fractions of this and that. They understand only Clydeside terms", meaning straight-forward P.B.R. schemes and differentials.

(he should be vested if possible, with structural, sapiential, personal and moral authority, but at the very least he must be vested with structural and moral authority; this depends partly upon the work group judgment, which has its basis in sociological structure);

(3) the sociological relations of the work-group in functional interdependence are not clearly defined,

(for on this depends evaluation of the morality of the scheme; this applies in the application of a group bonus scheme, but, as will be shown later, it holds for individual bonus schemes because, even then, the individual evaluation depends on the work group evaluation—"no man is an island");

(4) the scheme is not readily comprehended—in two ways,

(i) in arithmetical terms, for men tend to become suspicious of that which is complex and obscure—they like "Clydeside terms"; (this is not absolutely vital if the moral authority of the manager has already been established).

(ii) in relating the scheme to functional value of the man, that is reflecting the value of his rôle in the work-group.

It may not be amiss to wander aside to remark upon some of the difficulties that are frequently met by work study engineers and consultants, finding that their "scientific" schemes are rejected, or fail to produce the expected effects. The word "scientific" is used to imply 'rational' since mathematical methods are employed. But to be rational a scheme must take into consideration all those factors that are relevant to the work situation in which the scheme is to be applied. And if some of those factors are not measurable in mathematical terms and are therefore rejected, or are not considered because the instigators are unwilling to consider them, then the scheme is in no sense of the word rational, or scientific. I have yet to see in a textbook, descriptive of work study techniques and application of incentive schemes, any rational consideration of the kinds of factors that seem to have been in operation at Glasgow Ltd, and are well known, in empirical terms, to many now studying work. There is perhaps an exception in (1), the question of differential content in an incentive scheme, but even in such a case judgments on "fairness" have been those of the instigators, or of others external to the work-group, and have not been the judgment of the members of the group.

The fault lies in the failure of work-study engineers to recognise the difference between efficiency and performance, that what a man contributes to an enterprise is more important than what he can do in mechanical terms, that his function is more important than his operation. They seem to be unaware that men consciously or subconsciously value work as a function in life as well as a money-making operation, that work proper must be earned and is not labour that can be bought.

A method change, although logical to the instigator who is only concerned with, say, speeding up a process or reducing the physical effort required by the operative, may not be moral (in the sense used here) to the operative. For it may disrupt—and not replace—a sociological structure that provides a satisfying moral evaluation of work for the operative. An incentive scheme may seem to provide a much better chance of making higher earnings (with even little extra effort), and so be regarded as "fair" by the instigator—and he wonders why it is rejected by the operatives. He fails to see that his idea of "fairness" is not necessarily that of the operatives, that his morality is not necessarily theirs. Conversely, too often the success of an incentive scheme is ascribed wholly to the monetary 'carrot' or to "making gain easier", when it may quite well be that the scheme has been judged and found "good" or "fair", neither in terms of monetary reward *qua* money, nor of ease in labour, but in the moral terms that are consistent with the value system of a well-balanced, cohesive work-group, seeing the value of a man as a man and not as a money-making machine.

But, to the 'muttons' of this study—the third problem of the relation between the two production lines. This is a problem that comes under the general heading of communication—how does one group affect another? It would appear from what data are available that it was almost a one-way traffic, from the weepart to the bigpart line. There are three clear fields in which the weepart men influenced the bigpart, but there is no evidence of the bigpart men affecting the weepart men in similar fashion.

First, in the 'before' and 'after' periods the productivity of each line ran parallel, the general rate was about the same, and the increase was closely similar, Fig. 21. That the weepart line was the likely source determining these fairly fixed rates of effort is to be found in two pieces of negative evidence. When the bigpart men decided on a change of effort, 1951–52, and at the end of 1954 when they went on to the individual shift bonus scheme, the weepart men did not follow them.

Secondly, when the bigpart men made decisions to increase rate of effort, as in mid-1952, and in the attempt to increase holiday pay in 1953, the weepart men "restrained" them or otherwise obtained their consent to keeping their effort to a level acceptable to the weepart men.

Thirdly, although the bigpart men did not take part in the strikes of the 'before' period, and their productivity did not fall with the weepart productivity at these times, they took part in the strikes of spring 1952 and January 1953, even though these strikes were about a subject in which they had no concern. In Bulgin's time the bigpart men had once been "inveigled" into a strike, and Anderson thought the same about these two particular strikes.

The second case is the most easy to understand. In both cases of "restraining", weepart shop stewards made open approaches to the bigpart men, and, in the first instance in 1952, the "restraining" was not discouraged by

Macdonald, the union organiser. These were situations in which solidarity, in union terminology, was considered essential. If the bigpart men had persisted in their action, meal-time working in 1952, then the weepart case would have been jeopardised. But in the 1953 situation the weepart men were not fighting a case, they were restricting themselves to a rate, which restriction they felt would become untenable should the bigpart men work harder. The bigpart men were "taking a bait from management and changing their traditional practice for so little extra reward". The traditional practice was the "recognised" general level of effort.

This general level of effort, and its maintenance, was the subject of the first case. It seems that the weepart men established a rate of work after the inception of the first bonus scheme (influenced by bigpart production), a rate considered to be sufficient in the light of the external differential. Their attitude to the internal differential, between them and the bigpart men, was not that the bigpart men's earnings were too high or that they were working too hard, but that the weepart line bonus was not enough. The bigpart men were working hard and deserved their bonus, and the weepart men were working just as hard and not getting the bonus. Hence, if the bigpart men tried to increase their rate (which they could do easily) the manager could quite well point to this as an example. In such a situation the weepart men could readily convince the bigpart crews that they would be doing them a disservice. But the rate was decided upon by the weepart gangs not by the bigpart. Their decision was 'stronger' so to speak; and so it was in 1953, when the "traditional practice", only a few months old, was a weepart practice.

For this reason the bigpart men did not take part in the strikes of the "before" period. The battle was essentially a weepart affair, and the bigpart decision to conform to the general level was not affected by fluctuations in weepart productivity during the strike intervals. (See Chapter 20 on Strikes for an explanation of these fluctuations.)

The situation was changed during 1952. The solidarity with the weepart men in their reaction to the external differential was no longer necessary. Therefore the bigpart men could step up productivity, as they did immediately the new bonus scheme came into operation. But the complication of the new scheme (it was not in "Clydeside terms") and growing suspicion of Anderson at once aligned them with the weepart men. Productivity dropped towards the weepart rate and they went on strike as well. As said before, the ostensible cause, meal-time working, was a rationalisation on the suspicion; but the rationalisation came from the weepart men for whom the meal-time working, and foremen, were "traditionally" anathema. Here again the weepart line was 'stronger'.

In the January 1953 strike the bigpart men had no cause for joining in.

It was a weepart affair completely. The ostensible cause was illogical—the weepart men just would not work temporarily in N.A.P. and no reason was given. They weren't going to be "pushed around" by management. This reaction (and the deep-seated cause for it, to be analysed later) was a reaction which could well have appealed to the bigpart men. It is traditional on anti-authoritarian Clydeside. But locally it had its foundations in the weepart gangs who convinced the bigpart men of its justification. There was here, again, a 'power' or 'strength' in the weepart gang.

It would seem that the 'strength' of the weepart men, their higher 'potential' of opinion from which ideas, concepts, and decisions flowed out to the bigpart men, could only rest in the difference in structure of their groups, For the men, bigpart and weepart, were all of a kind and from the same social *milieu*. This difference was in the 'cohesion' of the weepart gangs, their being more 'group-minded' rather than individual-minded, more aware of 'we' than of 'me'; or more precisely, more aware of 'me' as being part of 'we'.

This could be put another way. Because of the closer proximity, better communication, and greater interdependence of function and operation, the weepart work-group tended to have a more clear-cut norm of behaviour and attitude towards productivity. Among the weepart gangs any tendency for a member to deviate more widely from the norm would meet more resistance from the rest, and, conversely, conformity with the norm would make group living easier, than among the bigpart men. This could be especially seen in two facets of group activity. Among the weepart men the individual deviation of the controller was reduced to a minimum, each gang saw to it that the other gangs in the shift did not slack off or "go to it" too much, and the three shifts did not vary widely in output. Among the bigpart men the controller's individual deviation was wide, for the assembly men could not restrain him easily, and different pairs of assemblers could "chivvy up" the others in front in the line, or slow down, to the exasperation of the others behind in the line—but within limits; just as there were limits of restriction among the weepart men. These limits might well be called permissible latitude of behaviour (P.L.B).

This general proposition of P.L.B around a norm being more restricted in a cohesive group could be expounded in the theoretical diagram, Fig. 33. If the horizontal co-ordinate represents attitude to productivity, and the vertical represents numbers expressing that attitude, it would be expected that a more cohesive group would show a narrower distribution around the norm than the less cohesive group; and it would follow, because of the nature of the distribution, that the P.L.B for the less cohesive would cover a wider range of attitude. This is a much simplified version of the reality supplied by the answers to the three questions, "What do you think is about a reasonable rate of work?", "What do you think is an unreasonably high rate of work?", and "What do you think is an unreasonably low rate of work?" The P.L.B norms thus obtained are much vaguer than represented here—the behaviour is much more specific, i.e., group behaviour and individual attitudes are not coincident. It is of interest to note that Maloney in the 'peace period' regarded a 70 rate of productivity as unnecessarily low, whereas in the "war period" this was a rate regarded as high, and certainly a 100 was thought of as impossible.

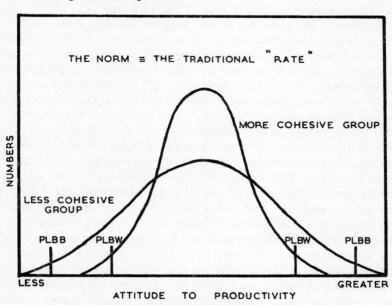

Fig. 33. To illustrate difference in group cohesion (theoretical).

This theoretical consideration is well borne out by a comparison of the weekly productivity for bigpart and weepart lines throughout the year 1954 when both were relatively stable in performance.

Table 11. *Distribution of Weekly Productivity Rates for both Production Lines for the Year 1954*

Rate	77	78	79	80	81	82	83	84	85	86	87	88	89	90	91	92	93	94	95	96	97	98	99	100	101	102
Big-part	2	—	—	—	1	2	—	1	5	7	4	4	3	4	1	2	—	1	4	3	1	2	—	1	1	1
Wee-part	—	—	—	2	—	1	5	7	2	4	2	7	6	3	1	2	4	1	1	1	—	—	—	—	—	—
Total	2	—	—	2	1	3	5	8	7	11	6	11	9	7	2	4	4	2	5	4	1	2	—	1	1	1

183

The median productivity is the same for each group, about 88, and the norm of the typical skew distribution towards the higher rate is about 86. The difference is quite distinct. The P.L.B for the weepart group ranged from 80 to 96, and for the bigparts from 77 to 102. The distribution for the two production lines together is as nearly ideal for a single group as would be expected in such circumstances; for though the techniques were the same in general, yet the number of parts coming off the line (rate), and the weights handled were of quite a different numerical order. This suggests that the 'core' effect of weepart decision-making was profound.

It is perhaps not surprising if the situation be seen another way. The smaller group, the bigpart, was not quite certain how it should decide to act, its P.L.B wide, and therefore the norm somewhat obscure. The members of the larger, weepart group were seemingly unanimous in their belief as to what constituted a "traditional rate of work", the P.L.B was narrow, the group's beliefs were expounded by exemplars certain of the rightness of their principles because the norm was clear, and the beliefs were thrust at the smaller group by aggressive exdomini, as sure as the exemplars of the rightness of their case. It was an example of the strength inherent in a morality democratically established by a group whose purpose was clear. There was no need for browbeating, threats or other measures that usually accompany authoritarian dissemination of morality not democratically established. There was no need for *potestas* as force, there was only *auctoritas*, the power based upon a democratic morality. And its effect was complete.

A similar process seems to have been in action in governing the relations of the weepart men with the rest of the factory. Up to the inception of the incentive schemes the indices for the rest of the factory show the same characteristics as those for the weepart line; but only the weepart line came out on strike. The 'after' period, succeeding the weepart change in autumn 1952, shows the same improvement and stabilising of performance. (The exceptions in N.A.P. were due to the introduction of the new product.) The change following the new bonus scheme of late 1951 affected immediately all those indices which were connected closely with earnings, productivity, spoilage, absenteeism and lateness. Labour turnover and accident rates altered finally with the changes in social and managerial factors.

It seems reasonable to assume that the production-line men, central to all factory activity, having decided on the morality of the bonus scheme—the differential content being eliminated—would communicate this decision to others in the factory, meeting them in the canteen, on the work floor, on the way out and into the factory, and through the union meetings of shop stewards. Then all P.B.R. schemes throughout the factory would become "fair", all methods of payment or of reducing payment for misdemeanours would become "fair", for the weepart men had so concluded. Unanimous in their decision, vociferous and bellicose through their exdomini shop stewards, their rightness expounded by the exemplars, they influenced the rest of the factory composed of groups of low cohesion, working mainly on individual P.B.R. schemes, or in pairs and not in gangs. If the weepart men regarded bonus schemes as "all right", then the rest would feel the same.

But the manager in 1952 was still suspect and not until, in addition, "Mr Anderson was all right" to the weepart men, could the rest of the factory be certain that he was; a certainty made doubly sure by his address in January 1953, and by Macdonald's support. This support was, in a way, a second-hand effect of the weepart men, for Macdonald was, by that time, voicing the opinion of the men for whom he had fought so long.

To me there does not seem to be any other possible explanation of the contemporaneous changes in groups and individuals carrying out entirely different kinds of operations, paid different rates, some of different sex, forming no obvious closed group related in any way other than in having functional duties towards an enterprise symbolised by one man, the manager. The only language common to them all would be that of morality, the rightness, justice, fairness of payment and government. And the changes that brought about alterations in judgments of this kind were made mainly in the weepart line. The judgments of the weepart men 'set the tone' of the whole factory for, in this case, they were the 'strongest', most cohesive group in it. They were the exemplar group for the operatives and, aggressive in their relations with the external agencies of manager and employer, they also took upon themselves the rôle of exdominus.

In other words I am suggesting that the process through which a small face-to-face group makes its common (democratic) judgments, and decisions on action on these judgments, has its parallel in the larger group. These small groups take, and are given, methectic rôles like those of individuals in the small groups.[1] It seems to be not outside the bounds of possibility that, in a large concern, action taken to better performance of the whole need be directed only at a part, that part which has been given and has taken the exemplar rôle. This, quite unconsciously, is what Anderson did. (See also the experiments in *Morale in War and Work*, cit.)

---

[1] This kind of methectics of large groups and associations I am proposing to call 'Collective Methectics' in a later, more extensive study of methectics generally.

CHAPTER 18

WAGE-EVALUATION AND LABOUR MOBILITY

It must not be thought that, because I have used the phrase "the operative is a man, not a money-making machine", I consider that money is not of prime importance to him. It is. He is a money-making man, but with the needs of a human being, and not the predictable, carrot-following propensities of an automaton. There is no more convincing experience than to sit with men, such as those of Glasgow Ltd, and listen to their talk that, between football, sport and politics, is liberally sprinkled with expressions such as "big money", "good money", "honest money" and "overtime". And with such talk comes news of jobs and job opportunities, labour mobility. So, to understand the meaning of some of the labour turnover characteristics of Glasgow Ltd history, I propose to analyse some hypotheses of wage evaluation. Such an analysis may throw light on motive in reaction to incentives and differentials, on wages and earnings, and on rationalisations on money that so often accompany disagreement in industrial relations.

A man makes an evaluation of his wage in what might be called an 'exponential' fashion—he places less and less importance upon the marginal earnings as the total earnings mount up. This can be roughly illustrated in Fig. 34, the way in which unskilled factory operatives of the type at Glasgow Ltd, use and value their income. What details hold in the City of Glasgow do not necessarily hold elsewhere, but the same *kind* of 'behaviour' would appear to be common to most industrial workers.

The horizontal co-ordinate represents income, increasing to the right; the vertical represents the 'importance' of that part of the income which is used to satisfy needs according to the enumerated list below. The 'importance', or 'value', is measured by the sequence in which the man apportions out his weekly wage packet, the first to be laid aside is the most highly valued, the last is the least valued. This doesn't mean to say that the last portion may not have the most obvious value to him as shown in overt action. It means that until the 'earlier' needs are satisfied (those of greatest 'value' to him) he does not, cannot, take overt action to satisfy 'later' needs.[1] (Unless, of course, he is a social delinquent; and that type is not being discussed.)

[1] What is of importance is not the amounts paid out. It is the order of what 'has to be seen to first' which is important. Indeed, a need group of low value might require much more money to satisfy it than a need group of greater value.

186

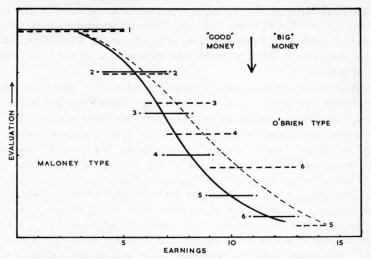

Fig. 34. To illustrate wage evaluation by unskilled operatives.

The unskilled man's needs fall into several groups, sequent in value, enumerated in the figure and tabled below (not complete, but indicative):

1. *Prime necessities:* food, clothing, shelter.
2. *Secondary necessities:* hire-purchase instalments on basic furniture (which lately adds television to radio); hire-purchase as subscription to clothing 'clubs'; education of the children, i.e. sending them to skilled trade apprenticeship (as Maloney did) or continuation school.
3. *Luxury necessities:* tobacco, cinema, football-pool money; and sometimes the Friday night glass of beer.
4. *Necessary luxuries:* beer and liquor on Friday and Saturday, holiday savings, football matches, and sometimes football supporters clubs (of Celtic football team for the Bridgeton district!).
5. *Domestic status needs:* instalments on special furniture, e.g. an electric kettle, saving for a 'better house' (with a bathroom), special clothes such as a hat in place of a cap for Saturday and Sunday, and a second dress "for the wife".
6. *Luxuries:* gambling on dogs and horses, other savings, conspicuous expenditure at pubs, taxis to football matches, etc.,[1] inexpensive hobbies.

The unskilled Bridgeton men fall into two broad categories, those like Maloney who look for a job with "good money", and those like O'Brien who look anywhere for "big money". In Fig. 34 the solid line represents

---

[1] This well-known item of conspicuous expenditure—especially among dock labourers—is occasionally not believed; but I have observed it myself.

the wage evaluation of the Maloney type, and the interrupted line that of the O'Brien type. The O'Brien type cuts down on secondary necessities and any form of savings, has practically no expenditure on domestic status, and has large outlay on luxuries. Conspicuous expenditure on the last is prestige-giving of a kind.[1]

Herein lies the basic distinction between "good money" and "big money". The Maloney type seeks a job whereby he can satisfy his particular needs which involve regular payments as necessities; he needs security. He has a larger capital investment, requiring its upkeep, and he seeks to enlarge it in 'things' or status. "Good money" is less than "big money", but it is a regular income from a "steady" job giving him enough for these simple needs. That is one reason why it is "good". "Big money" is irregular, for it can be obtained only in jobs that pay high time-rates for short intervals of extremely heavy labour, or in those that yield much overtime payments, which are also not very regular. The total annual income of a man like O'Brien is generally less than that of the Maloney type—he lives "on a hunger and a burst"; he moves rapidly from job to job seeking for "big money"; he is the "nomadic riff-raff" described by Anderson. Strangely enough O'Brien himself stayed an inordinately long time at Glasgow Ltd, probably because the earnings there were fairly high as well as being "good". This was the result of a steady piece-rate system of incentive payment.

Maloney and his ilk could be sure of taking home a weekly packet of the same size (very nearly) each week. It is not to be wondered that his type tended to seek a rate of work which off-set eventualities of most kinds by permitting speeding up if necessary. Hence the labour was not too heavy, as required for "big money", which was another reason for the earnings being "good". (There was a third, deeper, reason, to be discussed later.) Moreover, at Glasgow Ltd, earnings were secure and fairly high relative to earnings for unskilled labour in the area. So the problem of why there was a high labour turnover at certain times during the period discussed cannot be solved by reference to the external, *domestic* evaluation of the wage packet.

Comparison with the skilled and semi-skilled workers' evaluation of wage with that of the unskilled throws some light on the unskilled workers' attitude to the differential content in an incentive scheme. The skilled man's needs are somewhat distinct from the semi-skilled, and different from those of the unskilled.

1. *Prime necessities:* food, clothing, shelter.
2. *Secondary necessities:* hire-purchase instalments on furniture (which

[1] When a man gets his wage packet it is customary (among Bridgeton folk of Irish ancestry) that he extract that amount he considers essential for 3, 4, 5 and 6. Among those of Scottish ancestry there is a tendency for the wage packet to be handed to the wife who returns money for 3, 4 and 6, but not 5.

includes items such as carpet sweepers, sets of crockery, bedroom suites, regarded by the unskilled as rank-giving only); education of children to grammar school level and potentiality for professional education, but certainly technological or white collar education.

3. *Luxury necessities:* tobacco, cinema, 'pool money', holiday savings.
4. *Domestic status needs:* instalments on special furniture, e.g. washing machine, refrigerator, radiogram, etc., special 'good' clothing.
5. *Necessary luxuries:* beer and liquor money for Friday and Saturday football and also self-participating sports such as golf and bowls, inexpensive hobbies.
6. *Luxuries:* Savings, conspicuous expenditure in pubs, expensive hobbies such as photography, a motor-car, fur coat for 'the wife'.

A percentage of his earnings, higher than that of the unskilled, goes for groups 1, 2 and 4, about the same for 3, and this with 5 is all included in "good money". Secondly, only when he is making "big money" does he indulge in 6.[1]

The semi-skilled man (who might be called machinist, for he is generally trained over a period of months to be expert on a particular machine and has not gone through an apprenticeship) lies between the skilled and Maloney-type unskilled in his pattern of needs. He does not have to place domestic rank before necessary luxuries, but his earnings are now large enough for him to afford expenditure on these needs higher than would the unskilled, since his domestic rank is approaching that of the skilled. Secondary necessities overlap with his domestic rank needs. If he makes as much "big money" as the skilled man he tends to telescope 5 and 6 and enlarge on conspicuous expenditure.

Hence for the four categories of operatives:

(1) Unskilled, unstable men tend to seek "big money" alone (for irregular expenditure) through heavy labour, high time-rates, and through overtime.
(2) Partly skilled, stable men tend to seek mainly "good money" (for regular expenditure) through steady P.B.R. schemes at 'controlled' rates of effort, and "big money" not by extra effort but through overtime.
(3) Semi-skilled men, machinists, tend to seek both "good money" and "big money" through high rates of effort and overtime.
(4) Skilled men tend to seek mainly "good money" through skill differentials, and steady, 'controlled rate', P.B.R. schemes, and "big money" through overtime.

In Glasgow the skilled man's "good money" cannot be made by present skill differentials and P.B.R. schemes and overtime have become a necessity.

[1] Since the majority of skilled tradesmen in Glasgow are of Scottish ancestry there is a tendency for the wage packet to be handed to 'the wife' who apportions out money for 3 and 6. The woman may also look after the savings of all kinds.

Overtime payment is hardly "big money" to him any longer; but he declines to increase his productivity on a P.B.R. scheme because that would endanger his capacity to regulate his income to steadiness and hence endanger "good money". He would rather work longer at the same rate than faster over a shorter period.

The same holds for the stable unskilled man. As long as his needs are satisfied by "good money", he will be loath to alter his rate of work, and will rely on irregular overtime for "extras". He pockets these extras as his right, for expenditure under the luxury heading. Hence if the rising cost of living reduces his income below the "good money" level his union goes into action to raise the basic wage rate, and so retain the *status quo*. The basic wage rate is roughly that which a man requires for his prime necessities and some of the secondary. The "good money" level is reached by 'controlled rate' P.B.R. schemes, for which reason the two General Workers Unions (to which the unskilled men belong) demand opportunity to make at least 33 per cent, rising to 45 per cent, on P.B.R. schemes for their members. Similarly the skilled worker unions demand a rising basic rate, increased differentials and reduced need to work overtime, or if overtime is necessary, reduced standard weekly working hours so that the total number of hours worked to make "good money" at the regulated rate of effort is lowered— and there is more leisure to enjoy "good money".

The broad tendency in social change is for the exponential curve to move to the right, with wage demands accordingly. What is sought for is larger "good money" to buy more of those things which come under domestic rank needs. The movement is not only one of rising wages to meet rising costs of living (i.e. of primary and secondary necessities) but to meet a rising standard of living. Therefore "good money" needs are increasing, incomes are sought after that are regular and predictable. So the managers are faced with a problem of trying to obtain greater effort with P.B.R. schemes which a stable labour force will regulate in terms of effort rate, or instituting high time rates with guaranteed earnings to attract a stable force willing to work for "good money", at that rate, but prepared to make "big money" on extra effort. The relationship of prices of goods in the various categories of needs to the evaluation of "good money", "big money" and incentives is a problem for the social economist.

To return to the detailed problem of the unskilled men at Glasgow Ltd— since the external evaluation of the wage earnings was not the source of the major fluctuations in labour turnover, the source was most likely internal. This source may be economic, sociological, managerial, or combinations of them and of internal evaluation of wage earnings. The evidence for the wee-part line may be recapitulated:

(1) Before Anderson's arrival "dissatisfaction with wages" was as common

a stated reason for leaving as any other. After his arrival this was not given.

(2) During the first phase men rejected the conditions within days of coming; during the second phase fewer did this.

(3) The labour turnover seemed to increase at and about the times of strikes and go-slows.

(4) Even after the inception of the Anderson incentive schemes the labour turnover rose to a peak in autumn 1952, the time of sociological and managerial adjustment, whereafter it fell.

Since "dissatisfaction with wages" was not the cause of leaving during the period of greatest turnover, 1951, it can be assumed that the earnings were within the limits of "good money", as already suggested by comparing earnings at Glasgow Ltd with those generally earned locally. The major reasons for leaving rapidly, as so many men did, were "work unsuitable", "dissatisfied with job", "job too heavy", and dismissal for indiscipline (which was a rejection of the job as much as leaving voluntarily).[1] This dissatisfaction was greatest at times when those men not leaving showed some kind of dissatisfaction by strike or go-slow action—and they did not find the job too heavy or the work unsuitable. They, too, were guilty of indiscipline by striking and slowing down work. And this dissatisfaction and indiscipline continued after the start of the incentive scheme. For the rest of the factory, neither going on strike nor affected by the incentive scheme, the fluctuations in labour turnover are of the same kind. For them, too, the wages earnings were "good money" comparatively speaking.[2]

They had been comparatively peaceful and complained little from 1946 to 1950. Why should their labour turnover be like that for the weepart men if labour turnover were a matter purely of economics? Or, why should they leave a job with "good money"? If those leaving had all been of the "nomadic" kind, and they left only to seek "big money", it would be most unlikely that their pattern of leaving should be so close to that of the weepart men by chance. According to the analyses of the preceding three chapters it can only be assumed that the labour turnover rates were connected with changes of belief in the system of morality and authority.

But in that case a new problem is posed. After this system was satisfactorily adjusted for the weepart line in autumn 1952, why did the men work harder? And again, why did the bigpart men do the same at the appropriate earlier period? For, if the earnings had been "good money", or good enough up

---

[1] Some indiscipline is 'normal' in anti-authoritarian Clydeside, but dismissals on this ground at Glasgow Ltd were many fewer during the second phase.

[2] Their performance, as shown by all available statistics, improved after autumn 1952, so it seems permissible to assume that their work effort improved as well; and at the same time as that of the production lines.

to late autumn 1951 so that the existing bonus scheme did not inspire them to greater effort, then there is no clear reason why they should have worked harder. Moreover, under the new scheme, by continuing to work at the same rate they would make somewhat more than they had been doing, for the bonus began to operate at a productivity level of a 40 instead of a 50. One could well sympathise with Bulgin and Anderson who could not understand why the weepart men, presented with the chance of making greater earnings, did not do so when they could easily have done it. But one could be as equally surprised that the men should decide to increase their rate of effort when all the indications were that they did not feel an urgent need to make greater earnings.

This is not uncommon. For one example, in a large modern factory in Glasgow during this same period the manager was set a similar question. Semi-skilled men, in a department using machinery of a kind used in U.S.A., were placed on a P.B.R. scheme. They made regular earnings of about £14 a week, yet they refused to work harder even when it was shown to them that men in U.S.A., using the same machines, were constantly producing at a rate that, in Glasgow, would provide a regular pay-packet of over £20 a week. Indeed, they made a demand for a reduction of load with no loss of pay. "Why", said the manager, "did they not take this chance to make as much money as would provide them with far better living conditions?" My answer, that it was already "big money" for machinists, he would not accept. He never did get his increased productivity.

It would seem to follow that, at Glasgow Ltd, during the first phase, the weepart men, and presumably the rest of the factory, at intervals rejected, or were increasingly dissatisfied with, the system of morality and authority, and some left, not to seek better earnings but to seek better conditions in which to make comparable earnings; and that when the system improved in the second phase there was no need for them to go. But at that time there was no change in their domestic need to make greater earnings, and yet they did work harder. So it follows that the increase in productivity was not wholly an answer to an incentive to make more money for what money can give in the domestic (external) sphere of living, but was also connected in some way with the improvement in the work situation, and symbolised an improvement in the factory (internal) sphere of living. The men did not stay because they were making greater earnings, but they stayed and also made greater earnings for the same reason. As some said, they "were going to die there".

Therefore it would seem that the evaluation of wage earnings at the work place was different from the domestic evaluation. Since the increase in earnings for both bigpart and weepart lines was associated with the change in morality and authority, then within that change lies a clue to at least part of the factory wage-evaluation.

Because the wage earnings are a personal affair in the sense that they belong to the man, and their size depends on him, his capacities and the way he is regarded as an operative, the wage earnings are, in effect, a representation of the man in some way or another.[1] His evaluation of his wage is essentially an evaluation of himself. This evaluation is mainly one of worth, and must therefore be concerned with rank and prestige. Before reaching that element of the wage of importance to this analysis some general propositions can be put.

The factory evaluation of the wage is in three categories:

(1) *General occupational status element.* This is inherent in the basic rate now determined mainly by negotiation at national level. It is the external differential by which a man recognises the worth of his function to his fellow men generally. In society his job is valued at so much, therefore he is valued at so much. The large question of a national wage structure hinges on this evaluation.

(2) *Local occupational status element.* This is inherent in all rates paid by the firm to its own employees. It includes special payments of all kinds, but mainly rates for work done in the factory. It makes the internal differential the worth to the firm of the particular job the man is fulfilling. It is the worth of his function, and therefore of him, in the eyes of management and of his fellow employees. It was this differential which became of some importance to the weepart men when they compared their earnings with those of the bigpart. Since the employer/manager was concerned in the establishment of this differential the relationship with the manager, as making the first judgment of local occupational status, became of importance. So this element at Glasgow Ltd was tied up with the men's evaluation of the morality of the bonus scheme.

(3) *Local prestige element.* The third element of the wage-evaluation is concerned with the marginal amount, that is the fluctuating portion which depends upon the effort the man puts into his work. The more he gets the better he has performed his task, fulfilled his function, and therefore the value of him in his operation as well as his function. This operation is that for which he is self-responsible and, accordingly, as he operates to better fulfilling of his function so he will be given prestige ("kudos"). This is inherent in the marginal wage, what a man makes by variation of his own effort, by reason of how he happens to feel about the job and its environment. It is that element which measures how well he does his job, and symbolises the reward for serving the enterprise through his doing it well or

---

[1] It is of interest in this connection that many operatives in factories carefully guard the secrets of their wage card from each other if they are on individual rates. Miners on the Friday pay-out scan their wage card for mistakes, then carefully, very carefully, tuck it away or tear it to shreds. This happens even though their mates know nearly to a penny what their earnings are.

not. It is the only element of the wage which is completely personal in that no others share in it. This does not hold if his job is very much interdependent with others—as on weepart assembly where the gang must be regarded as an individual. On the bigpart line the work was less completely interdependent, therefore the individual evaluation of the wage became more important—as described in the preceding chapter.

Men seek prestige, some more than others. So some will work hard and others be regarded as lazy, capable of working harder (as were the weepart gangs), but not doing so. But it may be merely that they do not seek prestige, provided they have satisfaction of rank needs and domestic needs. It can be seen from the preceding discussion that if a man is making "good money" he may be satisfying all those desires that are external to the factory. If his earnings also satisfy his rank needs, then there is required only the balance between his domestic evaluation and the prestige evaluation. He has to seek with his mates a rate of effort around which there is a permissible latitude of behaviour, yielding earnings to symbolise his own conception of the balance of external needs and work prestige. He cannot seek prestige beyond these limits because he would then be losing prestige in another way—he would not be fulfilling his methectic function, his rôle, within the informal group of his mates. They have a morality, a code, which is in effect a protective weapon as over and against the external threat of the power of the manager, who may cut rates if they work too hard; that is, if he is not a moral man. Any individual behaviour which would endanger the group rate would be a negation of the value of the man's rôle, and that individual would lose prestige.

However, should the manager's morality be unquestioned, then there is no fear for the group or individual that their rates would be cut if they worked too hard. Therefore the group norm could rise and the individual's potentiality for hard work and need for prestige would have outlet, prestige as a worker fulfilling his function in the factory, and prestige as fulfilling his function within his group. So that to allow prestige drive scope for expression there are two prerequisites:

(1) a group sense of morality of rates of work dependent mainly upon group structure and external domestic needs;
(2) a group sense of the manager's morality in determination of the proper ranking of rates, and his adherence to them according to what the group considers is in a moral fashion.

These conditions were achieved in autumn 1952 for the weepart men. Their domestic needs of "good money" were already fairly well satisfied, their needs for prestige were now possible of satisfaction. And they did satisfy them, by increasing productivity.

Thus it seems that if the ranking differentials are equitable, and if the domestic needs for stability and security can be satisfied, security in the sense of steady income unthreatened by managerial immorality, then an incentive scheme will be effective in producing greater effort. This is the situation that holds in a period of full employment and of wages high enough to provide "good money", and not necessarily "big money". It seems to me that all I'm saying is that men will work better for a good manager or, as Maloney put it, "Mr Anderson just needed to ask us and we'd do it".

But to return to the marginal element which includes "big money". It can be seen now why the men unconsciously use the word 'big' for this element. It is relevant to the need for enlargement of the self. If a man has prestige he feels bigger.[1] It is self-gratification. Among stable men who seek "good money", it is self-gratification arising out of first having served in the rôle of providing "good" money to satisfy the needs of the domestic situation, and of rôle in the work-group. The money is "good" because it is a giving in service. Thereafter "big money" is satisfying in getting as well as giving. (The man pockets this as his reward, for he is "entitled" to it, as one put it to me.) He feels whole in so doing for he has served, and is now rewarded for having served well.

But there are the O'Briens who seek "big money" alone. They have self-desire only. They seek the plaudits of the pub-company by conspicuous expenditure, before seeking stability and security. They do not seek a balance of service and reward like the Maloney type. They are unbalanced, rootless, not knowing where they stand. Yet given a chance to make "big money" constantly some will remain fairly stable. This is what I think happened in the second phase at Glasgow Ltd. The stable men of the production-lines, having established with Anderson the requisite conditions for reacting to the bonus scheme, could then move from making "good money" into the "big money" region. This provided self-gratification for some of those who sought mainly that, and they stayed for more than a few days. The labour turnover of new entrants fell. But there were always those who sought the quick "big money", and were driven by the restlessness that would not allow their conforming to work-group discipline as well as managerial (Anderson now exerting strong structural authority). They came and went, as they did all over Glasgow.

It is now possible to give a tentative definition of what is meant in the expression "a fair day's wage for a fair day's work". The earnings in 1952 and 1951 were "good enough", but they were not "fair" because of the injustice of the differential. A "fair day's wage" is one which provides for a balance of domestic needs and occupational ranking, a balance of the "good money" and 'occupational element' of the wage-earnings. In general this balance is established by normative decision of the work-group, for the men

[1] If he has ranking he feels superior—higher.

of a particular work-group are almost always from the same kind of *milieu* with the same kinds of domestic needs, and from the same kind of occupation with the same ranking needs.

The wage became a "fair wage" at the end of 1951, that was what Maloney referred to in saying "it's a' richt—but". The "but" could be taken as implying that there was no accompanying "fair day's work". Work here implies function and the satisfaction in fulfilling function through operation. It is intimately tied up with the prestige element of the wage. The man who comes from his work and happily stretches his toes towards the fire and feels he has done a "fair day's work", has given to the general effort by fulfilling his function. In so doing he has received his reward, he has obtained "good money", and has also satisfied the prestige element. He is whole, and happily so because he has satisfied both of his basic needs to serve and to receive. There was no opportunity for this at Glasgow Ltd until autumn of 1952. Thereafter the increased productivity was the "fair day's work"; the men now had opportunity of establishing, through group decision, that which constituted their duty in the factory, that which was their function, which they felt obliged to do, and so 'right', 'proper', and therefore "fair". But this duty was intimately involved with the duty externally, which required a "fair day's wage". The total of a man's duties, and his rewards for fulfilling duties, is therefore implicit in "a fair day's wage for a fair day's work". When productivity leapt in 1952 the expression used for an increased output was "a good day's work". This was more than a "fair day's work", that is to say the men had done more than they felt obliged to do. "Fair" implies duty; "good" here implies beyond the bounds of duty.

CHAPTER 19

FRUSTRATION AND HEALTH

The chances of incurring accidents on the weepart line bore no relation to pace of work, nor to skill coming from experience, nor to age; and there is evidence that the fluctuations in productivity, spoilage and labour turnover were not related to accidents as causal, but as associated, in being reaction to the same cause or causes.

During the five-year period surveyed only one man seems to have been accident-prone, p. 99. That is to say he had such poor eye-muscle co-ordination that he had inadequate capacity for avoiding injury when he was placed in a dangerous situation. Some men had accident liability, in that their record over the period showed more accidents than most, but the distribution pattern of liability shows that their accidents could have been incurred by chance, just as the failure to have accidents by some men was also chance. The great majority of men were accident potential, that is to say, though they were not accident-prone they were potentially likely to get themselves into dangerous situations when their capacity for avoiding injury was not adequate;[1] as, for example, the careful car-driver of years' accident-free driving, incurring an accident because of behaviour under stress, such as unusual anger—he becomes careless.

An accident potential person, according to Alexander, tends to be anti-authoritarian, "decisive or even impulsive. He is apt to act on the spur of the moment. He likes excitement and adventure; he does not like to plan and prepare for the future. A large number of persons with the accident habit have had a strict upbringing and have derived from this an unusual amount of resentment against persons in authority. Briefly, they are men of action and not of planning, persons who do not interpolate much deliberation and hesitation between impulses and their actual execution. This impetuousness may have varied reasons but apparently rebellion against restriction by authority and all forms of external coercion is its most common origin. Planning and deliberation are potent factors which make one refrain from immediate rash action. The accident-prone person (meaning accident potential, T.T.P.) is essentially a rebel. He cannot tolerate even self-discipline. He rebels not only against external authorities but against the rule of his own reason and control."[2] On "Red Clydeside", and especially

[1] For enlargement on these definitions see Paterson, T. T., The Theory of the Social Threshold, The Social Aspect of Accident Causation. *Soc. Rev.*, XLII, 1950.

[2] Alexander, F., *U.S. Public Health Service Rep.*, vol. 64, 1949, No. 12.

in Bridgeton, the men are just such people. It would be small cause for wonder that, if the social situation at Glasgow Ltd were such as to incite anti-authoritarian feelings, there would be an increase in the number of accidents.

The close correlation of accident rate and labour turnover, Fig. 14, yields a clue to the process which probably led to an increase in the number of accidents at times when men were leaving in greater numbers than would normally be expected. According to the analysis of the preceding chapter men left because of non-satisfaction of the desires for "fair" differentials and for self-expression in work. Put in other words two complementary drives or motives were frustrated; and frustration led to anger, which led to leaving the firm (as well as to more than usual exhibitions of indiscipline— anti-authoritarian behaviour).

This was a situation which had close parallels with a war-time experience I have described elsewhere.[1] Fighter pilots in the Royal Air Force, frustrated in their desires to come to grips with the enemy showed consequent aggression in a high rate of accidents. By giving the pilots an opportunity to satisfy their desires the frustration was alleviated and accident-rate improved considerably. My analysis of the accident situation there could well be applied to Glasgow Ltd.

Men have two social drives, which I have called the service drive and prestige drive. In service drive the motive, deep-seated, is one of self-preservation through joining with others in activities or enterprises promoting survival. In prestige drive, the motive, also as deep-seated, is self-preservation through individual activity. In modern industrial society the enterprise is the firm (the community so to speak), and through working with others in such enterprises the individual gains a livelihood. But he seeks to serve the associational interests, as far as his capacities permit, in a "worth-while job", that is a job of recognised value in achieving the success of the enterprise, and hence a job of rank. The "job" has the rank, that is the man's function (his contribution to society and to his community) has rank, and he, filling the position, partakes of that rank. Accordingly as he fulfils that function (through good operation) to the benefit of the community so he is given personal prestige, and this he seeks as reflecting himself even more than his function, he "wants to be somebody", thus satisfying the drive to self-preservation through his own efforts. All men have these drives, but the relative importance of the two in each man is unique. Some seek to be happy only in the serving, and seem to be little concerned with prestige. Some seek prestige almost wholly, they are "self-seekers". The man who gets prestige by doing his best for the good of the whole group, the man with "team spirit" is the best balanced. But since the relation of these

[1] *Morale in War and Work*, op. cit.

198

drives is unique for each man, some men can be apparently balanced when not seeking prestige, some when they are apparently "self-seekers".

The service drive shows itself in several ways, one being the desire for rank which, in industry though not in some other fields of endeavour, is recognised by the money symbol, that is by the wage differential. The prestige drive shows itself in a desire to be well thought of, mainly by worker colleagues; and this often leads to conformity to the group standards, despite the individuality of the motive.[1]

Hence one could postulate that in the first phase at Glasgow Ltd the service drive was frustrated to some extent because rank was not recognised —the differential was not appropriate. It was not a "fair day's wage" for the rank of the job. The prestige drive could have expression only in conforming with the P.L.B of the work group, but that did not allow of expression through operation, that is, through working harder. Frustrated to some extent in both drives the Bridgeton labourer, anti-authoritarian as he was, became more aggressive, either "drew his books", cocked a snook at the foreman (and was "given his books"), or had an accident, being accident potential in a situation where that potentiality could have expression.

When the incentive scheme of winter 1951 evened out the differential, the service drive was satisfied to some extent, but the prestige drive was not. The sociological and managerial factors, now cleared of the economic, were still such that the work-group could not determine a new PLB for fuller expression of prestige drive. So, the accident rate, having improved on removal of frustration of the service drive, again rose in the failure of the system to give expression to the prestige drive. The men were still frustrated; some left and others had accidents.

Once the two drives were satisfied, by the successful outcome of the autumn 1952 crisis, then the weepart men could give expression to both drives; so labour turnover fell, productivity went up and accident-rate improved. The resulting balance of the two drives, with the satisfaction of external needs as well, produced what can only be described as "team spirit". Anderson could, and did, talk of his men as "my team" after that. I have deliberately avoided the words 'team spirit' and 'morale' so far, because these words are, I think, very much misused[2] and I wished to avoid confusing the issue.

[1] Hence in U.S.A. one finds the apparent paradox of the "freedom of the individual" with excessive conformity to group-standards; whereas in Britain 'team-spirit' is applauded and tolerance of eccentricity is a cultural trait. In U.S.A. there is competition and conformity; in Britain there is co-operation and individuality.

[2] An American definition of "morale" is concerned with "happiness" at work, and a generally cheerful air is called "morale" by some people on that side of the Atlantic. This leads to the kind of situation where men with so-called morale are found to have low performance at their work. Morale proper will always lead to better performance at work whether it be in war or peace.

This broad theoretical analysis of the peculiarities in the fluctuating accident-rate among the weepart men applies to the rest of the factory, whose general sense of the morality of the differential content of the incentive scheme, and of its instigator, their managerial co-worker Anderson, was so guided by the factory exemplar, the weepart line. Some might not themselves have felt frustrated in their particular function, but the factory tone having been set by the weepart group, they acted accordingly. There was too the depressing effect of working alongside frustrated men, "constantly grumbling" as a foreman said, which foreman finally became aggressive and took action (he was "brutally rude"), triggering off a strike. The way in which a small "bloody-minded" unit within a larger can influence the whole is no strange phenomenon to field officers in the services.

The setting of the 'tone' of the factory even affected health as shown in the appropriate indices—which may be analysed severally, and *in toto*. Involuntary absenteeism, it should be expected, would hardly be affected by 'political' and 'social' changes in the factory provided the physical conditions remained unaltered, as they did. Yet there was a pronounced change at the time of the inception of the incentive scheme, particularly so in the case of men. (But whereas the rate for men remained fairly constant thereafter, the loss of time for women showed a rise in 1952 parallel to the general behaviour of weepart indices.) There was no change in methods of recording. There was no change in general health in the community outside the factory. In the 'before' period there were marked fluctuations which were different for men and women—there were no marked fluctuations in the 'after' period. It can only be concluded that the change in the economic factors (plus changes in the social factors) produced a change in the pattern of involuntary absenteeism.

It could not be argued, and especially so for the weepart line, that, because of the new scheme, the men stayed off less in order to make more money. They did not increase productivity. If anything they could afford more easily to stay off because, at the same productivity, the earnings were greater. When broken down into time lost per absence the change is seen to be not in the numbers of operatives reporting sick but in the length of time they were sick. There seems to be no other conclusion but that the operatives were more able to throw off the ills that overtook them. Similarly (Fig. 30), even though more reported sick in 1954 the amount of time off per sickness was still further reduced.

If the arguments of the preceding chapter be accepted it would follow that general health of the factory as shown in absence through certified sickness was improved by removal of the inequity of differentials on the production lines, by removal of the sense of frustration of the service drive. This improvement was continued (as shown by the time off per person in the 'after' period) by removal of the negative social and managerial factors, by removal of the sense of frustration of the prestige drive, particularly so in the case of women.[1] It may not be surprising to some that frustration, even subconscious, can affect the bodily powers of recovery from sickness.[2]

Voluntary absenteeism, which may include minor sickness not with medical certification, appears to have been affected in the same way. The exception was that both numbers staying away and the length of time off were reduced. A striking characteristic was the remarkably steady voluntary absenteeism among the men (at 0·6 per cent of hours possible for work) during the years 1952 to 1954. The female absenteeism, also showing improvement during 1953 and 1954, was not so steady. This can be attributed, with some degree of certainty, to variation in domestic duties. Again the only possible explanation seems to be removal of frustration. But in the case of voluntary absenteeism it seems likely that frustration of the service drive was the only factor involved since the change took place in the winter of 1951 only.

It would appear that absenteeism, as percentage time lost, is not a very good index of the changes that may be taking place in a factory, nor of the general state of mind of its members. This is particularly highlighted by reference to lateness, Fig. 31. Lateness improved at the same time as absenteeism; but when the whole factory had reached a state of adjustment, and was, in general, a happier place with high productive effort, lateness soared. (Anderson didn't mind, for he was getting production.) This was contemporaneous with increase in the numbers absent with short-term sickness. As already said in Chapter 14, where productive effort is happily high men seem to think they can afford to take time off if they feel there is something wrong with them. They are working on the marginal value of the wage in both senses of wage-evaluation.[3]

Of the other indices of health, skin dysfunctions for the rest of the factory appear to have fluctuated as they did for the weepart line. For the rest of the factory there was a fall for the 'before' period, but it varied widely; the fall was continued for 1952 and then came the low, steady rate for the 'after' phase. On analogy with the weepart statistics it might be assumed that for the stable population of the factory (and those in contact with the allergenic materials), the situations of frustration-stress, and adjustment-alleviation of stress, were the causes of change. For the mobile population the same situations produced changes in gastric and other psychosomatic

[1] Earlier studies in another Scottish community, as yet unpublished, show that the Scottish women are generally more concerned with prestige in all ways than are their menfolk.

[2] Higham, T. M., Industrial Stress. *Soc. Dairy Technology*, x, 1957, p. 222.

[3] Whether this holds in the National Coal Board, for example, is debatable, for the published figures on absenteeism are inadequate.

conditions.[1] It may be argued that, for the latter index, a social process of selection was going on by which the proportion of stable 'types' was being increased by selected turnover; but the more probable explanation is that the environment of reduced stress led to fewer exhibitions of stress symptoms.

No more can be said than to hazard a general proposition. The changes that took place were such as to bring about an alteration from a socio-economic environment of stress to one of reduced stress; and stress appears to have affected different 'types' of people differently. Unstable 'types', that is nomadic, insecure, egocentric people reacted to stress either by getting out of the environment quickly and/or by exhibiting gastric and other psycho-somatic symptoms (usually not skin dysfunctions). More stable 'types', less nomadic, more secure, anti-authoritarian but comparatively less aggressive, incurred more accidents as well as worsening performance. The stable types also seemed to react in overt group activity of strikes and go-slows.

---

[1] Among the women of N.A.P. for instance, dysmenorrhoea does not appear (as a condition requiring treatment) during the 'after' period, though it appears in the 'before'.

CHAPTER 20

STRIKES

Between the beginning of 1947 and of 1953 there were thirteen stoppages and five go-slows. I have been unable to find an explanation for the men's decision to select one or other of these demonstrations, and so I propose to consider a go-slow as a strike, and to call all stoppages and go-slows 'strikes'. They are essentially the same in nature, withdrawal of labour.

They can be listed in sequence, with associated cause (*sic*), and with behaviour on the part of manager and the weepart men, thus:

1947

February. The men were suddenly told about the projected introduction of longpart manufacture. A short go-slow was neither preceded nor succeeded by changes in productivity. (Other indices are not available.)

March. A short strike was preceded by a four weeks' fall in productivity as longpart production was increased. But there was an immediate recovery, within one week, to a rate similar to that preceding longpart production, showing that the fall before the strike was not wholly conditioned by the new manufacture.

May. A short strike was apparently an expression of dissatisfaction at not being able to make the minimum bonus rate, and it was succeeded by an immediate improvement to that rate. (No mechanical changes were made.)

August. The manager began to cut longpart production. Productivity fell rapidly in the month preceding the strike, and thereafter rose steadily for the ensuing ten months. No changes of any kind were made.

1948

June. The men were told that longpart production was to be stopped, and they protested in a short 'down-tools'. Productivity fell away slowly.

August. The fall, succeeding the June strike, culminated in this strike. Thereafter productivity rose slowly.

November. A managerial decision to introduce 5 per cent longpart production was met by a short demonstration. There was little change in productivity.

1949

August. By this time there was no longpart manufacture. Falling productivity, and a very rapid increase of labour turnover to an extraordinary level, culminated in a strike ostensibly against Bulgin's introduction of meal-time working. After the strike productivity improved and labour desertion immediately dropped.

1950

February. The manager made a change on the machine-line for which the men did not think the bonus-reward was just. Productivity did not much alter before or after—nor was the bonus altered.

August. Falling productivity and rising labour turnover preceded this strike, which was followed by immediate and rapid recovery to a higher productivity and low turnover.

1951

April–May. Three strikes succeeded remarkable deterioration in productivity and labour turnover. There was recovery afterwards to nearly pre-strike level, though the men gained nothing as a result of the stoppages.

September. Again a remarkable deterioration in productivity and labour turnover culminated in two strikes succeeded by as rapid recovery. The new incentive bonus scheme was a result of the strikes.

1952

March. The ostensible causes were foreman behaviour and meal-time working proposed by the manager. There was a short fall in productivity of no great consequence, and little change in labour turnover.

July–August. Apart from rising accident-rate and falling spoilage there was little change preceding the strike but there was all-round improvement after it. There was change in the system of working, suggested by the men and introduced by the manager.

1953

January. No changes in trend heralded and succeeded this strike.

There appear to be two kinds of strike, those which were preceded by deterioration in productivity and labour turnover (and accidents, which index is closely correlated with turnover), and those which were not so preceded. Either kind of strike was generally followed by improvement in the indices even though the ostensible cause of the strike was not eradicated by agreement. Those which were not preceded by deteriorating indices were all related to managerial decisions. For these reasons I propose to call these two kinds of strike *manager-variable* and *operative-variable* strikes. (All the strikes here were unofficial in that they started without prior approval by union officials.)

Manager-variable strikes: 1947, February, May, August.
1948, June, November.
1950, February.
1952, March, July–August.
1953, January.

Operative-variable strikes: 1947, March.
1948, August.
1949, August.
1950, August.
1951, the April–May and the September complexes.

The operative-variable strike is typical of the 'wildcat' strike, as it is so aptly called in U.S.A., a stoppage that suddenly appears for no obvious reason, and that is apparently unpredictable because it is based so often upon what appears to be 'unreasonable' and 'illogical' causes. But such strikes are not unpredictable if this subdivision is correct. They are always preceded by changes in the performance indices, a pattern of changes that is fairly regular. They can be 'expected'. Indeed, the difficulty that faces managers in the avoidance of strikes does not lie in the operative-variable kind since they can be expected and so avoided (if the manager understands the deeper-seated causes). The difficulty lies in the manager-variable strike. He has to judge, or guess, whether his own decisions are likely to be regarded by the men as requiring demonstration in strike action. In other words he has to enquire into the 'morality' of his own decisions in terms of the men's frame of reference.

On the other hand he may be cynical enough about his position to decline to avoid an unofficial strike. Anderson acted this way in April 1951. He knew that the strike—concerning a rise of a penny per hour in the bonus—was going to come; and he did nothing to avoid it. "If they don't have it now, they'll have it sooner or later; let them get it out of their system." Practically the same words were said to me once by the manager of a coal mine when I pointed out to him that the statistics indicated the close approach of an unofficial strike. "Let them have it and get it off their chests, then get on with production." He knew two things. The strike was coming, as he *felt*, without reference to figures; electric lights were being smashed, and at dangerous places too; picks were being put through water cans and so on, and he also knew that once the strike was over productivity would rise. But he did not know how properly to avoid the strike. He could have given the men some sop or other, but he knew that that was no use—the real cause of the strike was unknown to him.

It is the recovery in productivity and other indices after a strike which is apparent to such managers. And they know that it is not due only to making up for a few hours lost-time money, because the recovery persists for some time. The strike allows the men to "get it off their chests", and "it" is the aggression that accompanies frustration. As a frustrated person may express aggression in some 'violent' activity and then "feels better for it", so the group strikes and, feeling better, recovers. But if the cause of frustration remains unaltered, the frustration reasserts itself leading to another desire for aggressive outlet, and this may be accentuated as a result of incomplete satisfaction in the previous outburst. This appears to have parallels in the 'before' period at Glasgow Ltd.

The sequence of operative-variable strikes, beginning in 1948 and terminating at the end of 1951, shows a steadily increasing 'amplitude' of action-reaction and speeding up of frequency. In 1951 the two groups of strike/go-slow complexes were the culmination of the process. The series suddenly terminated when the economic source of frustration was removed. Not only did the men reach a peak of aggression, so did the manager who himself threatened to strike—by proferring his resignation. (An extraordinary consequence of this was that Anderson became known at his Head Office, and among managers in industry generally, as "an appeaser". And this reputation remained even after he—and the men—raised annual production over 80 per cent. The state of mind of these "gentry" must be somewhat peculiar though, unfortunately, not unique.)

It seems that the operative-variable strike was a form of group aggression consequent upon group frustration. The individuals, as individuals within the group, reacted to frustration in a variety of ways—in lowering of performance indices. But the cause of frustration could not be removed by an individual (or several individuals) being sick, or absent, or late, or accident-liable, or a poor-quality worker. The removal had to be the effect of a group activity; which can be viewed this way:

The moral beliefs, the *mores*, of a social group do not come into being as a result of completely independent activity of the various members of the group. They are the result of social activity and, indeed, the existence of moral beliefs can be regarded as one indication of the existence of a group or groups. Moral beliefs represent the consensus of opinion of a group as to what is right or wrong, good or bad.[1] The inequity of the bonus scheme at Glasgow Ltd, that it was "not fair", was appreciated by the individual members of the group only as they became aware of consensus of opinion that it was unfair. A newcomer to the factory knew what his wage earnings were likely to be, before he began work. That was implicit in the contract of the hire of labour. He, as an individual, could regard it as "not very much", or "low wages", or "poor pay", but in taking on the job he could not make a judgment that it was "not fair". Immediately he became a member of the group and heard what it thought of the scheme he could then make comment upon its unfairness. His standard of reference was the group opinion, the group norm.

This can be put in a slightly different way. The members of the work-group, through interchange of ideas and through the mechanism of rôle-playing, set up a norm of belief with quite well-defined permissible latitudes of behaviour. This norm cannot be altered by the solitary activity of one member, or the separate solitary activities of several members. The norm can be altered only by group activity. Now, if the cause of frustration is to be

---

[1] Here I am well aware of how many intellectual toes I am treading upon, and of the enormous possibilities of argument on this point. I shall return to it even though it should be summarily.

PLATE II. Strike: the 'leader' talks. (This is not at Glasgow Limited)

removed, either the norm must be altered or else the environment which is antagonistic to the norm must be changed. In the first case a group activity is required. In the second case again a group activity is needed. This may not necessarily take the form of a strike. More frequent than the strike is action on the part of rôle-players, exdominus and exemplar, to get the environment changed. (Hence the approach to the manager of two such persons as a common method of getting questions of dispute settled.) Rôle-playing of this kind is a group activity, for its rôle-players cannot exist separately from the group. It was certainly tried enough at Glasgow Ltd prior to striking. Frustrated in this way the work-group had to be more overtly aggressive. The men must strike if the manager pays no heed to their sense of rightness and goodness. The traditional right of the working man to withhold his labour is a special case of the moral right to act as a group for moral reasons. That is why so many strikes are essentially "on matters of principle", even though the justification is frequently irrational, "cock-eyed".

A small diversion may be allowed here. To the activities of political *agents provocateurs* are ascribed many unofficial strikes. There is no doubt in my own mind, arising out of personal experience, that such agents are frequently active. But in no case that I have examined carefully do I find that these men actually started a strike in the sense that they have provided cause for striking. A cause always exists already, a question usually of 'right' or 'principle', and upon this these "factory politicians" work. Moreover, in those cases investigated I find the strike had already begun when they stepped in and, guiding the men, mob-like and less rational in their aggression, exacerbated passions and irrational arguments, making confusion worse confounded. I am open to believe that such a "politician" can actually trigger off a strike if he occupies the rôle of exdominus for his group. But I feel fairly confident that a cause has existed beforehand which has been a question of morality and is represented, not by the "politician", but by the exemplar. At Glasgow Ltd O'Brien was labelled "a Red", but he could lead only when the feeling of the weepart men was aggressive enough to require action, a feeling expounded by men like Maloney, dyed-in-the-wool "Labour men"—not "Red".

The difference in the strike activity of the two production lines illustrates another point in the relation of strike action to group morality. Even when frustration affected the bigpart line in the 'before' period they did not strike like the weepart men. They did not "push" Macdonald to question the external differential; wherefore it may be argued they had no complaint. But they reacted at once to the new incentive scheme, from which it has already been concluded that they had previously kept their work effort low. This rate-fixing was a reaction to the believed immorality, "unfairness", of the previous incentive scheme, a belief held more firmly by the weepart men

207

and more overtly expounded by them. That is to say the more cohesive, less individualist weepart group was more prone to strike than the less cohesive, more individualist bigpart group. The sense of the immorality of the incentive scheme, hence the sense of frustration and consequent aggression, was more intense in the cohesive group. The permissible latitude of behaviour was more restricted, the clarity of decision on what constituted "fair" and "reasonable", was enhanced; the belief was held more strongly; the sense of frustration was heightened.

A by-product of group cohesion is the security it brings, for the clearer the moral values of a group the greater the sense of security of the individual member.[1] This security is protected, and any attempt to disrupt it is resisted. Or, to put it another way, a group will tend to preserve and fight for its moral values and sense of security if it is threatened by external power and/or by internal change inspired by external power or influence.

In Chapter 5 (p. 37), Maloney described the situation in which Macrae took action in going to Anderson "for a bonus". The evidence suggests that the crew was not completely united on the matter of the rate to be worked. Maloney, the exemplar, was not at one with Macrae, exdominus. But both were at one on the matter of the reward. It seems to me that the permissible latitude of behaviour, the P.L.B, was widening, at least in one set of attitudes, and this insecurity added to the frustration arising out of the inequity of the differential. However, it may be that the approach of the strike was heralded by a tendency among members to question the rights and wrongs of the case in differentials and, as a consequence, in rates of work. Questioning of this kind in the bigpart group would be more permissible than in the weepart, and lead to no trouble unless the P.L.B became too wide. In the weepart group questioning was a threat to security since the group required unified action on a basic principle.

The January 1953 strike is a clearer case of resistance against threat to group security. That strike came about as a result of a shortage of personnel in N.A.P. at a time when the sales force was demanding much more from that department. Anderson proposed to use one of the three gangs of each shift on this work, each gang taking turn about, that is, once every three weeks. The gang so transferred was to be paid the same bonus as the pool on weeparts, so they would not drop earnings. The labour was much lighter than on weepart assembly; there was no loss of rank since the job was temporary, and only one week in three; Macdonald had been consulted, and raised no objections from the trade union point of view; indeed, the same earnings for less work struck him as a "good thing". He advised the men to try it and "see what it's like". Anderson had consulted the shop stewards and leading men a month before he proposed to start the scheme and, though

---

[1] I need not quote Fromm and such experts on this line of thought.

the first meeting was somewhat hectic because of his treatment of O'Brien, the second meeting went well. He put in front of them the difficulties he was faced with and asked, did not command, help. They agreed that his arguments were logical, but they refused to go on to N.A.P. No reason for the refusal was given. At the strike-meeting the shop stewards gave as some kind of reason that the manager was always using squeezing tactics to "suck more out of them for no extra"—which was a nonsensical argument in this case.

The only statement that had any validity as reason was "we want to be with our mates". The N.A.P. work was individual work which meant that the gang would be broken up. It seems that it was far more important to them that they stick together on a hard job rather than each get an easier job. (This may sound peculiar in the light of the oft-repeated statements that workmen today, especially unskilled, are work-shy.) There could be no other reason for the men's behaviour, as far as I could find out, other than the desire to stick together as a group. In the light of what has been said about work-group methectics this is understandable; the existence of the group satisfies certain needs and, among these, the need for security of belonging, in having a set of moral values for the work place. In the "job" itself lies a set of values for the workman, and these values are established for him through his membership of the group.

In the end the men went back to do what Anderson asked of them. But they went having heard Anderson's demand that they work *with* him. That is to say they could now undertake the temporary assignment as having job value within the total of the factory and not only within their gang, crew or pool. They became aware of the wider morality of the factory.

The strikes of 1952 were of a parallel nature. The go-slow of August that year was intimately connected with the creation of a new gang structure and, even though it was first mooted by the men, it became a manager-variable strike against a threat to their security and their existing sets of values. Then it would appear that the relationship of manager-variable to operative-variable strikes is in fact fairly close. In the one the security of the group is threatened, or need is frustrated, either by direct change of the group or by attack upon the moral values of the group, which values spring from its cohesion; and in the other, needs which spring from the morality of the group are frustrated, and hence that morality is threatened.

It could be said, at least for Glasgow Ltd, that, in general, if there is no frustration of the need for security as a group, and for the morality stemming from the group, then there is unlikely to be strike activity. If the group is threatened, and the need for security is hence frustrated (that is self-awareness within the group, such as is shown in prestige-seeking and role-taking), the strike aggression is of the manager-variable kind, triggered off by managerial action, and without preceding deterioration of performance. If the group morality is threatened, that is the needs arising out of morality of the group are frustrated, then the strike aggression is of the operative-variable kind with preceding deterioration of performance and, perhaps, a tendency to reduced cohesion (itself a threat to security, and also a cause of deterioration).

It would seem to follow that all these indices which did not again deteriorate after the winter of 1951–52 (that is, after the change in the economic factor) were indices closely related in some way to the sense of the morality (in this case the morality of the economic factor—the differential). That is to say they were indices which were governed by group standards rather than by individual standards. Productivity rates we know from many other observations to be so governed. Spoilage is not so clearly governed by group standards except in so far as it depends upon that which is generally called 'carelessness' and which is governed by group standards. Or, one would expect that any process which tended to reduce cohesion of the group would induce carelessness; and it seems that continued frustration of group needs might do this to some extent, with immediate recovery on release after strike aggression. Absenteeism and lateness are generally thought to be individualist behaviour symptoms, but here it seems they were subject to group standards; that is to say, men were absent or late accordingly as the group thought it right or wrong, good or bad to be absent or late.

On the other hand it would appear that psychosomatic complaints, accidents and labour turnover were not so closely governed by group standards. It requires no argument to understand why the first was not thus governed. As already postulated, these complaints are reactions by individuals to stress situations, and only in so far as group activity brings about release or increase of stress would the complaints alter. The problem of *accident* relationship to group standards is less easily understood. Like spoilage, accidents are attributable to 'carelessness' which can be increased by any process tending to reduce group cohesion, and by frustration of innate needs; accident potential individuals react in the main. In a situation where behaviour, which leads to accident, is governed by standards set up by the group, as for instance in motoring, flying, mining, the accident rate will show a relationship to group cohesion as well as to frustration. In those occupations where the group has no standards governing accident-producing behaviour there is likely to be no relationship to cohesion but only to frustration. This was the case at Glasgow Ltd. Spoilage, as distinct from accidents, was there governed by standards of behaviour, and hence was related to both cohesion and frustration.

A similar argument could be applied to labour turnover. As already analysed in Chapter 18, this index is dependent upon two sets of values, the external and internal evaluation of the wage earnings. The unskilled man moved accordingly as his needs (in terms of these values) were frustrated. (Indeed, labour turnover in coal mines has been called "the silent strike".) The external evaluation, or reaction to the standards of a group external to the factory, affected his stability, and therefore, in relationship to the factory, labour turnover was individual behaviour and not governed by internal standards. Accordingly as the internal evaluation affected his stability this was a reaction to standards of the work-group. But these were standards related to the egoistic—prestige—needs and hence would tend to be more 'individualist', and concerned less with cohesion-security than directly with frustration.

Returning again to the total picture—it might be conceived, as an argument, that during the 'before' period frustration of the need for security, and of satisfaction of moral standards, would have led to deterioration in performance until production finally stopped. However, this did not occur. Because of the deeper needs for preservation of self, and therefore of the work, the men went on strike in order to change the situation by group action, that is, a social method of self-preservation as distinct from an individual (by labour mobility). The strike had a cathartic effect in releasing the stresses occasioned by aggression arising from frustration, and performance improved temporarily. Hence, until the cause of frustration was removed, a recurring cycle of the operative-variable strike, increasing in amplitude and frequency, brought about fluctuations in performance—frustration/aggression/strike/catharsis/recovery/continuing frustration/aggression/strike/catharsis/recovery. The operative-variable strike provided the basis of fluctuation of indices.

Thus it would appear that, though the initial cause of trouble in the 'before' period was dissatisfaction and insecurity, the effect became cyclical as a result of the reaction in group activity through operative-variable strikes.[1] (The manager-variable strikes played little part in the cyclical process since they had no preceding deterioration. Nevertheless, these strikes had some cathartic effect in the succeeding improvement—to be lost again on approach of the operative-variable strike.) This gives cause for reconsideration of the wildcat strike generally, if this situation at Glasgow Ltd be taken as not unique in the character of its strikes.

Such strikes are generally decried on two grounds: they are irrational and they cause a loss in production, a loss usually calculated as a result of the

[1] Such a cycle seems to have been in operation in the docks in the few years after the war. Despite much speculation on basic causes to be found in the conditions external to the work place—and I do not disbelieve these factors were present as well—one basic reason, which appeared during Ministry conciliation, was frustration arising out of an agreement made as long before as 1924. Another, more intimate, cycle appears to have continued for some time in the Briggs Motor Car Body works in the years 1954–57.

time lost. This is the way in which Bulgin regarded the strikes in his time. Even Anderson, who saw the inequity of the bonus scheme, could not understand why the men were so irrational in their approach that they should strike. The loss of production during the stoppages was also a "bad thing" in his opinion. Strikes in docks, coal mines, and such like are usually considered in the same kind of way by the general public. But this attitude is not completely justifiable.

First the loss in production during time lost is fairly negligible compared with the loss in the preceding and accompanying deterioration in performance—and the strike is not the cause of that loss. Secondly the loss is made up by recovery in performance. The cause of loss in production is not the strike, it is the frustrating or aggression-producing factor; and this may well be the result of bad management. Their own bad management may not be recognised by the managers themselves, hence they cannot understand why the men strike; therefore for the managers the strikes are irrational—and so also for the public. The men, too, may be unaware of the real cause of their feelings of aggression, and, to justify their action, produce a reason which so frequently appears to be frivolous. So the blame for loss in production cannot be laid upon the strike, nor always upon the men striking, but upon the real cause of the aggressive action. (The judgment as to whether that cause has its right or not does not enter this discussion.)

Conversely there are those who point out that the production lost through wildcat strikes is negligible. In Glasgow Ltd this was certainly the case in most strikes (though not in go-slows). But to take this point of view is again a serious misjudgment of the case. Production loss can be quite serious as a result of preceding and accompanying deterioration of performance. This is the case in coal mines. The loss of coal output through strikes is comparatively small, the loss through bad performance is immense. And though miners may be castigated for striking, the real culprits are the agents who produce the frustrating and insecure situations. Who these culprits are is not for me to say, they may be Coal Board officials, Trade Union officials, *agents provocateurs* or the miners themselves. There can be no doubt, for one instance, that the differential content of the incentive schemes in mines was for long a source of discontent demanding, as it did finally succeed in obtaining, a review of the wage structure for occupations and regions. It might be the case in the coal-mining industry that the wildcat strike is 'good' for production (in the aggression-causing environment), for the cathartic effect of the strike, "it lets them get it off their chests", the recovery, makes up part of the leeway lost in the approach to the strikes.

How frequent the manager-variable strike may be in the coal mines is difficult to judge, but in the aggressive environment of the mines, a managerial mistake, however slight, is likely to cause a strike. The loss is then mainly through time not worked. The question then is "whose fault?" It may be ascribed to bad managerial decisions, or to the "bloodymindedness" of the men as a result of the environment. Judgment *ex cathedra* is not possible.

The implication of the manager in the strike-situation is of considerable importance. It is possible that had Anderson, in the 1952 August strike, allowed the men to start their four-men-three-gang shift as clearly their own willing, and had not taken upon himself to start the change by issuing commands as if the concept were his, the men would not have objected by striking. On the other hand the strike forced him into the position where he, too, had to take a stand, and express his structural and moral authority. Again it might be said he reacted in parallel with the men, as he did in 1951. But whereas in 1951 he figuratively went on strike against Head Office by threatening resignation, here he figuratively went on strike against the men by exerting power, i.e. a form of aggression. As a manager he had a set of threatened managerial values, but a different frame of reference from that for the men.[1]

What this seems to suggest is that the manager cannot be considered as unrelated to the striking group. The manager is the source of power in the power-group structure, as distinct from the non-power-group (informal structure), and the two types of groups must be integrated in a factory situation. Willy-nilly the two managers, Bulgin and Anderson, had to be more than officially involved. They were personally involved, each differently according to his standards or sets of values. Involved they were, so much so that their performance was affected. Both became aggressive because both were frustrated; both suffered, Bulgin to the extent of having a "nervous breakdown", and Anderson coming near to a "crack-up"; Bulgin was an involuntary absentee, and Anderson, a more aggressive type, almost deserted (labour mobility) by resigning; and both threatened 'strike' action by closure of the factory, i.e. a lock-out.

In such involvement managerial behaviour in the manager-variable strike becomes difficult to assess. To avoid such a strike two prerequisites are necessary. First, if the manager is already accepted by the men as having moral authority they are unlikely to question his decision—for then his decisions are moral. Secondly, if he does not have such authority then his decision must first be analysed by the men for their consideration of its morality. In the second case we have the basis for consultation. In the first case there is no need for consultation. Which is the same as saying that if industrial relations are not good consultation is valuable; and that if industrial relations are good consultation is of no value; or, if used, succeeds remarkably well—for the manager has moral authority.

[1] It is to my great regret that I have no studies of the foremen behaviour at Glasgow Ltd; their frame of reference was again different.

THE TRADE UNION

If the two major functions of a trade union official be 'to maintain and improve wages and conditions', and to represent the men in his charge, then Macdonald may fairly be said to have adequately fulfilled his duties. At no time did he fail to present the case for the operatives, and he was fully aware of the major cause of trouble during the first phase, the 'before' period. When, at last, the Head Office and the local manager permitted union organisation, Macdonald began his work by attempting to reach "gentleman's agreements" with the manager. His failure to do this with Bulgin's predecessor and Bulgin himself aroused, not unnaturally, considerable resentment in him, which showed itself at times in his use of expressions such as "monkey business as per Glasgow Ltd". It was not until the stage of confusion, stage 2, that he became confused himself. Here he took refuge in merely presenting the men's case without necessarily understanding what the case was—the men themselves not knowing. And finally, in the 1953 strike, he assisted, literally stood by, Anderson in convincing the men of the rightness of Anderson's decision to transfer weepart men to N.A.P. As far as I could make out from Anderson, his opinion of Macdonald was of a union official failing to see the situation as the manager saw it during the 'before' period, of being as irrational as the men he represented during the period of confusion, and being "a decent bloke" in the 'after' period. Their agreement that there should be "no more strikes come hell or high water" was a mark of that transition of opinion. From 1953 onwards Macdonald is reported to have said that if all managers were like Anderson there would be no need for union officials like him, and that the only thing he seemed to do on visiting Glasgow Ltd was to have a cup of tea with Anderson. This was merely a reflection of the men's feelings and therefore no change whatsoever in Macdonald's general behaviour.

The behaviour of the shop stewards was not so straightforward. In a general workers union the shop steward has no 'official' status such as that enjoyed in the engineering unions. That is to say, the general workers' shop steward who calls the men out on strike cannot negotiate with the manager as an officially recognised representative of the union, recognised by agreement between employer and trade union. Such a strike is 'unofficial'. Hence the reason for the immediate calling in of Macdonald by Anderson when trouble threatened or broke out. But Anderson could not understand why Macdonald apparently allowed these troubles to break out. As he wrote, "I would like to see the Shop Stewards at this Factory more closely controlled and disciplined than they are at present." "The Convener of Shop Stewards . . . should be a 'good man' . . . That was where Mr Macdonald blundered in the early Glasgow Ltd days and only by bitter experience did he learn that negotiation with me was virtually impossible unless his Convener was acceptable to me." He also talked at times about his being stronger than the trade unions, having more influence with the men than Macdonald. Finally, he was seemingly of the opinion that the shop stewards and Macdonald were the union, and "should never become so powerful that they can dictate to employers".

He was confusing shop steward behaviour with trade union behaviour. Macdonald did not. He was the union in the official, negotiated sense. The shop stewards were the men's representatives through whom should come the men's demands and requests for Macdonald to convey in negotiation with the manager. Anderson never was quite clear about these relationships, and he certainly did his reputation no good with Macdonald when, in 1951, he arranged with the shop stewards the men's bonus schemes, and did not consult Macdonald. The latter was more incensed at the stewards than at Anderson, but he was prepared to "pay out enough rope to let the manager hang himself". Which he very nearly did! But the shop stewards were, in a way, reacting to the decline in union membership at that time. Hardly any but weepart men were paying union dues about this time. There were only 55 members. Even so, when the union membership jumped to about 200 in the first quarter of 1952 the leading men and stewards 'negotiated' with the managers on spoilage fines without consultation with Macdonald. As far as I can gather Macdonald, during 1950 to 1952, was called to the factory only when production-line strikes had commenced or were about to commence, both operative- and manager-variable. (There was an exception in his negotiation on working conditions for N.A.P. and ancillary workers.)

It would appear therefore that the shop stewards were acting in two rôles. In one rôle, as union servants, representatives of the men to the union, they called upon Macdonald when in direct conflict with Anderson. In another rôle, as exdomini for the work-groups, they were representative of the men to the manager. It would follow that, since the union is a voluntary association, when the union organiser has no structural authority, the steward rôle of exdominus would supersede when no power 'politics' was required. But when force was involved then the stewards, in the rôle of union servants, would, as traditional, invoke the power inherent in the trade union, a power external to the factory and therefore additional to the power inherent in work-group strike action.

This would explain in part the irrationality of unofficial strike action when there exists a recognised system of collective bargaining negotiated by employers and unions. It stems from the fact that the steward rôle of exdominus, which is that involved in such strike action, is methectic and has an emotional basis alone. There is little rationality, only 'feeling'. It also accounts for the peculiar behaviour of men on unofficial strike, so led by exdomini, who can reject the union by such expressions as "What has the union done for me?", even when that union may have a long history of successful 'fighting' on their behalf.[1] It also explains the amazement of union officials that unofficial strikes can occur in spite of earnest and sincere union pleas not to strike. It does not seem to matter whether the union is strong in membership or not. The only relation of union membership to strike activity—and it may not be of consequence—is decrease at times of approaching operative-variable strikes, related perhaps to decreasing cohesion; and increase at times of manager-variable strikes, related perhaps to the need for the support of external power at these times.

[1] Paterson, T. T. and F. J. Willett, Unofficial Strike. *Soc. Rev.*, XLIII, 1951.

CHAPTER 21

OF MORALS AND INDUSTRIALISM

At several points I have used the words 'right' and 'good', especially with reference to moral authority. These abstractions, as I use them, now require some definition. The definitions I propose to give are not those that moral philosophers have pondered over for centuries, but are given in terms of social ethics and of reality, that is to say as they are used and felt by members of the community, which is the enterprise. The terms must be consistent with the relations that develop within the enterprise. In this sense I do not use 'right' and 'good' as absolutes; they are relative, and relevant only to the situation that is the enterprise, and one that is dynamic, in constant change.[1]

For a first example, in 1951 Anderson introduced an incentive scheme which Maloney called "fair"—"It was all right—but!" (p. 150). The "but" was removed when, in 1952, the weepart men were able, as a result of other changes, to express their prestige drive in increasing their productivity, that is to say in operation. Everything became "fine", and young men were prepared "to die there". The incentive scheme was 'fair' and 'just' in the eyes of the men, meaning that Anderson had carried out the introduction in a 'proper' manner, and that the scheme had due regard to the prevailing inequities of differentials. Since the differentials concerned status, they concerned functions. 'Fair' and 'just', hence "right", was therefore related to function, and to structural authority, since function implies responsibility, a responsibility which was implicitly assumed on hiring labour. The "fair day's work" was that which they felt obliged to do, their function, whereas "the good day's work" was more than the "fair day's work"; it was beyond the terms of their responsibility, it was beyond the bounds of duty (p. 196). They had bettered their operation, and so increased their contribution to the 'moral whole' of the enterprise.

Again, in a heavy engineering works in Glasgow, the manager introduced an incentive scheme without consultation with the shop stewards, union organiser, and men. The men reacted saying "It's not right", and, "The scheme is no good". These two expressions refer to two different aspects of

---

[1] This does not mean to say that I am denying absolute values, it is only that I am concerned immediately with the way in which men make judgments that govern behaviour in business and industrial enterprises. In this line of thought I have steered away from Ross's conception of right and good (*The Right and the Good*), but much of the argument is influenced by Moore's and Ewing's writings on the concept of utility and fittingness (*Principia Ethica* and *The Definition of Good*).

the case. "It was not right" for the manager to introduce the scheme without consultation; the scheme itself was "no good". The men did not say, "The scheme is not right", nor did they say, "The manager is no good". Here the manager had failed to recognise the contract in that he did not consult the men—he had 'no right' to do as he did. The scheme itself may have been 'right' in that it recognised status (functional) differentials, but it was referred to as "no good", because it did not permit operational flexibility in satisfying prestige drive; nor did it better the existing scheme of things.

A manager himself can be described in similar terms according to his behaviour. A manager of a bassoon factory, say, has the function of ordering and co-ordinating functions to achieve the purpose of profitably making bassoons. (It follows that they must be of a certain quality in order to sell to the customer.) If he does make a profit he has done right by the shareholders, who contributed their money to get a return in order to satisfy some of their personal needs. If, in the making of profit, he gives the operatives 'fair' wages, then he has done right by them, they having contributed their work and labour to get a return in order to satisfy some of their personal needs. He has done 'right', but he may not necessarily be called a 'good' manager. If, however, he improves his operations, bettering his functions beyond that which is his prescribed duty, and so increases profitability in such a way that shareholders and operatives get greater satisfaction of their personal needs, then he becomes "a good manager". So we have three common appellations for managers:

(a) "All right but no good"—fulfils his functions, carries out his duties, is fair and just, but no more.
(b) "Good"—fulfils his functions, is fair and just; and betters operations beyond his prescribed duties.
(c) "Bad"—neither completely carries out his duties, nor is fair and just, nor betters his operations.

It is impossible to conceive of a manager being called "all right but bad", or being called "incompetent but good". He may be called "a nice bloke but just doesn't know", "incompetent but decent (or nice)", when the last adjectives refer to personal attributes which have no relation to carrying out of his duties.

Another approach to the definition of 'right' and 'good' is partly theoretical. By contracting into the enterprise the operatives sanction the right of the manager to command and to expect and enforce obedience. That is, the operatives become responsible for their functions which, perforce, *must* be co-ordinated for the purpose to be achieved; wherefore the relations among functions must be regulated by one whose authority (structural) is sanctioned. In so far as the manager 'rightfully' uses structural authority (which necessarily implies his assumption of responsibility to the operatives) he is doing right. He is then fair and just, for regulation implies rule, and so law. The essence of law, according to Goodhart,[1] is that it is a rule of human conduct which is recognised as being obligatory; and responsibility implies obligation, which stems from the contract. The form of justice here involved is distributive justice.

Therefore, rightness concerns function, for it is in service to the enterprise (that is, in contributing to the achievement of purpose in the proper manner) that the manager is 'right' or his behaviour is 'right', the word 'proper' meaning appropriate to the achievement. Appropriateness of function is group-decided since all the members of the enterprise are involved in its purpose, and have needs which are satisfied through proper functioning. The manager has freedom of judgment in deciding what his 'right' behaviour may be, provided he safeguards the interests of all the members of the enterprise. Should some of these interests be endangered, then the determination of the duty and the 'right' cannot be left to the manager. To use a Kantian form of thought—he is subject to the legislation of the 'realm of ends' for the content of his judgment of what is right is that his operatives and shareholders are ends in themselves. To 'do right' is therefore obligatory, it is a 'perfect' obligation so to speak, since only through rightness can the purpose be achieved—a categorical imperative. The clash of conflicting obligations in terms of what is 'right' is one of the biggest sources of trouble for modern managers—it is not to be wondered that managerial neuroses and psychosomatic complaints are common.

A manager who 'does right', who is "all right", may also attempt to improve the way in which he does his managing, that is improve his managerial operations, so bettering the achievement of the purpose of the enterprise, even enhancing it. By adding this 'betteringness' to his rightness he becomes a "good manager". For example, the manager of a bassoon factory may be "all right" as far as his men and shareholders are concerned—he runs the factory and achieves the purpose. He then may organise the relations of the research and the engineering departments so that the factory produces better bassoons (in the eyes of the consumer) at a cheaper rate, so selling in greater numbers and increasing profit. He is then on the way to becoming a "good manager". Suppose, however, that he is not "all right" in that, say, he institutes incentive schemes that are regarded as inequitable ("unfair", "unjust"), then organises the two departments successfully with better and cheaper bassoons; he would not be regarded as a "good manager". That is to say a manager competent at organising (or competent in some technique), cannot become "good" unless he also is "just", so doing 'right'. He can be "right", but "no good", meaning that he does not better his operations.

[1] Goodhart, A. L., English Law and the Moral Law. *Hamlyn Lectures*, London, 1955.

Therefore, goodness concerns operation, for it is in the bettering of operations that the fulfilling of function is advanced, and the achievement of purpose enhanced. Since this improvement of operation is dependent upon the individual's self-responsibility, it is a self-decided activity; betteringness is not a duty since it is not group-decided. Nevertheless, to "*do good*" is *expected* of a member of an enterprise, since by so doing good the purpose is bettered and all members of the enterprise benefit—provided, of course, that the results of this bettering affect all members equitably. To better operations may, in come cases, be obligatory. For example, in a changing technical environment it may be 'up to' engineers to improve by application of new techniques. Nevertheless, as long as functions are fulfilled, and can be fulfilled without bettering of operation, this obligation remains imperfect, the choice still lying with the individual. Should a member of an enterprise better his operations he is going beyond the 'bounds of duty', that is, beyond what he is bound (obliged) to do.

A 'good manager' may become 'beloved' by his men; a manager who is 'fair' and 'just' alone may not be. This has its parallels in, say, the comparison between a physician and a judge. The physician is concerned with bettering the patient; he is concerned with 'goodness'; the judge is concerned with the law, with 'rightness'. The physician can become 'beloved', but never the judge; he can only become 'fair' or 'righteous'.[1]

We can now take the appellation of managers a step further:

(*a*) "All right but no good"—does only what he is obliged to do.

(*b*) "Good"—does what he is obliged and expected to do.

(*c*) "Bad"—does not do what he is obliged and expected to do.

At Glasgow Ltd, Bulgin was a 'bad manager' in the eyes of the men. His behaviour was not 'right' according to their beliefs; and he was not competent enough to better the enterprise. In the eyes of his managerial (Head Office) colleagues he was 'all right'—"a decent bloke"—but 'no good'. He behaved according to what they thought to be the managerial code in relation to the operatives; but did not improve the factory. To my mind his "nervous breakdown" was the result of his inability to resolve the conflict between his obligation to his employers (as he saw it) and his obligation to the men (about which he was vague). Anderson started his régime at Glasgow Ltd, as being "all right"—I believe the men reacted to this belief when he arrived. Later, 1951, his rightness became suspect and, despite his technical competence, he approached being a 'bad manager'. With his late-1951 incentive scheme he became "all right" again, "but" (as Maloney used that word) not yet 'good'. By the end of 1952 he was a "good manager", not just "the manager" but "Mr". In the eyes of his directorate and fellows of the same status he was not a 'good manager'. He was recognised as

[1] My colleague, Dr Osmond, brought this point to my notice.

competent enough in raising productivity, but he did not follow their code of managerial behaviour, he was not 'right', he was "an appeaser"; "He didn't make the grade", said one, and "It was only a flash in the pan", said another.

The relation of 'goodness' to 'rightness' is sometimes obscure, especially in a constantly changing environment (including a competitive) wherein the precise character of the purpose has frequently to undergo revision. The administrative function of the directorate is often taken up with revision of policy, not only as a result of, say, external changes in markets, but of internal changes in operations. The enterprise has to be dynamic in the sense of bettering its operations, and the imperfect obligation of goodness (utility) makes itself felt particularly at managerial level. (In a way this is the Kantian hypothetical imperative.) A manager cannot remain competent only in terms of fair and just administration (i.e. "all right"); he is then static not dynamic, and the survival of the enterprise is endangered.[1] He must become 'good'.

Yet this very goodness changes to rightness in time. The moral law (goodness) according to Goodhart, becomes the common law (rightness) through tradition in a cohesive society. For example, an old-established Scottish firm instituted a seniority system of placing men in higher status jobs (so higher earnings). This was 'good' at the time. Through traditional practice it became the rule, it became 'right', so much so that modern young managers in that enterprise are now inveighing against it as being 'no good'—it has become over-complicated in a situation of rapid technical changes. It is thought to be purely "traditional", "rote" and, finally, "union sponsored". The union, which had nothing to do with its inception, hold to the system as being "right", "fair and just", although in some ways the system is clearly not furthering the achievement of the enterprise. Negotiations are now on the way to "make the system better"; it is still 'right', and the changes will become 'right'—for they will become part of the social contract so negotiated.

In the modern world of rapid change this is one successful way (it would appear to me) to introduce changes in the social contract. The contract cannot be altered by unilateral action in terms of 'the right', that is to say the manager cannot introduce a new scheme, for instance of piece-rates, saying it is "fair". This is a matter of 'rightness', and, if the 'rights' of the operatives are, to their way of thinking, jeopardised, then what is 'fair' has to be decided by the members and not by the individual, the manager.

[1] There are firms in this country in which such an argument would be regarded as ludicrous. "What was good enough before is good enough now", strictly refers to the rule of the past as applying to the present. Goodness of the past has become rightness of the present, but is still seen as "good", and therefore still "betteringness", and not capable of being bettered.

On the other hand should the manager introduce a new scheme in the 'right' manner, that is to say, with due regard to the 'rights' of the operatives, he can say the scheme is "good" (omitting "fair"). At once, therefore, the scheme is in a different category of evaluation. As 'good' it will be examined more intently in terms of its betteringness than in terms of its rightness. As 'good' it is not 'law', and so is felt to be experimental, therefore liable to be discarded if found to be not good. If it 'betters', it becomes 'right' and then is transmuted into 'law'.

The bettering of operations comes through the use of competence, that is, sapiential authority. 'Goodness' cannot be ordered, it can only be directed, advised, or informed, for the obligation is imperfect. Structural authority is not involved in betteringness, since that authority is concerned wholly with rightness, with the proper organisation of functions, not operations. Hence there are two reasons why changes that concern operations (and hence so many methods of payment) must first be placed before the operatives in consultation.

(a) By reason of the implicit social contract; wherefor no change can take place without agreement to what is tantamount to a new contract. The operatives have a 'right', and this right is reflected in the moral authority of that manager who sees that his structural authority stems from the contract.

(b) By reason of the assumption that changes in operations are made to better the enterprise. This goodness, having its expression in the exercise of sapiential authority alone, cannot be ordered; sapiential authority does not entail the right to command, the decision is the self-responsibility of him who is to better his operations.

This, it seems to me, was the essence of the metamorphosis of August 1952 at Glasgow Ltd. Anderson put forward his scheme essentially as 'good', as an improvement in operations to be tested out in experiment. In his absence on leave a 'bad manager', Bulgin, took over, and treated the scheme in terms of 'the right', using structural authority. Anderson returned, again put it plainly that the scheme was essentially bettering the purpose of the enterprise, which included the benefit of the operatives. The scheme being accepted, it became right, whereupon Anderson's structural authority was sanctioned. He was vested with moral authority having used 'goodness' as well as 'rightness'.

A third way of looking at change is to see operations as affected by the manager's moral authority. He is responsible to the operatives for the means to fulfil their functions, that is to say, providing the 'how' of operations. They are responsible to him for their functions, that is to say, not the 'how' but 'how much'. Their operations they decide themselves, consistent with their fulfilling function and safeguarding the rights of other operatives in fulfilling theirs—hence managerial co-ordination. Therefore the manager has the duty of providing means for the men to operate, and is expected (of his 'goodness'), to provide means of bettering their operations. He cannot command a change in their operations, he can advise or tell them how to, since he expects them, like himself, to 'do good', bettering, in this day and age of rapid technical advance.

In this light it is now possible to examine, though in no detail, problems of instituting change that constantly confront our managers. First there is the situation wherein a change does not imply redundancy of operatives but merely bettering of operations—as, for instance, in change of methods. In so far as the operatives are already fulfilling their function, hence abiding by their contract, they cannot be ordered to adopt the change. If they adopt the change as being 'good' they are, in effect, accepting a new contract, and the good becomes the right, being contractual. They are therefore entitled to request that their reward, "a fair day's wage", be adjusted. A new 'rate for the job' has to be negotiated. This does not mean to say that *all* of the advantages (in money) should accrue to them, for their contract also involves their service to the enterprise as a whole. Should they so demand this total accretion to their wage then the change is 'not good' since it then becomes effected entirely for their benefit and not for the benefit of the whole. Moreover, the 'goodness' stems from the managerial contribution to the whole, the idea of the method.

Conversely, because goodness stems from a managerial idea, it is often considered that the operatives do not deserve benefit from it. This frequently happens in piece-rate working. A new method permits easier operative achievement of the rate, so managers consider that the new rate should be adjusted entirely in this light, that the men be paid for their labour and not their work. For example, at the coal face a miner's stint may be sixteen tons per shift. By better cutting and shot-firing the miner may be able to hew seventeen tons per shift with the same labour. The manager cannot ask that the new rate per shift, that is for seventeen tons, be the same as for sixteen. But, on the other hand, the miner cannot ask for his rate to be increased by the proportionate amount, by one-sixteenth.

Secondly, there is the situation where new machines can increase the productivity of the operatives. If, say, a new lathe can double a turner's output without extra labour the turner cannot ask that his piece-rate remain constant; nor can the manager order that the rate be halved because the labour content is unaltered (despite "scientific" arguments from work-study engineers). The new machine has to be paid for, certainly, and this has to be considered in the new 'rate for the job', the new contract, for the cost of the machine is borne by the whole enterprise. (Where new machines involve redundancy another consideration enters—to be examined below.)

This whole problem of constant change, of 'good' becoming 'right', is probably the 'good manager's' greatest source of concern. Not only are his conceptions of the needs of the enterprise to be considered; the men's conception of their needs in the changing external world have to be thought of as well. Costs and standards of living have their effects as much as business cycles, market fluctuations and fiscal policies of government. What were luxuries become luxury necessities; what were satisfactory cost-price ratios become inequitable. The change is so rapid that 'good' and 'right' are confused. "We ought to have a better machine", becomes "We must have a better machine"; there is little to discriminate between them. And the manager has to bear the burden. He has his responsibilities to his operatives below, and his responsibilities to his directorate above; the 'good' for the operatives becomes factory rule, the 'good' from the directorate, becomes his policy and purpose, hence right. Sometimes the two are compatible, at others incompatible; as happened to Anderson in 1951 when he battled with his Head Office, even threatened resignation in order to bring the directors' concept of right in line with the operatives'. Anderson having established a 'good' incentive, Head Office cheese-pared a $\frac{1}{4}$d. off the shilling bonus. It was correct actuarially speaking, it was wrong morally speaking. The directors had no sense of responsibility towards the men—they were too distant, socially and geographically. They demanded responsibility in Anderson's relationship to them, yet denied him the structural authority that must accompany responsibility. They asked him to 'do good' yet predetermined the 'right' that must automatically follow 'good'. In this position Anderson, like Bulgin, was near nervous prostration; unlike Bulgin he (unwittingly) found a 'good' that brought in its train a rightness acceptable to the directorate.

In similar conditions some managers come close to rebellion. Near Glasgow, in a factory famous for the so-called enlightened approach of its London-based managing director, who hired psychiatrists and developed a remarkably complicated consultation scheme, the men went on strike (manager-variable on a question of redundancy). The works manager found himself at variance with the managing director on what steps should have been taken and were to be taken, and the director approached the men directly—the manager was denied structural authority. He, and the other managers, banded themselves together to form an association comparable to a trade union. They sought to find authority (and with it, *auctoritas*) from an external source.

In the coal industry the colliery manager is responsible, in law, for the safety of his miners. He derives his authority from the state and not the Coal Board. Yet Coal Board officials, chaotically cluttered in an inverted pyramid of hierarchy above him, can order him to carry out activities which

224

may endanger his men. (The Coal Board is not the state though ostensibly responsible to the state.) This happened at a colliery near Glasgow, and, as a result, thirteen miners lost their lives. At the trial of the manager and of his superiors involved in the disaster, it became apparent that the difference between function and operation was unknown, that the forms of authority involved were unrecognised, and that none could distinguish between 'right' and 'good', most of all the colliery manager. The ensuing reorganisation of the Coal Board (Fleck Report) shows no sign of understanding of these basic concepts; colliery managers still lie between two millstone-like forces of 'we' and 'they'.

Nevertheless, these rapid changes which so bemuse our modern managers, also bring in their train a change which will, in the end, make their duties more easily comprehensible, and, at the same time, give a new character to their occupation, a character of professionalism in the quality of its ethical standards. Industrial economics of our society have altered considerably of late. One result is that capital (or the owners thereof) is less and less hiring managers; managers are more and more hiring capital for the purpose of conducting profitable enterprises, just as they hire men to provide labour and work.[1] Shareholders contribute their capital, operatives contribute their labour and work, and managers contribute their managing—the skilled function of ordering and co-ordinating—all to the joint enterprise. A second result is that managers are now more concerned with profitable-running, rather than with profit-making for the benefit of the shareholders; a manager conducts the enterprise to maintain himself and his men in a livelihood, to reward the shareholders for risking their money in the enterprise, and to serve the nation as being customers, and as being one large enterprise in itself.

"The change, of which managerial doubts are a sympton, may be described as a professionalising of management; the manager is beginning to recognise that he has a service to give to his men and to the nation. But this coming new profession is not the profession of technocrats, as Burnham would have it in his *Managerial Revolution*. The new managers' authority is not based on technical expertise. Their right to manage stems from their investment with and acceptance of moral responsibilities of the widest nature. They are becoming industrial humanitarians.

"Sir Hugh Beaver, a prominent industrialist, has said that what a manager requires most of all is 'to be a citizen'. Here we might well paraphrase Aristotle on such a matter. 'It is not the quantity or value of the work produced that ought to form the main object of management's care but the effect which producing of that work naturally creates on the mind and body

---

[1] I am now concerning myself with senior managers from whom, in any case, come the examples followed by junior managers, closer to the operatives. Most of my comments on management concern the activities of seniors.

of the workmen'; and again, 'The knowledge of the manager is in the proper use of his operatives, for the office of a manager lies in the employment not in the possession of operatives'. It seems to me that our managers are more and more reverting to this fundamental truth in citizenship—the enterprise exists for its members, the members do not exist for the enterprise. Management must take into consideration the total good of the enterprise, a good which applies to all its members, and if it makes a decision which fails to achieve that total good then it must be held responsible."[1] Total good is Bradley's moral whole.

Citizenship, as I see it, and as I think Beaver sees it, is the sense of the morality of one's membership of a community, and so behaviour.[2] It is often remarked that the economic objectives of so-called private enterprises are not identical with the objectives of the members of the enterprise, the shareholders, managers and operatives, wherefor the confusion of 'rights', and industrial war. The confusion of rights and the war are indeed facts; what is not so inescapable is the lack of identity of objectives, especially within the last few decades. Within this period has occurred a major revolution in social philosophy, a full recognition of the "rights of the common man". The Marxists would, no doubt, use the word 'proletariat'. I see merely a development of a philosophy which, to a Scotsman, is almost 'natural'—the realisation of the intrinsic value of a man in himself, whoever he may be, the equality of all men and the differences of all men. (Perhaps my Scottish upbringing—my frame of reference—is influencing my argument much more than I am properly aware of.) Humanism and humanitarianism, in the framework of citizenship, loom wide on the industrial horizon.

It is in the time-honoured means-end argument that we see this more clearly. Any business or industrial enterprise has a goal and a purpose. The goal is its function within the state enterprise, that which the enterprise contributes to the nation as the larger enterprise in the preservation and bettering of the life of the nation. The purpose is its operation in fulfilling its national function. The goal of a bassoon factory is profitably manufacturing bassoons for the benefit of the nation; its purpose is to make bassoons.[3] Since bettering of operation is 'good' then the bettering of purpose of the factory is good, that is to say a contribution to the moral whole for the nation—the total good. Hence the manager who seeks, through 'goodness', increasing performance of his enterprise is contributing to the 'total good'. Should a manager, however, seek, through 'goodness', the profit-making of his enterprise, that is to say, seek for profits for his shareholders alone, then

[1] T.T.P. in *The Listener*, 6 December 1956.
[2] The following *Philosophy of Industrialism*, which I teach my managerial students in more detail than is given here, appears to have good effect in practice.
[3] Note the -ing termination for function, and the infinitive—'action'—for operation.

he is contributing to a 'limited good', the benefit of a limited portion of the nation. A citizen is concerned with the total good.

Competition among enterprises, in so far as it promotes 'goodness' of the enterprise, and hence the total good, is compatible with citizenship. Since this good stems from operation, it is free in that it is a self-decided activity. This is the moral freedom of the enterprise, liberty to do its duty. If, however, the liberty is of the private enterprise, meaning liberty only for the limited good—hence with no concern for the total good—the liberty is not moral, there is no duty. Private gain is right when it stems from service to the moral whole, that is when satisfaction of the prestige drive comes from status arising out of function. Private gain is not right when it stems from self-interest, that is when satisfaction of the prestige drive comes from doing limited good. This I found to be the case in war.[1] When fighter pilots assumed prestige without having justified that prestige through fighting service, they became aggressive, accident potential, neurotic. Given the chance of fighting service, or its equivalent, and the prestige that ensued, they became thoroughly sound men, and formed powerful and cohesive groups—the essence of morale. In effect they were frustrated because they had assumed, without serving, the rights of those who had served, done the right; they had set themselves up as good without first having done the right—and so became sick people.

The question must inevitably arise, "Who judges whether right and good has been done?" The state decides whether enterprises are right for the nation in controlling (managing) by fiscal and monetary policies or even by downright financial support. Especially is this clear in war. The economic markets (at least in our western culture) decide whether enterprises are 'good' or not, by the purchase of their products, by the investment of capital and by the supply of labour. (In the U.S.S.R. the state decides on rightness and goodness.) It follows that in this macrocosmic system the good manager must have competence in economics, finance and technology, either in his own person, or in the persons of experts with sapiential authority whom he organises to advise him.

Shareholders, supplying capital, and operatives supplying work and labour, contribute to the total good through the enterprise; the total good becomes conterminous with the enterprise itself. Since the national enterprise provides all with livelihood and satisfaction of personal needs as a reward, so the business enterprise (as part of the nation) provides its members with livelihood or, at least, means of satisfaction of some of their personal needs. In this, therefore, the objectives of managers, shareholders and operatives are identical. This does not necessarily demand that their judgment of the right and good of the enterprise be identical; their judgments

[1] *Morale in War and Work.*

may be of the same kind, but different in degree according to their different frames of reference. Shareholders, for example, will be more concerned with good management which is likely to entail greater return for risking their capital; operatives will be more concerned with right management since their immediate livelihood depends upon this. The operatives must, of necessity, have a microcosmic view of the enterprise since the rightness of their financial reward is so intimately bound up with their daily living, its basic element for necessities, its marginal elements for satisfaction of status and prestige both internally and externally. The managers, concerned with macrocosmic forces of the economic markets, have therefore to be aware of the micro-cosmic forces impinging upon their operatives, have to think in large financial terms and in minute. It is small wonder that the manager often is exasperated by the industrial strife that may accompany the demand for a fraction of a penny per hour. But, to the operative, this is important. Its effect on his living is vital and immediate.

Here again the question must be asked, "Who judges whether right and good has been done in the factory?" Since there is a contract which involves rightness, and since this contract is the intimate concern of the trade union, it can at once be said that the function of the trade union is to question the rightness of managerial activity at factory level as far as it concerns opera-tives—"to maintain and improve wages and conditions", basic to the constitution of trade unions, implies holding to contracts and negotiating new ones. But the union is also involved in 'the good' in terms of the relation of the enterprise to the nation. Since a change of contract (say arising from method and technical changes) is the result of managerial good, then the union may consider this goodness in the negotiating of the new contract. It is indeed the duty of the trade unions to the nation to so consider the good of the enterprise while negotiating—at least that seems to be the general opinion as expressed in the cry for "trade union responsibility". (In the U.S.S.R. there is no need for trade unions since the state decides the rightness of the contract.) Managerial goodness at factory level is judged by the directorate, as representatives of the shareholders, and as shapers of policy which is concerned with the contribution to the national good.

As far as the rightness of organisation is concerned the manager judges for himself but, as I have said, only in so far as the rights of the members are safeguarded. It will readily be understood that if the union considers the directorate to be more concerned with the limited good and less with the total good, then the union cannot be expected to consider the limited good when negotiating the right. Adam Smith has said the same: "The proposal of any new law or regulation of commerce which comes from this order (i.e. self-interested business) ought always to be listened to with great pre-caution, and ought never to be adopted till after having been long and carefully examined, not only with the most scrupulous, but with the most suspicious attention. It comes from an order of men whose interest is never exactly the same with that of the public, who have generally an interest to deceive and even to oppress the public and who accordingly have upon many occasions both deceived and oppressed it.''

Here we have the genesis of industrial disagreement, dispute, and finally conflict. It is a clash between the good and the right. It will be more likely to occur when:

(a) the top management (administrative) is patently concerned with a policy of limited good.

(b) the senior management (executive) does not 'do right'.

(c) the senior management (executive) confuses good and right.

(d) the union does not consider the good in negotiating right.

In this age of rapid change, when top management is more and more hiring capital, and so becoming actively conscious of the need to consider the total good—spurred on by parliamentary and governmental exhortation —there will be decreasing tendency for the first factor to operate. There will be less of the cry for a larger "slice of the cake". Similarly, as unions become more aware of their wider duties, as a result of their successful battle for the rights of operatives at factory level, so the last factor will tend to be reduced in potency. As managers are more and more becoming 'educated' in management (as distinct from 'trained') the second factor will be less frequent in action. But, as technical and social changes speed up further, as they are now doing, the third factor will increase in importance. None of these factors will be eradicated; disputes at factory level in any case are liable to continue, for the reasons given in Chapters 15 and 18. However, there is hope that the social institution of collective bargaining will be so developed that dispute does not require to descend into conflict. I cannot, for my part, see that a jurisprudential system administered by the courts can possibly decide upon the difference between industrial good and right—that is a major difficulty in law as it is. Nevertheless, the provision of arbitration and conciliation courts and tribunals is a step in the right direction. There the difficulty is that there are so few precedents to go upon (as in common law, which is moral law). Some legal pundit will, no doubt, produce the required 'Institutions'.

But these arguments lead to the final conclusion that there can never be industrial peace. It depends upon what is meant by 'peace'. Moving from the deification of competition by the economists we are now faced by the psychologists' and sociologists' concept of collaboration and harmony— from "perfect competition" to "maximum collaborative participation". The economists lay stress upon the macrocosmic forces of business fluctuations, of the markets, and of the need for maximising economic advantages. The psychologists and sociologists lay stress upon the microcosmic forces of

229

individual personal needs, goals, status, leaders, groups, believing that in the "human relations approach" all will be the happiness of harmony in team-work. The 'war' of competition, the strikes that are Hicksian power con-flicts for example, is to be replaced by 'peace' that stems from cathartic treatment of individuals on the work floor, presented with psychiatric-type pills of works councils, consultations and counselling. But this, it would seem, is the distinction between the points of view of the manager, the macrocosmic reference, and of the operatives, the microcosmic. And from a philosophical angle it is accent upon the good (for the good manager, being concerned with the moral whole, is concerned with the macrocosmic eco-nomic forces), and it is accent upon the right (for the operative, being con-cerned about his daily living and his contract that means his contribution and reward, is concerned with the microcosmic forces). The two points of view cannot always be compatible. There will always be dispute about differences; and in this sense there can be no 'peace'. But this difference need not be resolved through strife that harms the enterprise—and so the total good; and in this sense there need be no 'war'.

In its very essence disagreement within industry, at least as it is now developing, is symptomatic of enhancement of the moral whole. The good is constantly becoming the right. The manager proposes his changes for the good; the men negotiate a new contract on this change, it becomes the right. This, in its turn, must be bettered. It is a step-like process up the ladder that is the nation's progress in well-being. If there were no changes for the good, then our society would become static and, as Toynbee shows, decadent. But conversely, if industrial strife ensues from the disagreement between good and right, then the nation's well-being is endangered, it is a slipping down the ladder of progress. It could well become catastrophic—the General Strike in 1926 was near to being that. (Strangely enough that same strike led to final recognition of the place of the union in society as the legitimate scrutinator of the labour contract, in itself an advance towards the moral whole.) What is required is recognition by management and union of the basic principles that govern this process of what I might call 'rightful bettering', so that differences need not lead to strife but to discussion, negotiation, compromise and agreement, wherein the total good remains the prime consideration. The result will be "sound men in powerful and cohesive groups" as Bartlett calls them. They will be moral men for they have con-sidered the right and the good.

In goodness they will have the individual liberty that is self-decision in operation. But this goodness will be directed towards promotion of the moral whole, which is rightness in group-decided responsibility, being duty. In short, men will have liberty to do their duty towards others; which is the essence of democracy.

What then is the part our managers can play, since from them come the guidance towards unwarlike resolution, in their own bailiwick, of this ever-reappearing dispute? Managers, as individuals, can take steps towards this resolution in a way that operatives (who act in groups) cannot.

The manager must have both the macrocosmic and microcosmic views, for, in his rôle, he lies between the greater, external world and his enterprise, the smaller, internal world. From his view of the external world he decides upon the policy to be followed—purposive decision—and from his view of the internal world he decides how to execute that policy. Sometimes these two functions are carried out by one person, such as a managing director, sometimes the functions are carried out by two or more persons. These we call respectively administrative and executive, the first being concerned with purposive-decision or policy-making. The executive has two major functions in implementing policy, one concerned mainly with the rightness of organisation, the ordering and co-ordinating of functions, and the other concerned mainly with goodness, that is, decision on bettering operations. A general manager is almost wholly executive and concerned with organisation of higher functions, a works manager, like Anderson, is more concerned with organising lower functions and bettering operations in order to implement administrative decision.

(1) *The Administrative View.* This view a senior manager must have, for here he sees his duty in subscribing to the total good. He relates the enterprise to the external world, and acts as the focal point through which his enterprise and the external world react.

He has to know something of economics, of all the pressures put upon his enterprise in a competitive system, business fluctuations, fiscal and monetary policies of government, export and home markets, the labour market, costs and standards of living and such like. He has to know something of accountancy, of the uses of capital, how to decide on cost-price ratios, budgetary control, cost control, inventory control, how to read a balance sheet, and so on. He has to know something of technology, what science and technology has to offer him to better the running of the firm, the use of machines, work-study, production engineering, office layout, and other methods and techniques. These are the tools of management. The manager need not be specialist in any one field, for he can always hire economists, accountants and technologists to advise him of their sapiential authority. What he does need to know is the kind of question to ask these members of staff.

But the really important questions are those he asks himself when he makes his judgments and decisions. There is no one he can turn to for the answers because the questions are moral, to be answered by himself alone as a moral man. "If I do not do such and such shall I have failed to do my duty in bettering the enterprise? Is what I propose to do right and good?

231

Will it have beneficial repercussions on my customers, my shareholders and my men? Or is it a limited good I propose—do my shareholders benefit at the expense of my customers and my men?" The answer to such questions is what I have called a primary judgment, one of principle, a judgment of the morality of the situation.[1] The manager implements this judgment in executive action.

(2) *The First Executive View.* Here the manager is concerned with rightness of his actions in organisation, that is, in relations which are static. This is a secondary judgment, one of action based upon the primary judgment of the situation. He has to ask himself the question, "Am I right in the doing of this?" Since this involves the functions of ordering and co-ordinating, hence responsibility, the manager *must know his duties*, that which is expected and required of him in his rôle. As a corollary, a duty is to see that his subordinates know their duties—for how can they be responsible if they do not? Duties require delineation of rôles. This is often misunderstood in textbooks on management—all of them stressing the delineation of functions (sometimes called 'responsibilities') or job definition. But to outline the function tells little about the relationships that must be involved; and the relationships are the essence of rightness in organisation.

The rôles that require delineation have not been examined in this book (except in the case of the relations of Anderson with his foremen), and one cannot delineate the rôles in the informal group situations since these rôles depend so much upon personal authority. Rightness of action is dependent upon the rôles of the formal situation, that is upon structural, sapiential and moral authority. In the foreman-manager case shortly described, the difference between responsibility and accountability as two relations was not recognised by either Anderson or his foremen. Indeed, it seldom is recognised in most modern enterprises even though it is of immense importance now that trade unions have established their right to scrutinise the rightfulness of managerial activity.[2]

(3) *The Second Executive View.* Here the manager is concerned with another secondary executive decision upon the bettering of operations; that is to say with decisions that are concerned with change of any kind, with the dynamic of the enterprise. Such decisions are the kind that have been mainly discussed in this book, becoming necessary in answering the need to alter work flow, to change techniques, to adjust rates, decisions frequently challenged by the operatives. Apart from purely technological decisions (which, in any case, can be made by a hired expert), these decisions are again a

---

[1] *Morale in War and Work*, p. 122.

[2] There are at least two more rôle relations over and above responsibility and accountability. These I have described in a cyclostyled paper, *A Methectic Theory of Social Organisation*, December, 1957, issued from the Department of Social and Economic Research, Glasgow University.

matter of moral judgment on the part of the manager. They are moral because they concern the operatives, the decision involving the contract, its change and reconstitution. They are decisions on actions which come roughly under a heading, frequently called "human relations", which can be summarised as *principles*.

PRINCIPLES OF HUMAN RELATIONS IN MANAGING MEN[1]

(1) *Men are to be regarded as equals in the social contract*—though all men are different. This means that subordinates are not to be treated as "cogs in the machine", but as men having intrinsic worth that has to be recognised. In many of the 'textbooks' of advice to managers ("How to be Human though a Manager"!) this is implicit in the exhortation to be "friendly", "to get on first name terms with subordinates", "be a mixer", "get to know them, their problems and their difficulties", and such like. To my mind these exhortations are not universally applicable, for they may involve a manager attempting to change the temperament aspect of his personality— which he cannot do; "He's not built that way". He may be the "naturally quiet type", "a strong worded man" (like Anderson), who could not do these things, being incapable of doing them. Besides, honest managers would reject it as false for them—and falsity of this kind would be very quickly discerned by the men. There need be only complete recognition and belief that the men are of worth in themselves. However a manager behaves, unfriendly or friendly, stiffnecked or genial, provided the content of his talk and behaviour involves this principle, the operatives will accord him the praise of "He's all *right*", or, as our American colleagues have it, "a regular guy".

(2) *It is the social contract which provides the right to command and to expect and enforce obedience*—that is the right comes from the moral law and not the laws of property. The social contract invests the position of manager (and so the manager) with structural authority; and hence, as a corollary, demands of him the exercise of moral authority. He must be aware of (and show) his responsibility to his subordinates. It is not enough that he gives them "welfare", he must provide them with adequate means to fulfil their part of the contract, and to advance the good of the whole through bettering of their operations. This is the basis of good morale and team spirit. Everyone becomes aware of the general purpose and of the part each has to play, wherefor there is not only the sense of responsibility to the superordinate but also the sense of responsibility internally, to one's self;

[1] Women are different social animals but, in the main, these principles apply to them as well. There are differences not considered here.

and from the knowledge that each and every one, manager and men alike, are aware of this responsibility, and so act, then there is team spirit.

(3) *The enforcement of commands must be right*—the rightness stems from the contract, hence all commands must be in terms of the contract. The manager cannot order the operatives to do other than that which they are obliged to do (by reason of the contract). What he orders are their functions; if he orders anything else then a new contract must be set up. Nor can he command a subordinate to do that which the subordinate is incapable of doing, and hold the subordinate responsible for failure to carry out the command.

This is the principle which is mainly operative in problems of demarcation. Immanent in the contract is that certain functions are the "right" of certain occupational groups, hence the manager cannot order functions which contravene this right. He has to negotiate a new contract. It is in this field particularly that trade unions are obviously scrutinators of the right. The unfortunate thing is that, so often in demarcation disputes, the unions forget to consider the good.

To fire a man is the extreme use of force; but it may be right. The members of the enterprise, manager and men alike, are committed to achievement of the purpose and therefore have, as a whole, the right to punish the parts of the whole for failure to fulfil functions. Such a punishment must be exercised through an agent, and the only agent satisfactory to all members is the manager, for he alone is able to judge the effect of punishment (such as the sack) upon the profitable running of the enterprise. There have been attempts to set up a body of operative peers to judge and punish an operative for misdemeanours, but in such cases their powers are derived from the manager. They cannot judge adequately for they cannot know the total effect of failure of the operative (therefore the extent of his misdemeanour) nor can they punish properly for, in punishing, they may harm the running of the business, being ignorant of it. (In a court of law a jury of peers may judge whether a person is guilty or not, but it is the judge—who knows the right—who determines the extent of and therefore the appropriate punishment for the crime. The authority and power of the judge is sanctioned by the peers.)

Here it is appropriate to consider the question of the sack as a result of technical changes (see p. 224) or of changes in the markets; what is known as redundancy. In the first case the operatives' presence hinders the dynamic of the firm. Here the manager can only present the need for good as justification for the sack; and since the man has not failed to fulfil his contract the trade union could well demand that the operative be retained on the payroll, and even deny the changes contemplated. This has happened frequently. A classic case is the introduction in the docks of new unloading machines

234

which reduce the required manpower considerably; no dockers are dismissed, the redundant men sit around while their working mates use the machines. The dock employers had forgotten this principle, and others (below).

In the second case, where reduced markets lead to redundancy, the problem is of the same kind. The labour contract is fulfilled but the good of the enterprise is in danger. Since the well-being of the operatives is part of the moral whole the right to work becomes a managerial responsibility. The Minister of Labour, during a strike as a result of redundancy dismissals in the motor-car industry, explicitly stated that organising jobs for the men is a moral responsibility of management. Arbitrary dismissal, that is without justification, without some care for the livelihood of the operative, is a denial of the moral whole: it is despotism. But since retention of redundant men would endanger the survival of the enterprise, and therefore the moral whole, the manager must retain the right to sack them; for the manager is held responsible for the survival of the enterprise and hence the livelihood of the men remaining. The men accept redundancy dismissal if they think the manager is not at fault. They seek to punish the manager if he is, if the redundancy can be seen to have arisen from incompetent administration. This has been thought to be the case in the motor-car industry some years ago, and the trade unions demanded an enquiry into its administration. This is a clear indication of the responsibility of the manager to the operatives.

(4) *The contract cannot be altered by unilateral action.* That is to say the manager cannot order a change which involves function and operation without consulting those subordinates whose functions and operations are affected. If he does so he breaks the contract wherefor the subordinates are entitled to use force in opposition, a force which has right on its side since it stems from reaction to unlawful use of force. This is the basis of operatives' contention that a manager-variable strike is "justified", it has 'right'. There is no need for the operatives to build up consensus of opinion on the right to strike in such a case, for the right is at once apparent.

On the other hand the operatives cannot alter the contract unilaterally. Here there *is* need for them to build up consensus of opinion on the right to strike—hence the longer approach to the operative-variable strike. But, just as they have right on their side in the manager-variable strike, so the manager has right on his side in the operative-variable. He would be justified in using the lock-out. However, the justification has to be weighed against the good of the enterprise, perhaps even its survival. This weighing of good against the right of the lock-out can properly be considered *before* the operative-variable strike occurs, since it can be forecast not only statistically but by the very clear evidence of operative approaches to the manager on the question of altering the contract. It is at these approaches that the manager has the duty to expound the 'good', and so why the contract cannot be altered if it is not in the interests of the whole.[1]

It seems to me that here is a very good reason why industrial relations, as a function of management, should have representation at directorate level—as is now common practice in U.S.A. The labour market is as much important as the selling, buying and financial markets normally represented at board level. It is only at this policy-making level that the purpose of the enterprise, and the rights and good of customers and shareholders can be appreciated. Hence it is only at this level that the good of the enterprise can be adequately weighed against the lock-out, or its equivalent in refusal to change the contract. Imminent operative-variable strikes should be reported to senior level for such decision; manager-variable strikes should be and can be avoided at the level of the manager causing the dispute.

(5) (a) *Proposals to change the contract, in the first place should be evaluated in terms of the good*—for change requires to be a bettering. (b) *The rightness, or fairness, of a change in the contract cannot be unilaterally judged*—the contract involves at least two parties.

Examples of this principle have already been given (p. 222 *et seq.*). However, the principle requires the meeting of manager and operative either in consultation, 5a, or in negotiating a decision, 5b. This involves two kinds of social institution which I define as the 'conference' and the 'committee', but which I cannot digress upon here.

(6) *Rôles, and therefore functions, must be defined as contractual*—that is, as duties. Functions of all subordinates, managerial and operative, should be defined as accurately as possible, for otherwise they cannot know that for which they are responsible, and so cannot be held responsible. To be held responsible for failure in a function not so defined is a gross denial of the right, and is a use of autocratic power. Such definition is also necessary to safeguard the enterprise which requires fulfilment of function. Moreover, a contract, in which responsibility for function is involved, is not valid if the function is not specified. For example, there is the case I have already quoted, of two shop stewards in the same factory, both dismissed. One was rightfully dismissed because he had failed to fulfil his function of turning crankshafts; the other was wrongfully dismissed because he had left his bench on trade union matters. In the second case the function of trade union officials should have been defined as part of the steward's 'job', his contribution to the enterprise.

Rôles, involving relationships in the exercise of structural and sapiential authority, must also be defined. With functions delineated the right is then

[1] The function of the trade unions in such situations cannot here be examined even shortly but, in my experience, it seems that trade union officials have not yet delineated the relations between union members and officials in the union enterprise itself.

apparent in the way functions are co-ordinated, and so the rights of others are safeguarded as well. The subordinates "know where they stand", they have security in belonging and serving. They have duties clear and explicit; which is the basis of loyalty, for loyalty can exist only when there is duty.

If a man works for himself having no sense of loyalty, then he cannot have high performance as service to the enterprise. (He may have high performance, in service to himself, in order "to make good", when the enterprise benefits as a secondary result.) Loyalty to the enterprise may offset external pulls on a man; he solves the problem of 'me versus work' more often in favour of the enterprise. For example, most everyone at some time or another feels he "cannot face" his work—most of voluntary absenteeism is of this kind. In such a case one man may be as lazy as another, but a sense of duty will bring him to work while the other, with no such sense, will stay away. Loyalty will also reduce labour turnover; loyal men stay by their enterprise despite attractive chances elsewhere—they are "firm's men".

As a corollary to this principle—*the reward for work and labour must be right and good*. The reward must be relevant to value of function (rank differential) wherefor it is right. The reward must take cognizance of personal effort beyond the bounds of duty, wherefor it is good. The reward must also have relevance to external pressures (such as costs and standards of living) since the purpose of the enterprise is conterminous with the total national good, and that is reflected in such pressures. The reward must also have relevance to internal pressures (not so readily uncovered) which lead to discriminating differentials regarded as right by the operatives. The benefits of loyalty to the enterprise may be reduced by incompatible rewards.

(7) *Operations cannot be ordered* for these are self-decided. The exceptions are: (*a*) Where functions may be affected, e.g. in care and use of machines; (*b*) Where relations with others have to be safeguarded.

If there is no liberty in operation men will become "cogs in the machine", and the first principle is denied. It is from the liberty in operation that goodness comes. If an enterprise is to be dynamic it must have this liberty, which should be fostered as much as possible. This is implicitly recognised in the many 'suggestion box' schemes that are promoted so as to "make the operative feel he is participating". The manager can't "make" the men feel this, he provides opportunity for them to do so in betteringness. But the essence of this betteringness is that it is for the whole and not for the individual—and almost all suggestion schemes are based upon individual benefit! An example of the opposite, and effective, kind of scheme is American, the Scanlon Plan, so-called after its originator. The quotations hereunder are from Whyte.[1]

The scheme is rather like our wartime Production Committee system,

[1] Whyte, W. F., *Money and Motivation*, Harper, New York, 1953, pp. 166–188.

when duty was clear within the explicit purpose of the enterprise towards the national war effort. On the work floor a committee of foreman and an elected union representative meet at intervals to discuss ideas put forward by the operatives. "The individual is expected to contribute his ideas for the benefit of everyone. He is rewarded of course but in a less tangible way . . . must receive a good deal of recognition from fellow-workers, union officers and management. Since he does not stand to gain on an individual financial basis, he is not caught between a desire to benefit himself and the possible adverse reactions of his work-group." Here is personal contribution towards the whole, and resultant prestige. The ideas are passed up to another management-union committee which suggests adoption and alteration. Management decides on adoption. From the opposite direction managerial ideas are passed to this upper committee for consideration and comment. Here is manager-originating change being put forward as 'good' (not 'fair'). "Management has not abandoned its customary managerial function of planning for technological and process changes. The difference is that management now *consults* the people who are most directly involved in the changes. This has two effects. On the one hand, it reduces or eliminates resistance to change. On the other hand, it makes possible the modification of the plan so that it will be more efficient in its technical as well as in its social sense."

The operatives are put on a time-rate and for "increase in productive efficiency as reflected in production values (an equivalent percentage of) participating bonus is paid to each employee working under the plan". (There are also other conditions, all 'equitable'.) In one firm 100 per cent of the labour cost improvement is paid out as bonus—"management expects to make its gains through spreading its overhead in increased production". All except top management share in the bonus. Here is recognition of the enterprise as existing for its members who contribute in required function and expected goodness. With technological changes and other alterations, such as basic wage-rates, the ratio of labour costs to production value changes, when management and union negotiate a new ratio. Here the union performs its function of holding and negotiating contracts, scrutinises the right while considering the good. "The Scanlon Plan objective is to devise a formula which will most adequately reflect the productive efforts of workers and management people as a whole." The Plan works well in some places with marked increase in productive effort.

To me, this Plan and its success, as well as the admiration accorded it in U.S.A., is somewhat of a new departure in managerial thought in that country. The Plan has the elements of what I have already suggested is the basis of democracy—in short, men will have liberty to do their duty towards others, for self-decided goodness will be directed towards promotion of the moral whole, which is rightness in group-decided responsibility, being duty.

With this concept of industrial democracy in mind one looks enquiringly from Bridgeton, close to the place where Adam Smith taught, outwards to the two wealthy nations, east and west. From U.S.A. comes the chant of "freedom of the individual", "free enterprise", adumbration of competition, and the cult of equality. Competition and hard work are "good". This is goodness, but it is not in terms of the right, the moral whole; it is in terms of a limited good, for one competes to "make good", that is, for one's self, and to "keep up with the Joneses". The wealth of the nation is a by-product of accent upon the prestige drive, the individual's desire for personal satisfaction. But here is the paradox—in so far as verticality is stressed the cult of equality demands horizontality. In the obsession with the prestige drive the service drive has outlet in overt horizontality, "team work", community, conformity; in other words equality becomes "sameness". The Americans are a nation of 'joiners' seeking "togetherness". And since the immense technical power of U.S.A. arises from prestige drive and not service drive, "it seems as if the most powerful people on the face of the earth are suffering from the worst case of jitters known". So says Selekman,[1] who sees the American dilemma as a result of the "conflict between a technical 'must' and an ethical 'ought'", which is our goodness as against rightness. Accent upon the freedom of the individual and upon equality without duty, accent upon 'goodness' without equivalent 'rightness', is a denial of the satisfaction that comes from liberty to serve the moral whole.

From the east comes the chant, "the state above all". Service to the state in U.S.S.R. is paramount. Here is a rightness in duty; but suppression of freedom of operation. Men work in service but are denied the liberty to choose how they serve. Again all are equal and the same. The 'norms' are set even though the stakhanovite is praised. In the obsession with horizontality and the service-drive the balance of prestige-drive appears in verticality, with adumbration of power, of *potestas* as well as *auctoritas*. Both good and right are decided by the state in which is vested all judgment. As I have already said, in U.S.S.R. there is no need for trade unions—nor for God for that matter.

In both nations conformity is stressed, in one competition, in the other co-operation, both denying (in the stress upon equality which becomes sameness) the liberty in operation and so contribution, that comes from difference. But who is entitled to say that U.S.A. is wrong and that U.S.S.R. is bad? They themselves call each other that; and claim that their respective "democracies" are the true. In the broadest sense the disputes of these two great agents are reflected on the factory floor at Glasgow Ltd—the dispute between the good and the right, a subject dear to the hearts of argumentative Clydeside Scotsmen, who spawned trade unionism as well as the *Wealth of*

[1] Selekman, B., *Power and Morality in a Business Society*, McGraw Hill, New York, 1956.

Nations. Perhaps, recognising the element of moral judgment that underlies this dispute, the U.K. has found no need for either Taft-Hartley Acts or industrial commissars. Perhaps the seeds of proper industrial democracy are sprouting, neither on the production-lines of Detroit nor in the shops of Stalingrad, but in the yards, the mines and factories of this old country.

INDEX

Absenteeism, rest of factory, 129; voluntary and involuntary, 131, 200.

Accidents, bigpart, 122; definition, 91; and labour turnover, 97; -liable, -potential and -prone, 197; and productivity, 93; rest of factory, 126; and skin dysfunctions, 107; and spoilage, 95.

Ackroyd, 53.

Administrative view, 231.

Agents provocateurs, 207, 212.

Alexander, F., 197.

Anderson, 17; and authority, 159; takes over, 33.

Arensberg, C., 13.

Auctoritas, 184, 224, 234.

Authority, 154, 163; definitions of line, moral, personal, sapiential, staff, and structural, 156 ff.

Bartlett, F. C., 230.

Beaver, H., 225.

Big money, 186, 188, 195.

Bigparts, 19; history, 115 ff; crew, 23.

Bloodymindedness, 75, 78, 200, 213.

Bonus, 22, 27, 34, 39, 43, 45, 51, 67, 147, 150 ff.

Bradley, F. H., 226.

Bridgeton, 9.

Brown, 50.

Bulgin, 29, 33; and authority, 154.

Burnham, J., 225.

Cairncross, A. K., x.

Carelessness, 75, 78, 95.

Catharsis, 211.

Causality, 3.

Celtic, 11.

Chalmers, 62.

Citizenship, 225.

Cohesion, 165, 174, 176, 182, 185, 208, 210.

Controller, 21, 165, 172, 176.

Dermatitis, 103, *see* Skin dysfunctions.

Differentials, and authority, 160; bigpart, 115, 117; definition, 145, 47; and health, 200; and wage evaluation, 188; weepart, 27, 29, 30, 33, 36, 38, 42;

Eccentric, rôle, 171.

Efficiency, definition, 113.

Evidence, 1, 2.

Exdominus, rôle, 171.

Executive, view, 232.

Exemplar, rôle, 171.

Ewing, A. C., 217.

Factors, definition, 112; economic, sociological and managerial, 112, 152; in stages, 140.

Fair holiday, 27, 71, 119, 145.

Fair and fairness, 15, 149, 159, 162, 175, 177, 184; day's wage, 195; day's work, 196; mores and norms, 206, 217.

Foreman, 21, 164.

Fromm, E., 208.

Frustration, and health, 197; and strikes, 206.

Function, definition, 167.

Gang size, 22, 23, 33, 34, 37, 38, 39, 41, 45, 50, 51, 162; and productivity, 152; weepart gang, 168; bigpart gang, 173.

Glacier Metal, 3.

Glasgow Irish and Scottish, 10.

Good, goodness, 16; manager, 217; money, 186, 188, 195.

Go-slow, 27, 33, 38, 39, 49, 55, 56; analysis, 203.

Goodhart, A. L., 219, 221.

Gregal, 15.

Group, definition, 167.

Hawthorne, 3, 176.

Health, definition, 101, 107.

Hicks, J. R., 230.

Higham, T. M., 201.

Horne, Dr., 103.

I.B.M., 3.

I.C.I., 26.

Incentives, and authority, 160; definition, 27, 34, 39, 40, 69, 117, 145, 147; and fairness, 149; and social conditions, 153; and wage evaluation, 188.

Indominus, rôle, 171.

Isolate, rôle, 172.

241

Date Due

JUN 21 '76			

Demco 293-5